concentration
unidirection
simplicity

Burlington
Vermont
Phone   4466
or
2959

Drama

Time must never be more than
                              24 hrs.

Only one plot
Place — one stage setup

Simplified French Review

SIMPLIFIED FRENCH REVIEW

Grammar and Composition

By

FRANCIS B. BARTON *&* EDWARD H. SIRICH

University of Minnesota

APPLETON-CENTURY-CROFTS, INC.

NEW YORK

Preface

Simplified French Review follows the same general plan as the authors' earlier grammars, but extensive modifications have been made in the presentation of the grammatical material. Some material previously included has been placed in the appendix, notably the tables of numbers, or has been eliminated entirely as unessential in a practical review grammar. Many rules have been restated to obtain greater simplicity or greater clarity. The lesson on personal pronouns has been divided into two to afford more ample drill on a difficult subject. The treatment of the past tenses, of the relative pronouns, and of the subjunctive has been thoroughly revised. The lessons on the past tenses and on the infinitive have been placed early in the book, and numerous other changes have been made in an attempt to meet more effectively the needs of the students for whom the book is intended.

The exercises are entirely new, and comprise, as heretofore, connected composition, largely in dialogue, dealing with French life, conversation, grammatical and replacement exercises, and verb drills. The exercises have been carefully graded, and anticipatory material has been excluded as far as possible. A series of review exercises has been provided for those who may desire additional material for classroom practice.

The authors wish to express their thanks to Professor George S. Barnum of the Lawrenceville School for many helpful suggestions, and to Professors Marguerite Guinotte and Emmert M. Brackney of the University of Minnesota, who read the manuscript and offered many useful recommendations.

F. B. B.
E. H. S.

Contents

Simplified French Review

LESSON I

The Articles — Prepositions with Names of Countries and Cities

THE ARTICLES

1. Forms of the definite and indefinite articles:

MASC. SING.	FEM. SING.	MASC. AND FEM. PL.	
le, l'	la, l'	**les**	the
du, de l'	de la, de l'	**des**	of the
au, à l'	à la, à l'	**aux**	to the
un	**une**		a, an

2. An article agrees in gender and number with the noun it modifies and is generally repeated before each noun in a series.

3. The definite article is required in French, contrary to English usage:

(1) before nouns used in a general sense and before abstract nouns;

Les hommes sont mortels.	Men are mortal.
L'amour de la patrie.	Love of country.

(2) before titles or adjectives preceding proper names, except in direct address; [1]

L'avocat Causse.	Lawyer Causse.
Le petit Alain.	Little Alain.
But:	
Bonjour, Docteur Martin.	Good morning, Dr. Martin.

[1] The definite article is not required after **monsieur, madame, mademoiselle,** etc., unless they are followed by a title. **Monsieur le président,** Mr. President.

(3) before names of countries and geographical divisions, except in certain cases after **de** and **en,** noted in §§ 6 and 7;

| Avez-vous visité la France? | Have you visited France? |

(4) to translate English *a* or *an* before nouns of weight or measure (but use **par** before expressions of time);

Dix sous la livre.	Ten cents a pound.
Vingt francs le mètre.	Twenty francs a meter.
But:	
Trente francs par jour.	Thirty francs a day.

(5) before the days of the week, to indicate repeated occurrence;

Il vient le lundi.	He comes (on) Mondays.
But:	
Il viendra lundi.	He will come (next) Monday.

(6) before the names of languages (all of which are masculine singular), except after **en.** The definite article is usually omitted also after **parler** standing immediately before the name of a language.

Nous étudions le français.	We are studying French.
Il parle couramment le français.	He speaks French fluently.
But:	
Je parle français.	I speak French.
Une lettre écrite en allemand.	A letter written in German.

4. The definite article is generally omitted after **de** in adjectival phrases and after **en.**

En avion. By airplane.	Une robe de soie. A silk dress.
En été. In summer.	Une leçon de français. A French les-
En ville. In town.	son.

5. The indefinite article is usually omitted in French, contrary to English usage, before an unmodified predicate noun (i. e., **être** + a noun) indicating profession or nationality.

| M. Robert est Anglais. | Mr. Robert is an Englishman. |
| M. Duval est avocat. | Mr. Duval is a lawyer. |

But:

Rodin était un sculpteur célèbre.   Rodin was a famous sculptor.

PREPOSITIONS WITH NAMES OF COUNTRIES AND CITIES

6. *To, in,* and *into* before names of countries and geographical divisions are translated by:

(1) **en** without the definite article before all feminine singular names;

(2) **à** with the definite article before feminine plural names and all masculine names;

(3) **dans** with the definite article before all names modified by an adjective or an adjectival phrase.
Names of countries ending in **-e,** except **le Mexique,** are feminine. All others are masculine.

En Europe; en Touraine.	In (to) Europe; in (to) Touraine.
Au Canada.	In (to) Canada.
Aux Etats-Unis.	In (to) the United States.
Aux Antilles.	In (to) the West Indies.
Dans l'Amérique du Sud.	In (to) South America.

7. *From* before names of countries and geographical divisions is translated by **de** without the definite article before all feminine singular names; by **de** with the definite article in all other cases.

Il vient d'Angleterre; du Mexique.   He comes from England; from Mexico.

8. *To, at,* and *in* before names of cities are translated by **à;** *from* is translated by **de.** The definite article is not expressed unless it is an integral part of the name.

A Paris; au Havre.	At (to) Paris; at (to) Havre.
Il part de Londres le dix.	He leaves London the tenth.

Un beau voyage

—Bonjour, Albert. Vous déjeunez tard ce matin.

—Bonjour, Raymond. Passez-moi le *Matin,* si vous l'avez lu. Tiens! Maryse Hilsz est rentrée. Je parie qu'il y avait un monde fou au terrain d'atterrissage du Bourget pour l'acclamer.

—Qui ça, Maryse Hilsz? J'ai bien remarqué dans le journal un cliché qui montrait une jolie femme à côté d'un avion, mais je n'y ai pas fait attention.

—Comment! Vous n'avez jamais entendu parler de la célèbre aviatrice?

—Ah! C'est une aviatrice?

—Parfaitement. Elle est partie de l'aérodrome du Bourget il y a deux mois pour l'Orient. Elle tentait d'enlever le record féminin de distance en ligne droite.

—Elle y a réussi, sans doute.

—Non. Mais elle a fait Paris-Saïgon en 92 heures 32 minutes.

—Paris-Saïgon? Où diable est Saïgon?

—Comment! Vous ignorez où se trouve Saïgon! Savez-vous, par hasard, que la Cochinchine, capitale Saïgon, est une colonie française en Indochine et que l'Indochine est une péninsule située à l'est de l'Inde et au sud de la Chine?

—Non. Je ne le savais pas. Ni vous non plus, avant de lire cet article-là.

—Bon, bon, Avouez, cependant, que c'est un beau raid que Mlle Hilsz a fait. Autrefois on mettait plus de temps pour aller de Paris à Londres.

—Combien d'étapes a-t-elle faites?

—Sept. La première à Alexandrie en Egypte, la dernière à Rangoon en Birmanie. Après une journée [2] de repos à Saïgon, elle est repartie pour la France. Mais, au retour, la malchance* l'a poursuivie. Une tempête l'a obligée à atterrir au milieu des déserts de l'Arabie, où des caravanes l'ont trouvée, assise près de son avion inutilisable.

---

[2] Jour, journée; soir, soirée; matin, matinée; an, année. The shorter forms name units of time. The longer forms stress extent of time—the whole day, a year full— or a period of time considered with regard to the events that fill it. Les jours fériés, holidays. Il y a un an, a year ago. Une belle matinée de printemps, a beautiful spring morning. Passer une soirée agréable, to spend a pleasant evening.

* Bad luck.

—Partir en avion et revenir à dos de chameau! C'est tout de même comique.

Conversation

1. Est-ce Albert ou Raymond qui déjeune tard? 2. Qu'est-ce que c'est que le *Matin?* 3. Quelles nouvelles y a-t-il dans le journal? 4. Qui est Maryse Hilsz? 5. Albert avait-il jamais entendu parler d'elle? 6. D'où est-ce qu'elle était partie? 7. Où voulait-elle aller? 8. Où se trouve Saïgon? 9. De quelle colonie française est-ce la capitale? 10. Où se trouve l'Indochine? 11. Nommez deux étapes que Maryse Hilsz a faites. 12. Où a-t-elle été obligée d'atterrir? 13. Comment son raid s'est-il terminé?

Composition

"Good morning, Albert. Aren't you ashamed to come down to the dining room at nine o'clock?"

"I always get up late on Tuesdays as I do not go to the university [in] [3] the morning. I am hungry. I'd like two boiled eggs and some toast."

"Impossible. There's only the breakfast that they always serve in France: a cup of coffee and a roll. We are not in the United States, you know."

"The coffee is good, anyway. Have you read the newspaper?"

"Here it is. There is an article on (à) the first page, which describes the landing of Maryse Hilsz at the airport of Le Bourget. You have heard of her endurance flight from Paris to Saïgon, haven't you?"

"Of course. On her return she landed in the desert to the south of Persia and lost her airplane. She ran across a caravan almost at once, and she came out of the desert on camel back."

"Have you ever been at Le Bourget? The airplane from Brazil arrives this afternoon. Do you want to go to see it land?"

"Gladly. Airplanes and airports interest me much. What line goes to Brazil?"

"Air-France. There are stops at Toulouse in southern France, at Casablanca in Morocco, at Dakar in Senegal, and at Natal in Brazil. They call this line 'le Mermoz,' in memory of the celebrated aviator

[3] Words enclosed in brackets, [ ], are to be omitted in translation; words enclosed in parentheses, ( ), are to be included in translation.

who disappeared with his plane in the Atlantic Ocean between Africa and South America."

"I should not like to be an aviator. The profession is too dangerous."

Drill Exercise

1. French is spoken in Indo-China as in all the French colonies. 2. The airplane for Brazil starts from Le Bourget airport on Wednesdays. 3. We are going to Europe this summer and expect to visit southern France, Switzerland, and Italy. 4. Our boat leaves Canada the fourth [4] of June. 5. My brother, who is a doctor, is going with us. 6. We shall land at Havre. 7. From there we shall fly to Marseilles in Provence, with a stop in Paris. 8. How long does it take to go from Paris to Marseilles by airplane? 9. He speaks German, and he reads Spanish and Italian rather well. 10. Our hotel is not expensive; we pay only forty-five francs a day. 11. He usually comes on Fridays, but next week he is coming on Saturday. 12. A French aviator made a nonstop flight from the United States to South America. 13. This meat costs eighty cents a pound. 14. What language is spoken in Canada? 15. Portuguese is spoken in Brazil, and English is spoken in the United States. 16. We shall be in town on Thursday. 17. We have a French class at the university at nine o'clock. 18. Good morning, Doctor Martin. Did you know that our friend Professor Duval has just arrived here?

Grammatical Exercise

Translate into French the words or phrases in parentheses:

1. Avez-vous jamais étudié (French)? 2. Non, mais je parle couramment (German). 3. Les (French lessons) dans ce livre sont très faciles. 4. Il vient toujours (on Mondays). 5. Combien d'étapes y a-t-il entre (France) et (Indo-China)? 6. Il est arrivé (at the airport of Le Bourget) à six heures. 7. Beaucoup de touristes viennent tous les étés (from the United States and Canada). 8. J'aime bien (France) et je passe toujours quelques semaines (in southern France). 9. (South America) et (the United States) sont maintenant de très bons voisins. 10. (French wines) ne sont pas très chers (in America). 11. Il est (a law-

---

[4] For numbers and dates, see §§ 57 and 158–160.

yer) et son frère, (Doctor Martin), est (a professor) à l'Ecole de Médecine.

Verb Review

Orthographic Peculiarities of the First Conjugation (cf. §§ 152–155)

commencer (à) [5] to commence	**jeter** to throw (away)
manger to eat	**appeler** to call; **s'appeler** to be named
espérer to hope	**geler** to freeze
préférer to prefer	**payer** to pay, pay for
acheter to buy	**essayer (de)** to try
se lever to get up	**nettoyer** to clean

1. I am buying this material at thirty francs a meter. 2. They were eating candy. 3. The aviator is trying to land. 4. The maids always clean the rooms on Thursdays. 5. At what time do we begin to play tennis? 6. I do not know him. What is his name? 7. They sent (*p. def.*) me this book. 8. Does he prefer to stay here with us? 9. How much does one pay for a railroad ticket from here to London? 10. I am hoping that she will not try to make a nonstop flight. 11. They always get up very early. 12. At what time do you get up? 13. Why does he throw that newspaper away? 14. It is very cold today; I hope that it will not freeze. 15. He began (*p. def.*) to study French in 1910.

[5] The preposition required by a verb before a following infinitive will be indicated in parentheses. Where there is no such indication, the verb is followed by a direct infinitive.

LESSON II

The Partitive Construction

THE PARTITIVE AS AN ADJECTIVE

9. Nouns may be used in two ways: (1) in a general sense, referring to an entire class of individuals or objects or to a whole; and (2) in a partitive sense, referring to some of the individuals that make up the class or to a part of the whole. When a noun is used in a general sense in English, *all, every, each,* or *the* is expressed or understood before the noun. When a noun is used in a partitive sense in English, *some* or *any* (in an affirmative sentence) or *no* or *not any* (in a negative sentence) is expressed or understood before the noun.

(All) automobiles are (The automobile is) a modern convenience.

(All) butter is expensive.

He has (some) friends everywhere.

10. Nouns used in a general sense in French are preceded by the definite article.

Les automobiles ne sont pas très chères.	Automobiles are not very expensive.
J'aime la musique.	I like music.

11. With nouns used in a partitive sense, the partitive idea (i. e., *some* or *any* expressed or understood before a noun) is regularly expressed in French by **de** + the definite article.

Avez-vous des amis à Paris?	Have you (any) friends in Paris?
Il y a de la viande et du pain sur la table.	There is (some) meat and (some) bread on the table.

8

12. The partitive is expressed by **de** alone:

(1) after a general negation; [1]
Nous n'avons pas d'argent.	We have no money.

(2) before a noun preceded by an adjective; [2]
Nous avons de bons amis.	We have (some) good friends.
But:	
Il a des livres français.	He has (some) French books.

(3) after nouns and adverbs of quantity, except **bien** *many* and **la plupart** *most,* which are followed by **de** + the definite article.
Une livre de sucre.	A pound of sugar.
Beaucoup d'amis.	Many friends.
But:	
La plupart des élèves.	Most (of the) pupils.

The commonest adverbs of quantity are:
assez enough	**peu** little, few [3]
autant as much, as many	**plus** more
beaucoup much, many, a lot	**tant** so much, so many
combien how much, how many	**trop** too much, too many
moins less, fewer	**un peu** a little

13. Both **de** and the article are omitted:

(1) after **ni ... ni;**
Il n'avait ni amis ni argent.	He had neither friends nor money.

(2) after **avec** before abstract nouns in adverbial phrases and after **sans;**
J'accepte avec plaisir.	I accept with pleasure (gladly).
Un homme sans expérience.	A man without experience.

---

[1] **Ne ... que** (*only*) is followed by **de** + the definite article. **Je n'ai que des livres anglais.** I have only English books.

[2] When adjective and noun are felt as an entity, the article is not omitted. **Des petits pois,** green peas. **Des jeunes gens,** young people, youths.

[3] *A few* is translated by **quelques. Nous passerons quelques jours à Paris.** We shall spend a few days in Paris.

(3) after many constructions composed of a verb, a past participle, an adjective, or a noun followed by **de.**

Une bourse pleine de monnaie.	A purse full of change.
Une table couverte de livres.	A table covered with books.
Il a besoin d'argent.	He needs money.

THE PARTITIVE AS A PRONOUN

14. The partitive (i. e., *some* or *any*) as a pronoun is expressed in French by **en.**

Il a de l'argent. Je n'en ai pas.	He has (some) money. I haven't
En avez-vous?	any. Have you any?

15. *Of it* or *of them* must always be expressed in French by **en** with numerals, adverbs of quantity, and nouns of quantity that are not followed by the nouns they measure.

Nous en avons six.	We have six (of them).
En avez-vous beaucoup?	Have you many (of them)?
Donnez-m'en une livre.	Give me a pound (of it).

Au restaurant

—Où dînons-nous ce soir? demanda Albert. La plupart des restaurants que je connais dans ce quartier-ci ne sont pas bien fameux.

—J'en connais un excellent, répondit Raymond. Seulement il est un peu cher. N'importe. J'ai reçu aujourd'hui de l'argent de chez moi et je vous offre un repas à l'Ecu de France.

—J'accepte toujours sans hésitation l'invitation d'un camarade qui a les [4] poches pleines d'argent. Nous prendrons un taxi, puisque c'est vous qui payerez.

Un quart d'heure plus tard les deux amis entrèrent dans un restaurant situé près de la Gare de l'Est et fréquenté surtout par de solides bourgeois français et par des Belges de passage à Paris. Ils montèrent au deuxième étage et choisirent une table près d'une fenêtre.

—Les hors-d'œuvre sont la spécialité de cette maison, dit Raymond. J'espère que vous les aimez. On en a de toutes sortes. On en a même

[4] For the use of the definite article, see § 101.

trop. Je n'en ai jamais vu autant ailleurs. Garçon, apportez-nous des hors-d'œuvre.

—Bien, monsieur. Et ensuite? Un bifteck peut-être? Ou est-ce que monsieur préférerait du veau aux épinards?

—Ni bifteck ni veau. Vous nous apporterez un poulet rôti et une bouteille de Sauternes. Aimez-vous les artichauts, Albert?

—Pas beaucoup. Je prendrai plutôt des petits pois et une salade de laitue après.

—Votre restaurant est épatant, dit Albert beaucoup plus tard, en redemandant du café noir. On y dîne très bien.

—Trop bien, répondit Raymond avec regret, en regardant l'addition que le garçon venait d'apporter sur un petit plateau d'argent. Nous avons mangé pour cent cinquante francs sans compter le pourboire. Espérons que vous avez de quoi payer un taxi, car il ne me restera plus que quelques sous.

Conversation

1. Qu'est-ce qu'Albert demande à son ami Raymond? 2. Où se trouve le restaurant dont parle Raymond? 3. Pourquoi Raymond paye-t-il le repas? 4. Comment Albert et Raymond vont-ils au restaurant? 5. Comment s'appelle ce restaurant? 6. Quels sont les clients qui le fréquentent? 7. Quelle est la spécialité de la maison? 8. Expliquez en français la phrase: 'spécialité de la maison.' 9. Nommez en français quelques hors-d'œuvre. 10. Qu'est-ce que les amis prennent après les hors-d'œuvre? 11. Que boit-on avec le poulet? 12. A combien s'élevait l'addition et qui l'a payée? 13. Est-ce que nos amis sont rentrés en autobus?

Composition

"Waiter! The bill, if you please. One hundred and ten francs. How much of [a] tip shall I give him, Albert?"

"Let's see. Ten per cent would make eleven francs. Give twelve to the waiter. He'll be satisfied (with it). Most Americans give too much. The dinner was excellent, wasn't it? I've never eaten so many hors-d'œuvre. We have them only rarely at my boardinghouse."

"It is the specialty of this restaurant. They serve thirty-two varieties (of them), and the bourgeois who come here are very fond of them.

By the way, what do you think of your boardinghouse? If you don't like it, you can find others without difficulty. The Latin Quarter with its thousands of students is full of them."

"I know it. There are lots of little bourgeois boardinghouses where for very little money one can obtain excellent meals and fairly good rooms. They have neither central heating nor bathroom, but students are never cold, and one can always go to a bathing establishment. Of course, that does not concern rich Americans like you, who rent furnished apartments."

"I am an American, of course. But I am not rich, and I haven't any apartment. My room is on (à) the fourth [5] floor, and there isn't any elevator. Fortunately for me, I have rich comrades like you who are always hungry and thirsty and can offer their friends delicious soups, fresh vegetables, beefsteaks and roasts, wines and coffee at restaurants like the Ecu de France."

"There's one thing that you have forgotten. I did not promise to take you back home, and we are far from the Latin Quarter. If you haven't enough to pay for a taxi, you will walk home, for I have only two francs left."

Drill Exercise

1. There are many good restaurants in Paris. 2. I know an excellent one near the Gare de l'Est. 3. Meals in my boardinghouse are not very good. 4. He has good friends in almost all the large cities of Europe. 5. Here is some writing paper, but I don't find any stamps. 6. This hotel has neither central heating nor elevator. 7. Very few Americans want to spend so much money for a room. 8. If he gives me any, I shall accept them with pleasure. 9. Are you going to order hors-d'œuvre, or do you prefer soups? 10. I am glad to have friends who have their (les) pockets full of money. 11. Are there any chops on (à) the bill of fare today? Order me two, well done. 12. A table in the dining room was covered with hors-d'œuvre. 13. I am spending a few days with relatives. 14. I shall take French pastry and black coffee. 15. If you like candy, I shall buy a pound. 16. Only French books are sold in this shop. 17. Most Americans speak only English. 18. As I do not eat meat, I am ordering only vegetables. 19. Are there

[5] In French: third. The ground floor is le rez-de-chaussée; the second floor, le premier étage, etc.

any interesting museums in Paris? Yes, I have already visited four.
20. I have enough butter; the waiter has just given me some. 21. Do
you like green peas? Yes, I shall order some green peas.

Grammatical Exercise I

Where necessary, replace the dash by the proper form of the definite
article or of the partitive as adjective:

1. Nous avons commandé — pain et — café noir. 2. Aimez-vous —
œufs à la coque? 3. On trouve ici — excellents hors-d'œuvre. 4. Je
prends — petits pois, — pommes de terre et — tomates farcies. 5. La
plupart — Français boivent — vin avec leurs repas. 6. Il n'y avait ni
— pain ni — beurre sur la table. 7. On nous attend avec — impatience.
8. Je n'ai pas — amis à Paris mais j'y ai — agréables connaissances.
9. Est-ce que — repas sont bons à votre pension? 10. Nous n'avons
pas besoin — argent. 11. Je n'aime pas — café au lait; je ne prends
que — thé. 12. Avez-vous assez — pain noir? 13. Très peu — Américains parlent bien le français. 14. Sans — argent, on ne peut rien faire.
15. Je ne vois pas autant — touristes que l'année passée.

Grammatical Exercise II

Insert **en** in the proper place and translate into English:

1. Je prends toujours le matin. 2. Donnez-lui sept. 3. Combien avez-
vous? 4. Nous n'avons que trois. 5. J'ai plus que lui. 6. N'y a-t-il pas
sur la table? 7. Je n'ai pas autant que vous. 8. Il ne leur a pas donné.
9. Elle a trop, mais nous n'avons pas. 10. Voulez-vous? Non, j'ai beaucoup.

Verb Review

être to be; cf. § 149
avoir to have; cf. § 148
  avoir chaud to be warm
  avoir froid to be cold
  avoid faim to be hungry
  avoir soif to be thirsty

avoir sommeil to be sleepy
avoir raison (de) to be right
avoir tort (de) to be wrong
avoir peur (de) to be afraid
avoir honte (de) to be ashamed
avoir besoin de to have need of

1. I am very [6] warm in this room. 2. They would be ashamed to arrive late. 3. What do you need? I don't need anything. 4. They were sleepy. 5. Were you cold when you got up? It was very cold in my room. 6. He is always right. 7. He does not want us to be afraid of it. 8. Will he need money? No, he will not need any. 9. They are afraid that he will be there. 10. Be good, and you will be happy. 11. Are you hungry? No, but I am very thirsty. 12. Let's be brave, and let's have patience. 13. I am very hungry. 14. They would be very cold here in winter. 15. You were (*p. indef.*) right to wait for him. 16. Marie Antoinette was (*impf.*) extravagant, and she always needed (*impf.*) money. 17. Have you been to England? 18. He wants them to be happy.

[6] **Très**—not bien—is now generally used to translate *very* with these idioms.

Adjectives: Formation of the Feminine and of the Plural, Agreement, and Position

FORMATION OF THE FEMININE OF ADJECTIVES

16. The feminine of adjectives is regularly formed by adding **-e** to the masculine singular. Adjectives ending in **-e** remain unchanged.

charmé, charmée delighted   **facile, facile** easy

17. Irregular formation of the feminine:

(1) Final **-er** becomes **-ère**; final **-et** becomes **-ète.**

cher, chère dear   **complet, complète** complete

(2) Final **-f** becomes **-ve**; final **-eux** and frequently final **-eur** become **-euse. Meilleur** and adjectives ending in **-érieur** form their feminine regularly.

neuf, neuve (brand) new   **causeur, causeuse** talkative
heureux, heureuse happy   **supérieur, supérieure** superior

(3) Final **-el, -eil, -ien, -on,** and usually **-s** and **-t** double the final consonant and add **-e.**

ancien, ancienne old, former   **gros, grosse** big
bas, basse low   **pareil, pareille** like, such
bon, bonne good   **sot, sotte** stupid
cruel, cruelle cruel

(4) Five adjectives have a double form in the masculine singular. The form ending in **-l** is used only before a masculine singular noun beginning with a vowel or **h** mute.

beau, bel, belle beautiful, fine   vieux, vieil, vieille old
nouveau, nouvel, nouvelle new,   mou, mol, molle soft
    another   fou, fol, folle mad

(5) The following common adjectives, not classified above, also
form their feminine irregularly:

blanc, blanche white   gentil, gentille nice
doux, douce sweet   long, longue long
faux, fausse false   public, publique public
favori, favorite favorite   sec, sèche dry
frais, fraîche cool, fresh

FORMATION OF THE PLURAL OF ADJECTIVES

18. The plural of adjectives is regularly formed by adding **-s** to
the singular; but adjectives ending in **-s** or **-x** remain unchanged
in the plural, those ending in **-eau** add **-x**, and those ending in
-al drop this ending and add **-aux.**

grand(e), grand(e)s tall, large   égal, égaux equal
gris, gris gray   heureux, heureux happy

AGREEMENT OF ADJECTIVES

19. Adjectives agree in number and gender with the noun or
nouns they modify. An adjective modifying two or more nouns
of different genders is masculine plural.

La fillette est très jolie.   The little girl is very pretty.
Des poésies et des romans intéres-   Some interesting poems and novels.
    sants.

POSITION OF ADJECTIVES

20. There is no invariable rule for the position of adjectives in
French, but the normal position of an adjective is after the noun
it modifies. In general, adjectives used in a literal sense to define
or to emphasize, such as adjectives of color, shape, nationality,

and religion, follow the noun. But adjectives used figuratively or to express a quality that is inherent or taken for granted usually precede the noun.

Une table carrée.	A square table.
Une église fameuse.	A famous church.
La fameuse cathédrale de Notre-Dame.	The famous cathedral of Notre-Dame.
Une porte étroite.	A narrow door.
Une étroite amitié.	A close friendship.
La République Française.	The French Republic.

21. The following very common adjectives usually precede the nouns they modify:

beau	gentil	joli	méchant	petit *autre*
bon	gros	long	meilleur	vieux *court*
grand	jeune	mauvais	moindre	vilain

22. Two or more adjectives modifying the same noun follow the above rules unless they are connected by **et**, in which case they both usually follow the noun.

Une jolie petite fille.	A pretty little girl.
Une grande maison verte.	A big green house.
Un jeune homme grand et beau.	A tall and handsome young man.

23. Certain adjectives vary in meaning according to position.

Mon cher ami.	My dear friend.
Un livre cher.	An expensive book.
Un ancien voisin.	A former neighbor.
L'histoire ancienne.	Ancient history.
Un nouveau livre.	A new (another) book.
Un livre nouveau.	A new (recently published) book.
Le pauvre homme.	The poor (wretched) man.
Un homme pauvre.	A poor (indigent) man.

24. Note the position of a predicate adjective in exclamations.

Comme (Que) Marie est jolie!	How pretty Mary is!

On marie Annette

Annette avait passé toute la matinée sur la plage. C'était une belle jeune fille svelte et vigoureuse qui aimait les sports et nageait comme un poisson. Elle songeait à ce grand garçon élégant en flanelle blanche et en chandail rayé, qui l'avait reconduite chez elle et qu'elle allait revoir le soir au Casino.

Tout à coup la porte de sa chambre s'ouvrit et sa mère entra.

—Ma petite fille, dit-elle, l'air mystérieux et solennel, tâche tout à l'heure d'être à peu près correcte, surtout au Casino où nous irons prendre des glaces. Ne danse pas tout le temps et ne va pas causer dans les coins avec tous les jeunes gens de ta bande.

—Pourquoi? demanda Annette, inquiète.

—Parce qu'on me propose un mariage pour toi, une affaire magnifique. C'est un ancien commerçant très riche et encore très jeune.

—Cela veut dire?

—Oh, il n'a pas l'air d'avoir quarante ans. Et puis il veut bien t'épouser sans dot.

—Alors il doit être affreux: gants gris, pantalon rayé, veston croisé noir, cravate noire, chapeau melon, l'air d'un banquier en retraite. Ce sera gai pour moi!

—Mais ma fille ...

—Oh, je sais ce que tu vas me dire. Les temps sont difficiles. Pour vivre il faut dépenser de l'argent. Pour dépenser de l'argent il faut en avoir. Or, nous n'en avons pas. Par conséquent, il faut que j'épouse quelqu'un qui en a. Amène-moi donc ce monsieur. Je tâcherai de ne pas être trop mal disposée envers lui.

Il vint. On l'examina. Il n'était vraiment pas trop mal. Il était même assez jeune. Annette ne regretterait pas trop le jeune homme au (*with the*) chandail rayé.

Conversation

1. Où est-ce qu'Annette avait passé la matinée? 2. Décrivez Annette. 3. Décrivez le beau garçon. 4. Qui est entré chez Annette? 5. Quels conseils sa mère lui a-t-elle donnés? 6. Pourquoi? 7. Décrivez le prétendant d'Annette. 8. Est-ce que la famille d'Annette était riche? 9. Expliquez en français ce que c'est qu'une dot. 10. Comment Annette

se représentait-elle le prétendant? 11. Croyez-vous qu'Annette regrette beaucoup le beau garçon? 12. Pourquoi pas?

Composition

Annette was not one of those happy and frivolous girls who pass their afternoons on the beach and who dance every evening at the Casino with young men in white flannels or in dinner coat[s]. Her parents were dead, and she lived with her poor old grandmother. She had no dowry, and in real life the Prince Charming of a girl without a dowry is usually a retired businessman who is (has) twice her age. Monsieur Dupont was, in fact, thirty-eight years old. He was [a] bachelor and [a] director in a government office. He had never had the time to think about marriage, but, when Annette entered his office one day to ask for a place, he began to think about it immediately. And Annette also. He was not bad-looking. He was even elegant when he came to see her, wearing gray gloves, a double-breasted black coat, and striped trousers. How happy she would be, if he asked her to marry him! But that was impossible, for he had found for her a place in the South.

"Aren't you sorry to leave Paris?" he asked her.

"Oh, yes, but I can't refuse this position, when times are so hard."

"And if I gave you a means of remaining in Paris? a heroic means?"

"I am courageous," she answered, looking at him with (de) her big blue eyes.

"Well..." He hesitated; then, very quickly, almost rudely, he added: "Will you marry me?"

A moment of silence.

"Do you find me too old? You seem frightened."

"Frightened? Oh, no; happy. It is too beautiful. I don't dare believe (in) it."

Drill Exercise

1. M. Martin has two very amusing little cousins (*f*.). 2. Marie is always gay and happy. 3. In the (**au**) center of the room there was a large square table. 4. The public schools are generally very good. 5. An ugly little man was seated near the narrow door. 6. He was

wearing gray gloves, a derby, and striped trousers. 7. The dear old lady was very talkative. 8. I like to read interesting books and plays. 9. I think you will find some in that blue box. 10. He is a very nice young man, and his little sister is beautiful and intelligent. 11. Don't be ill-disposed toward your old friends. 12. How charming she was when she received us! 13. She is buying a new dress and some silk stockings. 14. In front of us there was a high green house with a beautiful English garden. 15. Meals here are excellent: fresh vegetables, delicious meat, and good black coffee.

Grammatical Exercise

Replace the masculine singular form of the adjective given in parentheses by the correct form required in each case:

1. une manière (naïf)
2. une odeur très (doux)
3. une brise (léger)
4. une (fameux) cathédrale
5. une robe (neuf)
6. ma pièce (favori)
7. des feuilles (sec)
8. une (faux) alerte
9. mes (meilleur) amies
10. des pages (blanc)
11. mes (ancien) camarades
12. des leçons (facile)
13. une vie (actif)
14. des phrases (complet)
15. des fleurs très (cher)

Verb Review

aller to go; cf. § 156
  s'en aller to go away

envoyer to send; cf. § 156
  envoyer chercher to send for

1. Where did she go? 2. I sent them to Jean, but he had already gone away. 3. We are afraid that they may not go with us. 4. You will send them at once. 5. Don't go away now; it is too late. 6. He is sending us the presents tomorrow. 7. Send me some, but don't send me too many. 8. Do you want us to send them to Paris? 9. I would go with you if it were not so hot. 10. Why does she send for her? 11. She has already gone away. 12. He sent (*p. def.*) the books to me. 13. He used to send us fresh flowers every day. 14. They will not go away if it rains. 15. Where are they going? Who sent for them? 16. She was going to school then. 17. Last summer they went (*p. def.*) to France.

LESSON IV

The Comparison of Adjectives
Interrogative Word Order

THE COMPARISON OF ADJECTIVES

25. (1) The comparative of an adjective is formed by placing **plus** *more*, **moins** *less*, or **aussi** (**si** after a negative) *so* before the adjective and **que** *than, as* after the adjective. If a verb is used in completing a comparison after **plus ... que** or **moins ... que,** that verb is usually preceded by **ne.**

Il est plus (moins, aussi) grand que moi.	He is taller than (not so tall as, just as tall as) I am.
Jean n'est pas si fort en français que sa sœur.	John is not so good in French as his sister.
Il est plus riche que je ne le croyais.	He is richer than I thought.

(2) *Than* before an infinitive is usually translated by **que de.**

Il est plus facile de lire le français que de le parler.	It is easier to read French than to speak it.

26. (1) The superlative of an adjective is formed by placing the proper form of the definite article before the comparative form. If the adjective follows the noun, the definite article as a sign of the superlative must not be omitted.

La pièce la moins intéressante de l'année.	The least interesting play of the year.
La plus belle ville du monde.	The most beautiful city in the world.

(2) After a possessive adjective the article is omitted if the adjective precedes its noun.

Mes plus chers amis.	My dearest friends.
But:	
Mes livres les plus chers.	My most precious books.

(3) *In* after a superlative is usually translated by **de.**

Le meilleur élève de la classe.	The best student in the class.

27. The following adjectives are irregularly compared:

bon good	**meilleur** better	**le meilleur** best
mauvais bad	**plus mauvais** ⎫ worse **pire** ⎭	**le plus mauvais** ⎫ worst **le pire** ⎭
petit small	**plus petit** smaller **moindre** lesser	**le plus petit** smallest **le moindre** least

Le plus mauvais élève de la classe.	The poorest student in the class.
Un criminel de la pire espèce.	A criminal of the worst sort.
De deux maux, choisissons le moindre.	Of two evils, let us choose the lesser.
Marie est plus petite que vous.	Mary is smaller than you are.

INTERROGATIVE WORD ORDER

28. Subject pronouns (also **ce** and **on**) follow the verb, as in English, and are joined to it by a hyphen.

Sait-il votre adresse?	Does he know your address?

29. Subject nouns (or possessive, demonstrative, or indefinite pronouns) stand before the verb and are repeated after it by the suitable conjunctive pronouns.

Vos parents demeurent-ils ici?	Do your parents live here?
Cela est-il vrai?	Is that true?

30. After certain interrogative expressions such as **qui, que, quel, combien, comment,** and **où,** noun subjects frequently follow the verb, except in compound tenses.

Où sont vos livres?	Where are your books?
Comment s'appelle ce monsieur? ⎱	
Comment ce monsieur s'appelle-t-il? ⎰	What is that gentleman's name?
Quand Molière a-t-il écrit "L'Avare"?	When did Molière write "L'Avare"?

31. Est-ce que *is it that,* placed before, or **n'est-ce pas** *is it not so,* placed after, any declarative sentence, forms a question without changing the word order. **Est-ce que** followed by the declarative word order may also be used after the interrogative expressions **qui, combien, où,** etc.

Est-ce que Joseph les lui a donnés?	Did Joseph give them to him?
Joseph les lui a donnés, n'est-ce pas?	Joseph gave them to him, didn't he?
Combien est-ce que vous avez payé ces livres?	How much did you pay for these books?

32. The interrogative order is also used in explanatory statements after direct quotations and frequently after the adverbs **aussi** (*so, therefore*), **peut-être,** and **à peine,** if they stand at the beginning of a clause.

—Prenons un autobus, dit Marie.	"Let's take a bus," said Mary.
Peut-être a-t-il oublié son billet.	Perhaps he has forgotten his ticket.
But:	
Il a peut-être oublié son billet.	He has perhaps forgotten his ticket.
Peut-être qu'il a oublié son billet.	Perhaps he has forgotten his ticket.

Aux Deux Magots

—Les cafés parisiens, dit Raymond, comme vous l'avez certainement remarqué, ont des tables en plein air et les Parisiens aiment y aller vers le soir prendre un apéritif et voir passer le monde des boulevards. Voici un des cafés les plus caractéristiques du Quartier Latin, celui des Deux Magots. Il doit son nom à deux grotesques figures chinoises qui en ornent la grande salle. Asseyons-nous un moment à la terrasse. Ce sera moins fatigant que de continuer notre promenade.

—Je veux bien. D'ailleurs, j'ai très soif.

—Que prenez-vous alors?

—Je prendrai une tasse de thé avec des petits fours. Je préfère le thé aux meilleurs apéritifs.

—Vous avez sans doute raison. C'est une boisson aussi agréable que digestive. Moi, cependant, je préfère la bière.

—On est bien ici en plein air, dit Albert. Mais que font toutes ces personnes qu'on voit à l'intérieur du café? Comme distraction, il n'y a pas même d'orchestre.

—On écrit des lettres, on cause avec ses amis, on lit les journaux. Les cafés sont abonnés aux principaux journaux et aux meilleures revues. Ce sont de véritables clubs, où les habitués viennent tous les soirs.

—Et cette pile de soucoupes que je remarque devant ces trois messieurs là-bas, qu'est-ce que c'est?

—Ces soucoupes représentent le nombre de consommations qu'on leur a servies. Quand un client s'en va, il paie le montant des prix marqués sur les soucoupes. Ces messieurs-là ont été moins sages que nous. Je n'ai que deux soucoupes devant moi et vous n'en avez qu'une.

—Garçon, l'addition. Non, n'insistez pas, dit Albert, ou je vous en voudrai. C'est moi qui paie. Dix francs cinquante. C'est moins cher que je ne le croyais.

Conversation

1. En général, où se trouvent les tables des cafés parisiens? 2. Pourquoi est-ce qu'on place les tables en plein air? 3. A quoi le café des Deux Magots doit-il son nom? 4. Pourquoi les amis s'asseyent-ils à la terrasse? 5. Qu'est-ce que Raymond décide de commander? Et Albert? 6. Que font les personnes à l'intérieur du café? 7. Expliquez la pile de soucoupes devant ces trois messieurs-là. 8. Comment le client sait-il ce qu'il doit payer? 9. Combien de soucoupes est-ce que Raymond a devant lui? 10. Comment dit-on en français: "Waiter, the bill"?

Composition

"Five o'clock already," said Raymond. "It is later than I thought."
"Will you sit down on (à) the terrace of the Deux Magots? It is.

the best café in this quarter and not much more expensive than the others."

"I am willing. I should rather take a cup of tea here than go back to the boardinghouse."

They sit down at a table. The waiter removes a pile of saucers, representing the number of drinks served to the last customer, and brings them tea and cakes.

"Do you see those two gentlemen over there?" said Raymond. "Weren't they here yesterday?"

"Doubtless. Every café has its habitués. At the Dôme you will see artists as grotesque as the Bohemians of (the) comic opera. La Régence is the rendezvous of the most famous chess players in Paris."

"The Emperor Joseph II of Austria went there once. He was not so proud as his sister, Marie Antoinette, and one day, in order to avoid the crowd that was waiting for him at the Palais-Royal, he entered that café. The barmaid served him his coffee in the empty hall. 'That cursed emperor is stealing all my customers,' she explained. 'Have you ever seen him?' asked Joseph. 'No, but I'd like to see him,' she answered. Joseph got up and threw a louis on the table. 'What a beautiful coin!' said the barmaid. 'It is the head of our good Louis XVI.' 'Yes, madam,' said the stranger, 'and here is the head of the emperor.' He took off his hat (in) smiling, bowed, and left, without waiting for his change."

"Well," said Albert, "we shall not be as polite as the emperor. I have not the slightest intention of leaving without counting my change."

Drill Exercise

1. He is taller than I thought. 2. It is more interesting to write a book than to read it. 3. Here is the most interesting café in the quarter. 4. She is the most intelligent pupil in the class. 5. Where do her parents live? Perhaps they live here. 6. I hope that this story will not be so long. 7. Those two boys are not so rich as you think. 8. How much did you pay for these cakes? 9. Doesn't John want to go with us? 10. What is her friend's name? His name is Alan. 11. She is taller than he, but she is not so tall as her sister. 12. Your best friends live in Paris, don't they? 13. It is easier to read French than to write it. 14. He is the best friend that I have. 15. He speaks French

much better than English. 16. You have chosen the worst moment to (pour) find a seat (place). 17. Are French newspapers as interesting as French reviews? 18. To how many reviews do you subscribe? 19. To listen to a good orchestra is one of his greatest pleasures. 20. These are my most valuable books. 21. Shall we sit down on (à) the terrace or inside the café? 22. New York is the largest city in the world. 23. She is much more intelligent than you believe. 24. He is just as old as I [am]. 25. How much did Mary pay for that hat?

Verb Review

vouloir to wish; cf. § 156
  en vouloir à to be angry with, have a grudge against, be put out with
  vouloir bien to be willing to, be kind enough to; (condl. tense) should like very much to

ouvrir to open; (intrans.) s'ouvrir; cf. § 156
couvrir to cover
découvrir to discover
offrir (de) to offer
souffrir to suffer

1. I am sorry that he does not wish to go with us. 2. John and Mary would like very much to be here. 3. Do they want to see us now? 4. At what hour do the doors open? 5. Columbus discovered (p. def.) America in 1492. 6. What did he offer to do? He offered to go with me. 7. The ground was covered with (de) snow. 8. If he suffered as much as that, he would go to see a doctor. 9. He does not want us to open the door. 10. I don't want him to offer me that. 11. He opened (p. def.) the door, entered (p. def.) the room, and began (p. def.) to read. 12. They do not want to stay here. 13. I shall open the door. 14. He has not offered me what I wanted. 15. We are sorry that he suffers so much.

The Present and Future Tenses
The Plural of Nouns

THE PRESENT TENSE

33. The present tense is used in general as in English. It translates all three forms of the English present tense.

Il travaille.   He works (does work, is working).

34. The present tense is used in French with **depuis, depuis quand, depuis que,** and **il y a...que** to denote an act or a state that began in the past and is still going on. English usage here usually requires the progressive form of the present perfect tense, *has (have) been + -ing.*

Depuis quand êtes-vous ici?	How long have you been here?
Je suis ici depuis trois jours.	I have been here for three days.
Depuis que je suis ici, je n'ai vu personne.	Since I have been here, I have seen no one.
Il y a huit jours qu'il ne travaille plus.	He hasn't been working for a week.

THE FUTURE AND FUTURE PERFECT TENSES

35. The future and future perfect tenses are used in general as in English.

36. The future and future perfect tenses are used, however, in French to translate the English present and perfect tenses after such conjunctions as **lorsque** *when,* **quand** *when,* **aussitôt que** *as soon as,* and **dès que** *as soon as,* when futurity is implied.

Je le lui donnerai, quand je le verrai.	I shall give it to him when I see him.
Quand je l'aurai acheté, je vous l'enverrai.	When I have bought it, I shall send it to you.
Dites-lui de venir me voir, aussitôt que vous le trouverez.	Tell him to come and see me, as soon as you find him.

When futurity is implied, the verb in the main clause of the English sentence is in the future tense or is an imperative. *When* in the sense of *whenever* does not imply futurity but refers to an habitual act. In such clauses, **lorsque** and **quand** are used in French with the present tense.

Je le vois tous les jours quand je suis à l'université.	I see him every day when(ever) I am at the university.

37. *Will* denoting volition and not futurity—that is, when it implies willingness or unwillingness—is rendered in French by the proper tense of **vouloir.**

Il ne veut pas venir.	He will not (refuses to) come.
Il ne voudra pas venir.	He will not (be willing to) come.

THE PLURAL OF NOUNS

38. Some exceptions to the regular plural in -s are:

(1) Nouns in **-s, -x,** and **-z** remain unchanged in the plural.
   le bras, les bras the arm(s)
   la voix, les voix the voice(s)

(2) Nouns in **-au** and **-eu** and certain nouns in **-ou** add **x** to form the plural.
   le château, les châteaux the castle(s)
   le jeu, les jeux the game(s)
   le bijou, les bijoux the jewel(s)
   But:
   le sou, les sous the cent(s)

(3) Most nouns in **-al** and a few nouns in **-ail** change to **-aux.**
  le cheval, les chevaux the horse(s)
  le journal, les journaux the newspaper(s)
  le travail, les travaux the work(s)
  le vitrail, les vitraux the stained-glass window(s)
  But:
  le bal, les bals the dance(s)

(4) Note the following irregular plurals:
  le ciel, les cieux the sky (skies)
  l'œil, les yeux the eye(s)

39. Unhyphenated compound nouns are treated as a single noun. In the case of hyphenated compound nouns, usage varies according to their formation. The following common nouns should be noted.
  la grand'mère, les grand'mères the grandmother(s)
  le grand-père, les grands-pères the grandfather(s)
  le chef-d'œuvre, les chefs-d'œuvre the masterpiece(s)
  le (les) porte-monnaie the coin purse(s)
  le (les) tête-à-tête the private interview(s)

40. Names of persons and families are generally not pluralized.
  Les Duval the Duvals

L'aventure d'un touriste

Monsieur Parker est à Paris depuis six mois et il n'est guère sorti de la capitale. Il a bien vu les fameux vitraux de la cathédrale de Chartres et il a perdu pas mal de billets de cent sous aux courses de chevaux à Auteuil, mais il ne connaît pas la province.

—Prenons notre valise, se dit-il un jour, et allons voir les châteaux de la Loire.

Monsieur Parker prend donc son pardessus, son chapeau et sa valise, hèle un taxi et se fait conduire à la Gare d'Orléans où il demande un billet d'aller et retour pour Tours. Trois heures plus tard il dîne tranquillement dans un hôtel de l'ancienne capitale de la Touraine.

Tout à coup il lève les yeux et aperçoit devant lui trois sergents de ville.

—Qu'est-ce qu'on me veut? se demande-t-il. J'ai déjà montré mon passeport et ma carte d'identité au gérant de l'hôtel.

—Monsieur, lui dit un des agents, vous serez bien aimable de passer au bureau du gérant.

Très inquiet et assez curieux de savoir de quoi il s'agit, monsieur Parker suit les deux agents.

—Voulez-vous bien ôter votre veston?

Inutile de protester. Monsieur Parker enlève son veston et son gilet.

—Votre chemise aussi.

Les deux agents examinent soigneusement son dos ainsi mis à nu.

—Mille pardons, monsieur. Nous nous sommes trompés.

Les agents se confondent en excuses.

—Expliquez-moi, au moins, . . . supplie monsieur Parker. Pour qui me prenait-on?

—Vous avez le malheur, monsieur, de ressembler à un meurtrier que nous recherchons depuis longtemps. Un voyageur a cru vous reconnaître dans le rapide de Paris. Le meurtrier a une marque de naissance à l'épaule gauche, mais vous n'en avez pas, heureusement pour vous. Nous sommes désolés de vous avoir incommodé.

Conversation

1. Depuis quand est-ce que M. Parker est à Paris? 2. A-t-il visité la province? 3. Comment a-t-il passé son temps? 4. Où se trouve la Touraine? 5. Pour quels monuments la Touraine est-elle fameuse? 6. Savez-vous les noms de quelques châteaux tourangeaux? 7. Qui vient interrompre le dîner de M. Parker à Tours? 8. Où veut-on emmener M. Parker? 9. Que faut-il qu'il fasse? 10. Pourquoi examine-t-on le dos de M. Parker? 11. Expliquez en français la phrase: une marque de naissance.

Composition

"Hello, Albert. I've been looking for you since yesterday. Will you go to Tours with me tomorrow?"

"I should like to visit the famous châteaux of Touraine with you, but I am expecting the visit of an old classmate, who will land Friday at Havre."

"Come along (**Venez donc**). Your friend will spend a lot of time in Paris. You will be able to see him when you come back from Tours."

"Impossible. He does not know Paris, and he will be angry with me if he does not find me at the station Friday evening. Besides, I promised to take him to his hotel. By the way, when you arrive at Tours, go to the Faisan d'Or. It is a little more expensive than most of the hotels, but you will not regret the few extra pennies that you will spend there. I always go there when I am in Tours."

"Thank you. I shall follow your advice."

"An amusing adventure happened to my friend Parker at Tours. He was sitting in a café when two policemen asked him to go to the manager's office. They tell him to take off his coat and his shirt, and they examine carefully his bare back. Then they make profuse apologies. They have been seeking for a long time a murderer who has a birthmark on (**à**) his right shoulder. They have made a mistake. They are very sorry. Poor Parker, who does not speak French well, was very scared. He did not understand the explanations of the policemen, and I believe that he does not yet know what it was [all] about."

Drill Exercise I

1. We have been studying French for two months. 2. I shall tell him that when I see him. 3. As soon as they see us, they will recognize us. 4. How long have you been waiting for me? 5. We saw them two weeks ago. 6. Stars resemble jewels in the (**au**) sky. 7. The Parkers do not want to come with us. 8. Whenever I see a beggar, I always give him a few cents. 9. Horses and dogs are the animals I like the best. 10. They have been working for hours in the garden. 11. Explain that to him when he arrives. 12. Since we have been here, we have not seen many of our friends. 13. When he lands in Havre, he will send us a post card. 14. We went to Chartres a week ago to see the marvelous stained-glass windows. 15. He did not want to go to Tours with us.

Drill Exercise II

1. When I have visited Tours, I shall go to Orleans. 2. When I saw John, he was working in the garden. 3. My grandmother will be eighty years old next week. 4. As soon as you see her, tell her what I said. 5. How long have you been sitting here? For an hour. 6. The newspapers in this city are very interesting. 7. I have been here since yesterday. 8. The Martins will be waiting for us, I am sure of it. 9. When I see him, he is always studying French. 10. The most beautiful stained-glass windows are in Chartres. 11. When you arrive in Paris, go to see my cousin. 12. We have been studying our lessons for two hours. 13. I shall tell you what he thinks, when he has left. 14. Since he has been in France, he does not write to me any more. 15. How long have they been speaking French? For three years.

Verb Review

croire to believe, think; cf. § 156   **dire (de)** to say, tell; cf. § 156

1. Believe what (**ce que**) he tells you. 2. Say what you believe, and we will believe you. 3. When I tell him that, he will be put out with me. 4. He doesn't believe us. 5. If he knew you, he would believe what you say. 6. They will tell us not to stay here. 7. I shall believe that when I see it. 8. I am sorry that he does not tell me what he wants. 9. It is necessary that we believe them. 10. If he had believed that, he would not have said it. 11. He believed (*p. def.*) what they told (*p. def.*) him. 12. Let him say what he will (*fut.*), I shall not believe it.

LESSON VI

The Past Tenses

THE IMPERFECT TENSE

41. The imperfect tense is used:

(1) to express an action going on or a condition existing at a certain moment in the past [usually rendered in English by the progressive form of the past tense, *was (were) +-ing*];

Il entrait dans un magasin, quand je l'ai vu.	He was entering a store when I saw him.
Il était très malade, quand nous sommes arrivés.	He was very sick when we arrived.

(2) to express repeated or customary action in past time (frequently translated in English by *used to* or *would* + an infinitive);

Il chantait pendant qu'il travaillait.	He sang (used to sing) while he worked (was working).
J'allais le voir tous les jours.	I used to (would) go to see him every day.

(3) as a descriptive tense in past time;

La nuit était belle.	The night was beautiful.
Elle portait un chapeau gris.	She wore a gray hat.
Le jeune homme était grand et mince.	The young man was tall and slim.

(4) to express a mental or emotional state of indefinite duration in the past with such verbs as **croire, penser, savoir, désirer, espérer, pouvoir,** and **vouloir;**

| Je voulais lui écrire, mais je ne savais pas son adresse. | I wanted to write to him, but I did not know his address. |
| Nous espérions le revoir bientôt. | We hoped to see him again soon. |

(5) with **depuis, depuis quand,** and **il y avait…que** [1] to denote an action or a condition previously begun and still continuing at a given moment in the past (English usage here requires the progressive form of the pluperfect tense, *had been + -ing*).

Il y avait un an qu'il le disait.	He had been saying it for a year.
Depuis quand m'attendiez-vous?	How long had you been waiting for me?
Je vous attendais depuis une heure.	I had been waiting for you for an hour.

THE PAST DEFINITE

42. The past definite tense denotes an act or a condition entirely completed in the past. It is essentially a narrative tense in contra-distinction to the imperfect, which is essentially descriptive. The past definite is a literary tense and is replaced in conversation by the past indefinite.

Il travailla dix heures ce jour-là.	He worked ten hours that day.
Il entra, ôta son pardessus et s'assit à son bureau.	He went in, took off his overcoat, and seated himself at his desk.
La guerre éclata en 1939.	War broke out in 1939.

THE PAST INDEFINITE

43. The past indefinite tense is used:

(1) in conversational style in place of the past definite (the past definites used in § 42 would be replaced in conversation by past indefinites);

| Je ne l'ai pas vu hier. | I did not see him yesterday. |
| La guerre a éclaté en 1939. | War broke out in 1939. |

[1] For the use of **depuis,** etc. with the present tense, see § 34.

(2) to translate the English present perfect tense, *have* (*has*) + a past participle.

Je ne l'ai pas vu aujourd'hui. I have not seen him today.

THE PLUPERFECT AND THE PAST ANTERIOR

44. The pluperfect tense is used in general as in English, except for the cases noted in §§ 41 (5) and 45.

Je lui en avais déjà parlé. I had already spoken to him about it.

45. The past anterior is a literary tense rarely used except after **après que, aussitôt que, lorsque,** and **quand.** It is avoided in informal writing by turning the sentence in some other way.

LITERARY

Quand il eut fini son travail, il partit. When he had finished his work, he left.

INFORMAL

Son travail fini, il est parti. His work finished, he left.
Après avoir fini (Ayant fini) son travail, il est parti. (After) having finished his work, he left.

LITERARY

Aussitôt qu'il fut parti, nous nous couchâmes. As soon as he had left, we went to bed.

INFORMAL

Nous nous sommes couchés tout de suite après son départ. We went to bed immediately after his departure.

La sauce mayonnaise

C'était en 1756. Le maréchal duc de Richelieu, un des plus fameux généraux de Louis XV, faisait depuis deux mois le siège de Port-Mahon, petite ville de l'île Minorque. Le duc, qui était gourmet et gourmand, commençait à trouver assez fades les repas que lui servait son chef. Surtout les sauces, dont il était très friand et qui semblaient avoir perdu leur goût.

Un soir il rentra affamé à son camp. Comme d'habitude, son cuisinier vint lui demander ce qu'il voulait pour son dîner. Le duc fit plusieurs recommandations et finit par s'informer de la sauce qu'on comptait servir avec les viandes froides.

—Mais celle que monsieur le maréchal voudra, répondit le chef. Il sentit, au ton sec du maréchal, que son maître était de mauvaise humeur. Depuis deux mois il lui offrait toujours les mêmes plats et il se rendait compte que le maréchal allait bientôt se fâcher.

Le maréchal réfléchit un moment. Puis, il demanda si on avait des œufs.

—Pour la première fois depuis huit jours nous en avons, répondit le chef.

—Si on essayait quelque chose de nouveau, alors! Battez un jaune d'œuf avec du sel, une pincée de poivre et un peu de moutarde. Ajoutez ensuite de l'huile d'olive et un filet de vinaigre, en tournant toujours. Servez-moi ça avec les viandes froides.

Le chef sortit.

Quand au dîner on apporta la nouvelle sauce, le maréchal, qui avait déjà mangé un potage médiocre et un poisson exécrable, était d'une humeur massacrante. Il goûta délicatement la sauce. Aussitôt son visage rayonna.

—Superbe! s'écria-t-il.

C'est ainsi qu'Armand, duc de Richelieu, petit-neveu du Grand Cardinal et maréchal de France, inventa la fameuse sauce mahonnaise, qu'on a appelée depuis—on ne sait pas pourquoi—sauce mayonnaise.

Conversation

1. Quelle est la date de cet incident? 2. Où se passe-t-il? 3. Qui était le roi de France à cette époque? 4. Que faisait le duc de Richelieu? 5. Expliquez en français la différence entre "gourmand" et "gourmet." 6. De quoi le duc était-il friand? 7. Donnez en français un synonyme de la phrase "être friand de." 8. Pourquoi le duc n'était-il pas content de son cuisinier? 9. Avec quels plats est-ce qu'on sert ordinairement la sauce mayonnaise? 10. Expliquez en français la préparation de la sauce mayonnaise. 11. Quelle est l'origine du nom "mayonnaise"? 12. Qui était le grand-oncle du duc de Richelieu? 13. Que savez-vous de lui?

Composition

Translate first in formal style, using the past definite as your narrative tense; then replace all past definites by past indefinites.

The Duke of Richelieu, great-nephew of the famous cardinal, was born in 1696 and died in 1788. He played a brilliant role at the court of Louis XIV and became, under Louis XV, one of the best generals in France. He accomplished one of the finest military feats of the century and invented mayonnaise dressing.

War had broken out in 1756 between the French and the English, and the French had decided to seize Port-Mahon, which had belonged to England since 1708. For two months the French army had been besieging the city without success. The forts which defended it seemed to be impregnable, and the defenders evidently did not lack provisions. The situation was becoming desperate. The duke was in [a] bad humor, and the miserable meals that his cook served him rendered him almost unbearable, for he was both (à la fois) [a] gourmand and [a] gourmet. The day came when (où) he lost his temper. He sent for his chef and told him that his meats were bad and that his sauces were still worse.

"If monsieur le duc would be willing to make a few recommendations, I should be glad to follow them," the chef suggested timidly.

"Very well," answered the duke. "For once I consent to become (me faire) [a] cook. It is certainly easier to concoct a sauce than to handle my soldiers." For a few moments he remained silent; then he dictated the famous recipe that the entire world has made use of since under the name of mayonnaise dressing.

It would be rash to affirm that the English lost Minorca because a French gourmet invented a new sauce for cold meats. The fact is, however, that the duke found his sauce superb, forgot his bad humor, and took Port-Mahon the next day.

Drill Exercise

1. I would see him every evening at half past eight o'clock. 2. How long had he been sleeping? For half an hour. 3. Night was falling, and they were reading in the living room. 4. He was talking when we entered the room. 5. They could not receive him when he arrived.

6. I have never seen him before. 7. We often used to talk about that when we were in Paris. 8. As soon as he had left Paris, he went to England. 9. We have not seen John recently, but we have been expecting him here for a month. 10. I hope that you were not disturbing him. 11. I had been hoping for some time to find an opportunity to (de) write to you. 12. When the cook had prepared the dinner, he went to the movies. 13. John did not think that she would be busy. 14. He did not know that you were working when he called you up. 15. I was fifteen years old when I saw him for the first time. 16. It was cold; the ground was covered with snow, and we were amusing ourselves at home. 17. The cook wanted to serve him the same sauce. 18. They thought that she would be glad to see us. 19. The French took Minorca in 1756. 20. Why was the duke always in a bad humor?

Grammatical Exercise

Replace the infinitives in parentheses by the appropriate past tenses:

Orso s'étant retiré dans sa chambre, Colomba (envoyer) coucher Saveria et les bergers, et (demeurer) seule dans la cuisine où se (préparer) le potage. De temps en temps, elle (prêter) l'oreille et (paraître) attendre impatiemment que son frère se fût couché. Lorsqu'elle le (croire) enfin endormi, elle (prendre) un couteau, (s'assurer) qu'il était tranchant, (mettre) ses petits pieds dans de gros souliers, et, sans faire le moindre bruit, elle (entrer) dans le jardin.

Le jardin (toucher) à un terrain assez vaste où l'on (mettre) les chevaux, car les chevaux corses ne connaissent guère l'écurie. Colomba (ouvrir) la porte du jardin, (entrer) dans l'enclos et, sifflant doucement, elle (attirer) près d'elle les chevaux à qui elle (porter) souvent du pain et du sel. Dès que le cheval noir (être) à sa portée, elle le (saisir) fortement par la crinière et lui (fendre) l'oreille avec son couteau. Le cheval (faire) un bond terrible et (s'enfuir) en faisant entendre un cri aigu. Satisfaite alors, Colomba (rentrer) dans le jardin.

D'après Mérimée

Verb Review

dormir to sleep; cf. § 156
  s'endormir to go to sleep
mentir to lie
partir to go away, leave
sortir to go out

servir to serve
  se servir de to use
sentir to feel; se sentir to feel (*of health*)
consentir to consent

Note: All the verbs above are conjugated like **dormir**.

1. What time did he leave? 2. She was leaving when I telephoned. 3. John went to sleep very late last night, and he did not sleep very well. 4. She did not use that recipe. 5. When is dinner served in this hotel? 6. They used to serve it at half past six o'clock. 7. I am sorry that he is not feeling well. 8. Go to sleep early. 9. We shall leave soon. 10. He would feel much better if he had slept more (**davantage** [2]). 11. I am glad that she is leaving. 12. Ordinarily he sleeps very well. 13. Let's not use that book. 14. I am using the book that he gave us. 15. They left (*p. def.*) at eight o'clock. 16. What did they serve (*p. def.*) for (**au**) lunch? 17. They are leaving tomorrow at noon.

[2] **Davantage** (not plus) is used to translate *more* when no expressed comparison follows. It usually stands at the end of a clause.

LESSON VII

Avoir *and* Etre *as Auxiliary Verbs*
Reflexives — *The Passive Voice*
The Agreement of Past Participles

AVOIR AND *ETRE* AS AUXILIARY VERBS

46. Avoir is used to form the compound tenses of all transitive verbs and of most intransitive verbs.

47. Etre is used as the auxiliary with (1) the passive, as in English; (2) all reflexive verbs; and (3) some intransitive verbs.

48. The most common intransitive verbs conjugated with **être** are:

(1) **mourir** *to die,* **naître** *to be born,* and **rester** *to remain;*

(2) the following intransitive verbs indicating a change of condition or motion, but not stating the kind of motion: [1]

aller to go	**rentrer** to re-enter, go (come) home
arriver to arrive	**retourner** to return, go back
descendre to descend	**revenir** to come back
devenir to become	**sortir** to go out
entrer to enter	**tomber** to fall
monter to go up	**venir** to come
partir to go away	

---

[1] Intransitive verbs which state the *kind of motion,* such as **courir, marcher,** and **voler,** are conjugated with **avoir. Monter** and **descendre** are also conjugated with avoir in such sentences as **Elle a descendu la rue** and **Il a monté l'escalier.**

40

But the transitive verbs **monter** *to carry up*, **descendre** *to carry down*, **entrer** *to carry in*, and **sortir** *to take out* are conjugated with **avoir**.

Napoléon est mort à Ste Hélène.	Napoleon died at St. Helena.
Il est monté à sa chambre.	He went up to his room.
But:	
Le concierge a monté les malles.	The janitor carried up the trunks.

REFLEXIVE VERBS

49. Reflexive verbs are verbs the object pronoun of which (whether direct or indirect) refers to the same person or thing as the subject. Most transitive verbs may become reflexive. All reflexive verbs are conjugated with **être**.

Elle a bien amusé les enfants.	She amused the children well.
Il s'est bien amusé.	He had a good time.
Nous nous sommes parlé.	We spoke to each other.

THE PASSIVE VOICE

50. The passive voice is formed in French, as in English, with **être** + the past participle of a transitive verb. The agent is usually denoted by **par** in the case of a specific act, by **de** when the action is habitual or when it represents a condition or an emotion.

Jean était accompagné par son ami.	John was accompanied by his friend.
Elle est toujours accompagnée de sa mère.	She is always accompanied by her mother.
Il est aimé de tout le monde.	He is liked by everyone.

51. The passive voice is used less frequently in French than in English. When the agent is not expressed, the passive is often replaced by:

(1) an active verb with the indefinite pronoun **on**;

On vend des timbres ici.	Stamps are sold here.
On m'a volé.	I have been robbed.

(2) a reflexive construction.

Cela se dit souvent.	That is often said.
La sténographie s'apprend facilement.	Stenography is easily learned.

THE AGREEMENT OF PAST PARTICIPLES

52. Past participles of intransitive verbs conjugated with **être** and of verbs in the passive voice agree with the subject in gender and number. Past participles of intransitive verbs conjugated with **avoir** are invariable.

Marie est sortie à trois heures.	Mary went out at three o'clock.
Ces cravates ont été choisies avec soin.	These neckties were chosen with care.

But:

Nous avons marché très vite.	We walked very fast.

53. Past participles of all reflexive verbs (auxiliary, **être**) and of all transitive verbs (auxiliary, **avoir**) agree in gender and number with a preceding direct object. If there is no preceding direct object, the past participle is invariable. The past participle never agrees with **en,** whatever the antecedent of **en** may be.

Voici les fleurs que nous avons achetées.	Here are the flowers we bought.
Elle s' (*direct object*) **est blessée sérieusement.**	She injured herself seriously.
Elle s' (*indirect object*) **est fait mal.**	She hurt herself.
Elle s' (*indirect object*) **est lavé les mains.**	She washed her hands.
Je vous ai rendu votre argent.	I gave you back your money.
Il en a acheté.	He bought some.

En lisant

—Les romans que vous lisez ne sont pas précisément nouveaux, dit Albert en voyant un volume de Cherbuliez sur la table de Raymond.

—En effet. Mais en lisant celui-ci, j'ai trouvé un passage curieux.

—De quoi s'agit-il?

—Eh bien, Ladislas, le héros de ce roman, après s'être promené un jour au Bois, est entré se rafraîchir dans un café. Là, il a rencontré un vieux Polonais, professeur de langues, qui s'était battu autrefois avec les Russes. Fort impressionné par l'aspect de ce vieillard, Ladislas songeait toujours à lui, quand, une heure plus tard, il a remarqué par hasard à la devanture d'une librairie un livre qui portait en lettres rouges le titre: *Mes Souvenirs*. L'auteur, Conrad Tronsko, était le vieillard qu'il venait de voir. Il a acheté le livre, l'a fourré dans sa poche et est rentré chez lui. Il a allumé sa lampe, a pris le livre et s'est mis à le feuilleter. Il a commencé à lire, assis sur le bord de sa table. Tout à coup sa pendule a sonné neuf heures. Il a eu un tressaillement, car il avait manqué d'oublier un rendez-vous important. Il s'est levé, a fait rapidement sa toilette et puis, le chapeau sur la tête, il s'est rassis et s'est remis à lire. Dix heures ont sonné. Il a levé la tête, a réfléchi un instant et est sorti. En arrivant au bas de l'escalier, il s'est arrêté. Après un instant d'indécision, il a remonté l'escalier, a jeté à terre son chapeau et s'est enfoncé dans un fauteuil. A la pointe du jour il lisait encore.

—Je ne vois rien de bien remarquable dans cet incident, dit Albert. Il me semble plutôt banal.

—Eh bien, moi, j'en ai été frappé, parce qu'il m'est arrivé la même chose la première fois que j'ai ouvert un volume de Poë.

Conversation

1. Qui est l'auteur du roman que lit Raymond? 2. Qui en est le héros? 3. Où est-ce que Ladislas se promenait? 4. Qui a-t-il rencontré? 5. Où s'est-il arrêté ensuite? 6. Qu'est-ce qu'il y a vu? 7. Comment s'appelle le vieillard qu'il vient de voir? 8. Racontez ce que Ladislas a fait en rentrant chez lui. 9. Qu'a-t-il manqué d'oublier en lisant le roman? 10. Qu'a-t-il fait quand il s'est rappelé son rendez-vous? 11. De quel incident est-ce que Raymond se souvient en lisant le roman de Cherbuliez? 12. Qui est Poë? 13. Savez-vous les titres de quelques œuvres de Poë?

Composition

"A curious thing happened to me last night," said Raymond. "I was taking a walk on the boulevard Saint-Germain, and I stopped by chance in front of a bookseller's window in which (où) there were some small volumes of Maupassant. I bought two of them. I thrust them into my pocket, and I forgot [about] them completely."

"Haven't you read Maupassant?"

"I knew only the short stories that everyone has read. Anyway, I went home and went up to my room. I had an appointment with George at nine o'clock, and I was wondering what I would do in the meantime, when I suddenly remembered the volumes I had bought. I took them from [2] my pocket, I sat down on the edge of the table, and I began to turn the leaves of the smaller [one]. It contained *La Peur* and other short stories that I had already read, but I reread several of them. Then I picked up the other volume. It was *Le Horla*. You know the story, doubtless."

"Yes. Maupassant describes in it (y) a monster created by his imagination, which often tormented him during his sleep."

"Well, I sat down in an armchair and began to read. Ten o'clock struck. Absorbed in the story, I had forgotten my appointment with George. I was beginning to feel a little uneasy, and I dared not raise my [3] head. When the monster passed through the wall, entered the chamber, and threw himself on poor Maupassant, I almost uttered a cry of terror. I got up, I undressed, and I went to bed, but I did not go to sleep before daybreak."

"What do you expect? You can't read Maupassant at eleven o'clock at night [4] if you want to sleep afterward."

Drill Exercise I

Reread the composition, making the narrator feminine.

Drill Exercise II

1. She came into the living room and sat down. 2. The flowers you gave me are fresh. 3. They would have stayed if they had had a good time. 4. When she fell, she hurt herself. 5. They had already gone to

---

[2] **dans.** After **prendre** in the sense of *to take, pick up, from* is translated by a preposition indicating the location of the object in question. **Il a pris sa montre dans sa poche (sur la table, sous un journal).** He took his watch from his pocket (from the table, from under a newspaper).

[3] **la.** See § 101.

[4] **du soir.** For expressions of time, see § 106.

bed. 6. French is spoken almost everywhere in Canada. 7. We did not walk so fast as you think. 8. Why did you hurry to leave us? 9. They wondered when we would leave. 10. Remember what I say, and don't hurry to see them. 11. Mary and John went to the movies last night, and they had a very good time. 12. You don't remember [5] me, do you? 13. We went to bed very early and got up at seven o'clock. 14. The doors are opened at eight o'clock. 15. Did you remember that they had left before dinner? 16. I would have given them to John, but he did not need them. 17. If I had known them, I would have introduced them to Mary. 18. Even after having seen her so many times in France, I did not remember her. 19. They came in and went upstairs to wash their hands. 20. French books are found in almost all bookstores. 21. Your valises, which the janitor carried upstairs, have been opened. 22. I hope that she slept well and that she was not disturbed. 23. The lesson had already begun when we entered the classroom. 24. Won't you sit down? Mary has gone up to her room, but she will come down soon.

Grammatical Exercise

Replace the infinitive in parentheses by the correct form of the past participle:

1. Nous sommes (arriver) de bonne heure hier soir. 2. Est-ce qu'ils les ont (voir) quand ils sont (partir). 3. Pourquoi est-ce qu'elle a (courir) si vite? 4. Savez-vous ce qu'elle est (devenir)? 5. Quoiqu'ils se soient déjà (coucher), on peut toujours les réveiller. 6. Quand Jeanne et Marie sont (entrer), ils étaient déjà (sortir). 7. Nous nous sommes (dépêcher) de les trouver. 8. Marie et Hélène ont (marcher) très vite pour éviter la pluie. 9. Est-ce qu'elle s'est (rappeler) cette histoire? Oui, elle se l'est (rappeler). 10. Je sais très bien qu'ils ne se sont pas (souvenir) d'elle. 11. Elle est (entrer), s'est (asseoir) et s'est (mettre) à étudier. 12. Marie a été (accompagner) par son amie. 13. Qu'est-ce qu'elles se sont (dire)? 14. A quelle heure sont-ils (revenir)? 15. L'histoire qu'ils lui ont (raconter) n'était pas vraie.

[5] Use se souvenir de. Se is direct object. Se (indirect object) rappeler *to recall, remember* is more frequently used for referring to things than to persons and cannot be used with me, te, nous, or vous as direct object. Je me le rappelle. *I remember it (him).* But: il se souvient de moi (toi, nous, vous).

Personal Pronouns (I)
Dates

54. Table of the conjunctive and disjunctive personal pronouns:

	CONJUNCTIVES			DISJUNCTIVES
SUBJECT	DIRECT OBJECT	INDIRECT OBJECT	REFLEXIVE	
je	me	me	me	moi
tu	te	te	te	toi
il, elle	le, la	lui	se	lui, elle
nous	nous	nous	nous	nous
vous	vous	vous	vous	vous
ils, elles	les	leur	se	eux, elles

CONJUNCTIVE PRONOUNS

55. Conjunctive pronouns are used as subjects or objects of verbs, i. e., are conjoined with the verb.

56. Position of conjunctive pronouns:

(1) All conjunctive object pronouns, and also **y** and **en,** precede the verb (in compound tenses, the auxiliary), except the affirmative imperative, which they follow and to which they are joined by a hyphen.

(2) The order of conjunctive pronouns before a verb, or before an auxiliary in a compound tense, is:

me								
te		le						
se	before	la	before	lui	before **y**	before **en**
nous		les		leur		
vous						

Il nous les donne.	He gives them to us.
Je le lui ai donné.	I gave it to him.
Ne leur en donnez pas.	Don't give them any.
Vous l'a-t-il donné?	Did he give it to you?

(3) The order of object pronouns after the imperative affirmative is: verb, direct object, indirect object, **y, en. Moi** and **toi** replace **me** and **te** except before **en** and **y.**

Donnez-le-moi.	Give it to me.
Donnez-nous-en.	Give us some.
But:	
Donnez-m'en.	Give me some.

(4) When the direct object of a verb is **me** (**moi** in the imperative affirmative), **te** (**toi** in the imperative affirmative), **se, nous,** or **vous,** the indirect object is translated by a disjunctive pronoun preceded by **à** and is placed after the verb.

Il s'est présenté à moi.	He introduced himself to me.
Présentez-moi à elle.	Introduce me to her.
But:	
Présentez-la-moi.	Introduce her to me.

DATES

57. Date expressions:

Quel jour du mois est-ce (sommes-nous) aujourd'hui?	What day of the month is it today?
C'est (Nous sommes) aujourd'hui le quinze mai.	Today is the fifteenth of May.
Il y a huit (quinze) jours.	A week (Two weeks) ago.
Samedi passé.	Last Saturday.
D'aujourd'hui en huit.	A week from today.

La semaine prochaine.	Next week (*in the future*).
La semaine suivante.	The following week.

Au téléphone

—Alors, c'est convenu, dit Albert. Nous passons une journée à la campagne dimanche prochain. Mais où me menez-vous?

—J'ai envie de visiter la vallée de Chevreuse, répondit Raymond. L'abbaye de Port-Royal s'y trouve—c'est à dire les quelques pierres qui en restent—et je pourrai vous la montrer en passant.

—Port-Royal? On en a parlé dans mes cours de français mais je ne m'en souviens plus. Attendez. Ne me le dites pas. Je me le rappelle maintenant. C'est là, n'est-ce pas? que le jeune Racine a été élevé par des savants jansénistes qu'on appelait les Solitaires.

—C'est ça. Les Solitaires y dirigeaient les Petites Ecoles de Port-Royal, où ils enseignaient la logique, la grammaire et les langues étrangères. Malheureusement, ils ont été dispersés par ordre de Louis XIV et l'abbaye a été détruite en 1710. Mais vous y verrez les ruines d'une vieille tour carrée, de beaux jardins, et un petit musée où on conserve des souvenirs de Racine et de Pascal. D'ailleurs, le site est magnifique comme l'est, du reste, toute la vallée de Chevreuse.

—Allons-y alors. A propos, pourquoi ne donnez-vous pas un coup de téléphone à Marcel? Peut-être qu'il voudra nous accompagner.

—Bonne idée. Voyons s'il se trouve à son bureau. (*Il décroche le récepteur du téléphone.*) Allo! Mademoiselle, allo!

—(*L'employée des téléphones*) J'écoute.

—Rivoli—vingt-huit, cinquante-deux, s'il vous plaît ... Allo! Marcel? Ici Raymond ... Pas mal, merci. Et vous? ... Tant mieux ... Dites donc, nous allons à Chevreuse dimanche. Voulez-vous nous accompagner? ... Comment! Vous avez demandé un congé? ... Et on vous l'a accordé en cette saison-ci? Mais c'est épatant! ... Dans le midi? ... Et vous reviendrez quand? ... De vendredi en quinze? ... Mais non, je n'ai pas besoin de mon guide. Je vous l'enverrai cet après-midi ... Il n'y a pas de quoi ... Oui, vous pouvez me les adresser chez Madame Bernard ... Au revoir et bon voyage. (*Il raccroche le récepteur.*)

—Marcel est très travailleur, dit Albert. Il a bien gagné son congé. Je suis content qu'on ne le lui ait pas refusé.

Conversation

1. Où Raymond et Albert comptent-ils passer la journée de dimanche?
2. Quelle fameuse abbaye se trouve dans la vallée de Chevreuse? 3.
Port-Royal évoque les noms de quels écrivains? 4. Quand les Petites
Ecoles de Port-Royal ont-elles été détruites? 5. A qui est-ce que Raymond et Albert donnent un coup de téléphone? 6. Pourquoi? 7. Pourquoi Marcel ne peut-il pas les accompagner? 8. Quand est-ce que
Marcel reviendra? 9. Comment dit-on en français "to unhook the
receiver" et "to hang up the receiver"? 10. Que savez-vous de Racine
et de Pascal?

Composition

ALBERT: Raymond, you are wanted (**on vous demande**) at the
telephone.

RAYMOND: Don't hang up. I am coming at once. (*Taking the receiver*) Hello! This is Raymond. Oh, hello, Marcel.

MARCEL: Hello, Raymond. You are going to be angry with me
but I can't accompany you Sunday to the valley of Chevreuse, as I
promised (it to) you.

RAYMOND: That's too bad. We were counting on you to act as our
guide.

MARCEL: I know it, but here is what has happened. You know my
cousin, Martha. I introduced you to her, when she was here last
winter. You remember it, don't you?

RAYMOND: Of course, I remember it.

MARCEL: Well, Martha is going to be married next Tuesday. I
have asked for a leave at the office, and they have granted it to me.
I am leaving this evening for Avignon.

RAYMOND: Have a good time, and don't fail to present my respects
to your cousin. When shall you return to Paris?

MARCEL: A week from tomorrow. In any case, I'll write you a note
from Avignon. By the way, I have a guidebook of the surroundings
of Paris. I'll lend it to you if you wish it.

RAYMOND: Many thanks. Madame Bernard has one, and she will
be glad to lend it to us. Until next week, then, and [have a] good
trip. (*He hangs up the receiver.*)

ALBERT: How do you know that Madame Bernard has a guide-book?

RAYMOND: She showed it to me the other day. But I shall not ask her for it. We shall not need it. We'll take the train as far as Chevreuse, and from there we'll go on foot to Port-Royal. The abbey was destroyed two centuries ago, but we can still see the old tower and the gardens. As for the souvenirs of Pascal and Racine, the museum attendant will explain them to us. If you give him a small tip, he will tell you the history of the whole seventeenth century.

Drill Exercise

1. You ought not to give him any. 2. We did not find them there; did you give them to her? 3. There are not any in my room; look for them elsewhere. 4. Send me some, but do not send him any. 5. If you succeed in it, I shall be very glad of it. 6. I did not find any there. 7. John did not give them to me; he left them there. 8. Don't send me three; I need only two. 9. If he had had any, he would have sent some to me. 10. He did not send it to her last Saturday; he sent it to us. 11. I gave him seven a week ago, but he has lost them. 12. Don't send them to her; send them to me. 13. I should not give them any even if I had a lot. 14. Today is the sixteenth; I expect to be there a week from today. 15. Let's send them some; they are very fond of them. 16. He arrived on Thursday the thirteenth, and the next week he left for London. 17. Tomorrow will be the fifteenth. 18. I shall be in Paris two weeks from today. 19. Give us some, but don't give us too many. 20. They were here two years ago, but I was in France.

Grammatical Exercise

Insert in the correct place the French equivalents of the words in parentheses, being careful to make the past participle agree when necessary:

1. Je n'ai pas trouvé (*them there; any there*).
2. Il donnera (*some to her; them to me; it to us; some to you*).
3. N'envoyons pas (*them to him; any to her*).
4. N'a-t-il pas envoyé (*any to them; them there; it to us*)?
5. Il n'a pas expédié (*them to us; it to you; any to them*).

6. Il ne va pas donner (*her any; it to me; them to us*).
7. Présentez (*her to us; us to them; yourself to him; them to her*).
8. Elle veut donner (*some to me; him some; it to us; them to you*).
9. Donnez (*me some; it to her; us some; them to them*).
10. Ne donnez pas (*him any; them to her; them six; us so many*).

Verb Review

connaître to know, be acquainted with, meet; cf. § 156
   reconnaître to recognize
savoir to know, know how; cf. § 156

1. Do you know how to cook? 2. I know how to prepare a good meal. 3. Know what you want. 4. I did not know that you knew them. 5. We used to know the Martins in the United States, but we did not recognize them yesterday. 6. We are sorry that you do not know where he is. 7. Will you recognize him when you see him? 8. Do you know Mademoiselle Renaud? 9. We shall know what it will be necessary to do. 10. We met (*p. def.*) them in 1937. 11. I shall not recognize him. 12. I am afraid that he does not know them very well. 13. I thought that he would recognize us immediately. 14. We hoped that he would know how to help you. 15. If they had known then what they know now, they would not have done that.

Personal Pronouns (II) — En *and* Y — *Age*

DISJUNCTIVE PRONOUNS

58. The disjunctive pronouns (see § 54) are used:

(1) absolutely, without a verb;

Qui vous a dit cela? Lui? Non, elle.	Who told you that? Did he? No, she did.

(2) after ce + être;

C'est lui, elle, moi, etc.	It is he, she, I, etc.

(3) after all prepositions;

Avec moi; sans eux.	With me; without them.

(4) in compound subjects or objects when one or both of them are pronouns;

Jean et moi (nous) sommes allés en ville.	John and I went downtown.
Je les ai vus, lui et elle.	I saw him and her.

(5) in place of a conjunctive subject pronoun if the subject is separated from the verb by any word except **ne,** pronoun objects, **y,** or **en;**

Lui seul va avec nous.	He alone is going with us.

(6) for emphasis, with or without **même.**

Il a fini le travail lui-même.	He finished the work himself.
Moi, j'ai fini le travail.	*I* finished the work.
Lui jouait du piano, eux travaillaient.	*He* was playing the piano, *they* were working.

EN AND *Y*

59. En is equivalent to **de** (= *of, from, with,* etc. + a personal pronoun *(it, them)*.

(1) It is used partitively, as a pronoun, to translate *some of it* *(them)* or *any of it (them)*. In this case it may refer either to persons or to things. (Cf. §§ 14-15.)

Avez-vous des amis ici? Oui, j'en ai.	Have you (some) friends here? Yes, I have (some of them).

(2) It is used as a pronoun standing for a noun governed by **de** or for a construction introduced by **de.** In this case, **en** refers to things only. To refer to persons a disjunctive personal pronoun must be used.

Il a visité Paris et il en admire les monuments.	He has visited Paris, and he admires its public buildings.
Vous venez de Londres? Mais j'en viens aussi.	You come from London? But I come from there also.
J'en suis très content.	I am very glad of it.
Je m'en souviens.	I remember it.
But:	
Je suis content de lui.	I am satisfied with him.
Je me souviens d'elle.	I remember her.

60. Y is equivalent to **à** (= *to, at, in,* etc.) + a personal pronoun *(it, them)*. It refers only to things. As an adverb, **y** translates the English *there* and, when so used, refers to a place previously mentioned.

Voici la liste. Que faut-il y ajouter?	Here is the list. What must be added to it?
Est-il à l'université? Oui, il y va tous les jours.	Is he at the university? Yes, he goes there every day.

AGE

61. Age expressions:

Quel âge a-t-il?	How old is he?

Il a dix-huit ans. Il est âgé de dix-huit ans. }	He is eighteen years old.
Il est plus âgé que moi.	He is older than I am.
Il a trois ans de plus (moins) que moi.	He is three years older (younger) than I.

Anecdote historique

François de Bonne, seigneur de Lesdiguières, appartenait à une famille ancienne et aussi pauvre que le village qu'elle habitait. François comprit de bonne heure qu'on ne pouvait pas faire fortune en province. Sous prétexte d'aller voir un parent, il emprunta à l'hôtelier du lieu un cheval, promettant de ne le garder que deux ou trois jours, et disparut.

Vingt ans plus tard il retourna, comme gouverneur du Dauphiné, à son village natal et s'apprêta à passer la nuit dans une superbe maison qu'il y avait fait bâtir. Il était sur le point de se coucher et interrogeait ses domestiques sur ce qu'ils avaient vu et entendu, quand l'un d'eux lui dit:

—J'ai entendu un brave homme dire, en voyant passer Votre Seigneurie: "Le diable emporte François de Bonne qui m'a causé tant de mal." Je me suis informé de lui. C'est un hôtelier qui prétend que Monseigneur, en quittant le pays, lui a emprunté un cheval et qu'il ne le lui a jamais rendu. Le cheval n'était pas à lui et le voisin qui en était le propriétaire lui a fait un procès qui dure depuis vingt ans.

—Ma foi, dit Lesdiguières, c'est Charlot. Je me souviens de lui. Faites-le venir à l'instant.

Charlot arriva tout tremblant.

—C'est bien toi qui m'envoie au diable, lui demanda Lesdiguières, le jour même où je rentre dans mon pays natal?

Le bonhomme se jeta aux pieds du gouverneur.

—Monseigneur, j'ai eu tort. Je m'en repens.

—Tu as eu raison. Voilà cinq cents écus pour le mal que je t'ai fait. Maintenant va-t-en et recommande-moi à Dieu, sur qui, j'espère, tu auras plus d'influence que sur le diable.

Conversation

1. Pourquoi François de Bonne a-t-il quitté son village? 2. Qu'est-ce qu'il a emprunté à l'hôtelier du lieu? 3. Sous quel prétexte? 4. Pendant

combien de temps a-t-il été absent de son village? 5. Quelle était sa situation en y revenant? 6. Où est-il descendu? 7. Que lui a raconté son domestique? 8. Qu'est-ce que François de Bonne a fait alors? 9. De quelle façon est-ce que François de Bonne a récompensé l'hôtelier? 10. Quel conseil lui a-t-il donné?

Composition

"Let's go for a walk in the quarter of the Bastille. You have been promising me for a long time to show it to me."

"You and I will go there today. You will like the old houses that date from the seventeenth century. One of them, the Hôtel de Sens, belonged to Henry IV."

"According to my guidebook, it belonged to Henry's former wife, Marguerite de Valois."

"Henry lent it to her. You recall the story, don't you?"

"No. You know the history of France better than I. How narrow these streets are!"

"I shall show you some that are still narrower. Here is the rue Lesdiguières."

"Did Lesdiguières live here?"

"Yes, in a hôtel built by the Italian financier Zamet, who sold it to him. But what do you know about him?"

"An interesting anecdote. I have read several of them recently."

"Tell it to me."

"Lesdiguières, when he left his native town to seek his fortune in Paris, borrowed a horse from the local hotelkeeper and did not return it to him. Some years later he went back there."

"And of course the first person that he met . . ."

"(It) was the hotelkeeper. Poor Charlot had lent a horse that was not his and had been obliged to pay for it. 'The devil take these great lords who cause us so much trouble!' he grumbled."

"Did Lesdiguières get angry?"

"On the contrary. He took five hundred écus from his pocket and gave them to him. 'Go back home,' he said; 'go to bed and commend me to God. You certainly have no influence on the devil, since I have owed you money for twenty years.' "

Drill Exercise

1. Who introduced you to them? He. 2. It is I who asked him for it. 3. He and I will call for you early. 4. Without them (*m.*), he alone can do nothing. 5. She introduced herself to us; then we introduced her to them. 6. It is she who is going with us. 7. We were thinking of her when she came in. 8. You and I will wait for him there. 9. Didn't you remember her? No, but I remembered him. 10. He sent John and me some post cards from France. 11. On returning there, he found John with her in the salon. 12. They did not remember me when I saw them there. 13. When Henry and he arrive, I shall introduce you to them. 14. She saw us both there, but she did not remember us. 15. *They* were playing cards, *he* was reading. 16. How old was your sister then? 17. She was eighteen years old; she will be nineteen years old next Wednesday. 18. My brother is two years older than I.

Verb Review

faire to do, make, have (done), order, etc.; cf. § 156
  faire froid (chaud, frais, beau, mauvais, etc.) to be cold (hot, cool, fair, stormy, etc.)

se faire tard to be getting late
se faire à to get used to
faire venir to send for

1. It is warmer here than in France. 2. It is getting late. 3. It will be colder tomorrow. 4. They did (*p. déf.*) their duty. 5. We never got used to it. 6. Do what you wish. 7. I should not do that if I were in (à) your place. 8. She is afraid that he may not do what she asks. 9. I was taking a walk when I met her. 10. It was (*p. indéf.*) very warm yesterday. 11. It was getting late when he arrived. 12. What he does, does not concern me. 13. Let's take a walk. 14. I shall send for him immediately. 15. I am sorry that he has done that.

LESSON X

Negation

Ce *and* Il *as Subjects of* Etre

NEGATION

62. The most common negatives used with verbs are:

ne ... pas not
ne ... point not
ne ... jamais [1] never
ne ... guère scarcely
ne ... plus no more, no longer
ne ... que only

ne ... personne [2] no one, nobody, not ... anyone
ne ... aucun [3] none, no one, no
ne ... rien nothing, not anything
ne ... ni ... ni neither ... nor

63. **Ne** always precedes the verb and any pronoun objects.

64. **Pas, point, jamais, plus, guère,** and **rien** stand immediately after the verb in simple tenses and immediately after the auxiliary in compound tenses. They usually precede the infinitive and its pronoun objects.

Je ne l'ai pas vu.	I have not seen him.
N'a-t-il rien fait?	Has he done nothing?
Elle n'y va plus.	She does not go there any more.
J'ai envie de ne pas le faire.	I have a mind not to do it.

65. **Personne** usually stands after a past participle or an infinitive.

Je n'y ai rencontré personne.   I met no one there.

---

[1] Jamais used without **ne** means *ever;* used without a verb and without **ne**, it means *never.* **Avez-vous jamais été en France? Jamais.** Have you ever been in France? Never.

[2] Personne in the sense of *nobody* is masculine, but in the sense of a *person* or *individual* is feminine. **Personne n'est venu.** No one has come. But: **Quelques personnes sont déjà arrivées.** A few people have already arrived.

[3] For aucun as an indefinite, see § 122.

66. Ni, the **que** of **ne ... que,** and the negative adjective **aucun** stand directly before the words they modify.

Il n'y a que deux livres sur la table.	There are only two books on the table.
Je n'ai aucune envie de voyager.	I have no desire to travel.
Il n'a trouvé ni amis ni connaissances à Paris.	He found neither friends nor acquaintances in Paris.

67. Aucun, rien,[4] and **personne** may be used as subjects of a verb. **Ne** must be used before the verb.

Personne n'est arrivé.	No one has come.
Aucune de ses amies ne lui a écrit.	None of her friends has written to her.

68. If the verb is omitted, **ne** is also omitted, the complementary negative retaining full negative force. **Pas,** however, must be supported by some other word.

Qu'avez-vous vu? Rien.	What did you see? Nothing.
Est-ce que le président est arrivé? Pas encore.	Has the president arrived? Not yet.

CE AND IL AS SUBJECTS OF ETRE

69. Il(s) and **elle(s)** are used before **être** to translate *he, she,* and *they* when the verb **être** is followed by an adjective or an unmodified noun.

Ils sont amis.	They are friends.
Elle est Française.	She is French (a Frenchwoman).
Il est médecin.	He is a doctor.

70. The invariable pronoun **ce** is used before **être:**

(1) to translate *it* or *that* when the verb is followed by an adjective or an adverb referring to an idea implied or expressed in a previous word or phrase (if reference is to a specific noun or pronoun, **il(s)** or **elle(s)** must be used);

---

[4] For the use of **rien** + an adjective, see § 128.

| Je suis fatigué. C'est vrai. | I am tired, It is true. |
| Votre travail est terminé. C'est bien. | Your work is done. That is well. |

But:

| Comment trouvez-vous cette comédie? Elle est très intéressante. | How do you like that comedy? It is very interesting. |

(2) to translate *it, this, that, he, she,* or *they* when **être** is followed by (a) a modified noun, (b) a pronoun, (c) a proper name, or (d) a superlative.

(a) **Ce sont des amis de mon frère.**	They are friends of my brother.
C'est une Française.	She is a French girl.
(b) **C'est moi, vous, elle; ce sont (c'est) eux.**	It is I, you, she; it is they.
(c) **Ce sont les Chamard.**	It is the Chamards.
(d) **C'est le plus beau de ses romans.**	That (It) is the finest of his novels.

Comment travaillait Balzac

En 1839 le grand Balzac, qui n'avait jamais d'argent, résolut d'aborder le théâtre et, ayant besoin d'un collaborateur, s'adressa à Lassailly. C'était un jeune auteur qui écrivait des romans que personne ne lisait et qui ne mangeait pas tous les jours. Balzac l'emmena aux Jardies, petite propriété qu'il possédait près de Versailles. Arrivé là, il expliqua à son collaborateur que chez lui on ne vivait que la nuit et que le jour on dormait, excepté lui, qui dormait peu et qui avait des affaires en ville. "Mais vous avez encore de vieilles habitudes, ajouta-t-il; pour ce soir couchez-vous. Je vous ferai réveiller quand il le faudra."

Lassailly se coucha. Deux heures après, un domestique le réveilla et le mena dans le cabinet du maître, où l'attendait une énorme pile de papier blanc. Quand sept heures du matin sonnèrent, Balzac lui conseilla de regagner sa chambre et lui-même s'en alla gaîment vers Paris.

Le lendemain on recommença et le surlendemain. Au cours des séances de travail, les yeux du collaborateur se fermaient sous le regard étonné du maître, qu'aucun effort ne semblait fatiguer. Ce dernier renvoyait le pauvre diable à sa chambre, puis une demi-heure plus tard le faisait rappeler. Lassailly allait et venait par la maison, traversant vingt fois les mêmes salles sombres et désertes. A la fin de la semaine il demanda un congé mais comme la besogne n'était pas terminée, Balzac refusa et verrouilla la porte.

La nuit suivante, par un beau clair de lune, un homme pâle comme un spectre, les vêtements en désordre, sans chapeau, escaladait [5] le mur du jardin avec tous les signes du plus vif effroi et de la plus grande précaution. C'était Lassailly qui s'enfuyait des Jardies.

Conversation

1. Quand Balzac a-t-il commencé à écrire pour le théâtre? 2. De qui avait-il besoin? 3. Comment s'appelait celui qu'il a choisi? 4. Est-ce que Lassailly était déjà auteur? De quoi? 5. Comment savez-vous qu'il n'était pas riche? 6. Où est-ce que Balzac l'a emmené? 7. Où se trouvent les Jardies? 8. Décrivez la vie qu'on menait chez Balzac. 9. Est-ce que Lassailly a pu facilement se faire à cette vie? 10. Qu'est-ce qu'il a demandé à Balzac? 11. Pourquoi Balzac a-t-il refusé sa demande? 12. Comment Lassailly est-il sorti des Jardies?

Composition

Balzac, author of *The Human Comedy,* made a great deal of money, but he never had a (le) cent. Nothing discouraged him, however, not even his enormous debts, which he would never be able to pay. In order to work without being disturbed by anyone, he had in Paris and in the vicinity numerous dwellings where neither his friends nor his creditors could find him. There he often worked all night, eating nothing and drinking only black coffee.

In 1839, being in great need of money, he decided to tackle the theater and sent for four of his friends, with the intention of asking them to help him. Gautier arrived (the) first at the Jardies, where Balzac had been hiding for several weeks. A servant led him through somber, deserted halls to the master's study.

"There you are at last!" cried Balzac. "I've been waiting for you for

[5] Note the use of the imperfect for vividness, a use comparable to that of the historical present in English. The reader is not merely informed of what happened; he is made an eye-witness of it.

an hour. I am reading tomorrow to Harel"—he was a theater manager—"a drama in (en) five acts."

"And you want our opinion?"

"No, the play isn't written yet."

"Then it will be necessary to postpone the reading for (à) six
weeks."

"No," replied Balzac. "The play must be finished for tomorrow."

"Between now and (D'ici à) tomorrow, it is impossible. We should
hardly have the time to recopy it."

"The matter presents no difficulty. You will do one act, Ourliac
another, Laurent-Jan the third, de Belloy the fourth, and I the fifth,
and I shall read the drama tomorrow at noon, as I promised (it)."

"Tell me the subject, outline [for] me in a few words the charac-
ters," implored Gautier, "and I'll do my best."

"Ah, if it is necessary to tell you the subject," exclaimed Balzac,
"we shall never have finished."

Drill Exercise

1. We did not find anyone there. 2. They have never given us anything. 3. No one has ever said anything to me about it. 4. They are
Americans, but she is a Frenchwoman. 5. That is the most beautiful
of his paintings. 6. Never have I seen so many flowers. 7. We don't
go there any more. 8. She is poor, but she is a very intelligent girl.
9. Have you ever seen *Le Cid?* No, never. 10. There is neither bread
nor butter on the table. 11. No one has come since your departure. 12.
That was my cousin whom you saw. 13. The novels of Dumas are
doubtless very interesting, but they are not so interesting as Hugo's
novels. 14. We have only five francs. 15. They scarcely had (the)
time to talk with us. 16. He hasn't any more of them; he had only
four. 17. I have no desire to see them again. 18. I hope not to meet
them here. 19. She is always very well dressed. 20. What has happened today? Nothing. 21. This is the hat I always wear to the theater.
22. None of their friends lives here. 23. I am sorry that no one recog-
nizes us.

Verb Review

mettre to put, put on; cf. § 156
  remettre to put back, postpone
  permettre (de) to permit (*indirect object of the person*)
  promettre (de) to promise (*indirect object of the person*)
  se mettre à to begin

prendre to take, get; cf. § 156
  apprendre (à) to learn
  comprendre to understand
  aller (venir) prendre to go (come) and get, call for (*a person*)

1. What is he promising to do? 2. Where did she learn to speak French? 3. He is getting them at Mme Martin's. 4. She began to run very fast. 5. Don't put them there. 6. I shall take you with me in my automobile. 7. We shall postpone our trip until (à) next year. 8. They did not permit him to stay. 9. We do not understand what you are saying. 10. Where does he want you to have coffee? 11. I am afraid that she does not understand us. 12. We are glad that you are beginning to study more. 13. He took (*p. def.*) the money from (sur) ⁶ the table and put it back (*p. def.*) in his pocket. 14. Even if he calls for us, I shall not promise to go with him. 15. They were always promising to come to see us. 16. I had put them (*f.*) there before my departure.

⁶ Cf. page 44, note 2.

LESSON XI

Conditional Sentences
Uses of Devoir

CONDITIONAL SENTENCES

71. (1) Conditional sentences follow the same tense sequence as in English, except that, unlike the English, **si** meaning *if* may never be followed by a conditional or future tense. For the English future in an *if* clause, use the present indicative in French. For the English conditional in an *if* clause, use the imperfect indicative in French.

S'il est en France cet été, je le verrai.	If he is (will be) in France this summer, I shall see him.
Je le ferais, si j'avais le temps.	I should do it if I had the time.
Je l'aurais fait, si j'avais eu le temps.	I should have done it if I had had the time.
S'il vous envoyait une invitation, vous ne l'accepteriez pas.	If he sent (should send, were to send) you an invitation, you would not accept it.

(2) Si meaning *whether* is followed by the same tense as in English.

Il ne sait pas s'il pourra venir.	He does not know whether he will be able to come.
Il ne savait pas s'il pourrait venir.	He did not know whether he would be able to come.

72. *Should* and *would* in English do not always indicate the conditional tense in French. Distinguish carefully between the following:

63

(1) *Should* (= *ought*) implying duty is rendered in French by the conditional or conditional perfect of **devoir.**

Vous devriez étudier davantage.	You should study more.
Vous auriez dû venir plus tôt.	You should have come sooner.

(2) *Would* implying volition is rendered in French by the appropriate tense of **vouloir.**[1]

Il ne voulait pas étudier.	He would not study (habitually).
Il n'a pas voulu le faire.	He would not (refused to) do it.
Il ne voudrait pas vous prêter son auto.	He would not (be willing to) lend you his automobile.

(3) *Would* indicating an habitual action in the past is translated by an imperfect tense.[2]

En été, je le voyais tous les jours.	In summer I would see him every day.

USES OF *DEVOIR*

73. **Devoir,** besides meaning *to owe,* translates:

(1) *must, to have to,* expressing duty or obligation;

Je dois l'aider.	I must help him.
Je devais l'aider.	I had to help him (regularly).
J'ai dû (je dus) l'aider alors.	I had to help him then.
Je devrai l'aider.	I shall have to help him.

(2) *must,* expressing probability;

Il doit être riche.	He must be rich.
Il a dû manquer le train.	He must have missed the train.

(3) *be to, be expected to, be supposed to* (present and imperfect tenses);

Je dois partir demain.	I am to leave tomorrow.
Il devait partir hier.	He was to leave yesterday.

[1] Cf. § 37.
[2] Cf. § 41 (2).

(4) *should, ought* (conditional and conditional perfect tenses).

Je devrais l'aider.	I ought to (should) help him.
J'aurais dû l'aider.	I ought to have (should have) helped him.

Un complot politique

Les complots politiques qui troublent l'Europe depuis quelques années ont souvent leur côté comique. L'arrestation en 1937 du prétendu fasciste, Eugène Deloncle, fait penser à une aventure de roman policier.

Après la découverte de son complot, Deloncle avait dû se cacher, en attendant l'occasion d'envoyer un mot à un chef militaire de ses amis qui devait le sauver. Il écrivit enfin une lettre au militaire, sans donner d'adresse mais expliquant comment on pourrait arranger un rendez-vous.

Malheureusement cette lettre tomba entre les mains d'un commissaire de police qui imagina un moyen de s'emparer du conspirateur. Utilisant les renseignements fournis par la lettre, on ferait savoir à Deloncle que le chef militaire, recherché lui-même par la police, n'osait pas se montrer dans la rue; qu'il enverrait à sa place un homme sûr (rôle que jouerait le commissaire, bien entendu), qui conduirait Deloncle auprès de son camarade. Cet inconnu, qui porterait à sa boutonnière une étoile rouge, se trouverait le 24 novembre à 21 heures du soir à la terrasse d'un café des Champs-Elysées. Il expliquerait à Deloncle ce qu'il devrait faire.

Deloncle reçut le message mais au lieu d'aller lui-même au café, il y envoya un émissaire, à qui l'homme à (*with*) l'étoile rouge donna ces instructions définitives: Deloncle devait se trouver le lendemain à minuit, seul, dans un taxi rouge, place Vauban.

Deloncle aurait dû se méfier; mais comme il ne savait pas même les noms de la plupart de ses camarades, il dut penser que l'inconnu était quelque membre de la bande. Il se rendit donc au rendez-vous, comme on le lui avait recommandé. L'inconnu du café ouvrit la portière du taxi, monta et s'assit à côté de lui. "Impossible ici, expliqua-t-il, c'est à un petit hôtel du quartier que doit avoir lieu l'interview avec le chef."

Dix minutes plus tard le taxi stoppe devant l'hôtel. Deloncle descend le premier. Son compagnon, derrière lui, fait un signe rapide.

Deux hommes surgissent et le personnage mystérieux redevient le commissaire de police.

—Eugène Deloncle, dit-il, je vous arrête. Veuillez me suivre à la Sûreté.

Si vous écriviez un roman policier, pourriez-vous trouver un meilleur dénouement?

Conversation

1. Depuis quand est-ce que des complots politiques troublent l'Europe? 2. Quand a-t-on arrêté Eugène Deloncle? 3. Pourquoi avait-il dû se cacher? 4. Pourquoi voulait-il trouver ce chef militaire? 5. Qui a imaginé un moyen de l'attraper? 6. Où est-ce que Deloncle devait se trouver? 7. Qui lui expliquerait ce qu'il devrait faire? 8. Que savait Deloncle de ses camarades? 9. Où est-ce que l'interview devait avoir lieu? 10. Quand Deloncle est descendu du taxi, qu'est-ce qui est arrivé? 11. Expliquez en français ce que c'est qu'un roman policier.

Composition

"You ought to have gone to the theater with me last night."

"I should have accompanied you gladly if I had known that you were to go (there)."

"I don't know whether you would have liked the play. It was a detective play, and you don't like detective stories."

"You ought not to say that. I am suspicious of French detective stories, for, in general, they are rather mediocre, but I must confess that I have read the adventures of the famous detective, Monsieur Lecoq, half a dozen (of) times."

"The play that I saw was rather curious and very improbable. The victim was speaking into (à) the dictaphone when the mysterious assassin entered his office, and the dictaphone recorded the murderer's voice also. If you had written the play, would you have imagined as ingenious an ending?"

"Your mysterious personage reminds me of the arrest of the fascist, Eugène Deloncle, a few years ago."

"Yes, I remember it. While he was hiding from the police, he was informed that a stranger whom he would find at a Parisian café would save him. He did not know whether he ought to follow these instructions or not, but he went to the rendez-vous."

"And the stranger took him in a white taxi to a hotel where the interview with a military leader was to take place."

"But the stranger was a police inspector, as Deloncle should have suspected (it). He must have been stupid."

"Not necessarily. If you will read the report of his arrest, you will notice that each member of the band knew only his own leader. Put yourself in (à) his place. You would doubtless have done the same thing."

Drill Exercise

1. I must leave now; I am to be at the station in an hour. 2. Were we supposed to stay here? 3. If Mary had (the) time, she would wait for us. 4. I should not have gone with them. 5. How much did he owe you? 6. We had to study in order to pass our examinations. 7. She was not here yesterday. She must have been ill. 8. I do not know whether he will come or not. 9. If we should go to Paris, we should be glad to call on your friends. 10. You ought to study more if you want to learn French. 11. They were supposed to arrive this morning at half past nine. 12. As he would not give me any money, I had to stay at home. 13. You will have to read this novel even if you do not like detective stories. 14. He telephoned me every morning when I was sick. 15. John ought to have waited for us there; he must have forgotten our appointment. 16. She would not have left if she had known that he was coming. 17. Are we to wait for them here, or should we go to their house? 18. I had to go to town in order to find what I wanted. 19. He ought not to have gone away without going to see them. 20. He did not know whether he ought to take a taxi or not.

Grammatical Exercise

1. He is expected to be here. 2. He ought to have come. 3. If he sent me that, I should not accept it. 4. When are you to leave? 5. I shall have to help them. 6. She must have been sick. 7. He will wait for me if it is not too late. 8. They were to leave at six o'clock. 9. One must not do that. 10. He must be very rich. 11. They would have come with us if they had not been busy. 12. John had to stay there. 13. We ought not to have gone away. 14. I am sorry that he must leave

so soon. 15. Had I had the time, I should have gone to see him. 16. They ought to send them to John. 17. At what time will he have to leave? 18. He did not know whether he should come. 19. They have had to wait for him.

The Infinitive

THE INFINITIVE AFTER OTHER VERBS

74. Verbs in French may be followed by an infinitive without a preposition, by **de** + an infinitive, or by **à** + an infinitive.

(1) The following common verbs govern an infinitive directly without a preposition:

aimer [1] to like	**oser** to dare
aimer mieux to prefer	**paraître** to appear
aller [2] to go	**penser** to think
compter to intend	**pouvoir** to be able
croire to believe	**préférer** to prefer
désirer to desire	**se rappeler** to recall
devoir must	**regarder** to look at
entendre to hear	**savoir** to know (how)
envoyer to send	**sembler** to seem
espérer to hope	**valoir mieux** to be preferable
faire to do, make	**venir** to come
falloir to be necessary	**voir** to see
laisser to let	**vouloir** to wish

(2) The following common verbs take **de** before a following infinitive:

cesser to cease	**décider** to decide
commander [3] to order	**défendre** [3] to forbid
conseiller [3] to advise	**demander** [3] to ask
craindre to fear	**se dépêcher** to hurry

[1] May also be followed by **à**.

[2] The other verbs of motion listed in § 48 (2) also govern an infinitive without a preposition.

[3] Takes indirect object of the person. **Il demande à Jean de l'aider.**

dire ³ to say, tell
empêcher to prevent
essayer to try
être obligé to be obliged
éviter to avoid
finir to finish
manquer to fail, come near
offrir to offer
oublier to forget

permettre ³ to permit
prier to pray, request
promettre ³ to promise
refuser to refuse
regretter to regret
remercier to thank
se souvenir to remember
tâcher to try

(3) The following common verbs take **à** before a following infinitive:

accoutumer to accustom
aider to help
apprendre to learn, teach
chercher to seek
commencer to begin
consentir to consent
continuer to continue

décider to induce
se décider to make up one's mind
inviter to invite
se mettre to begin
obliger to oblige, compel
réussir to succeed

A OR *DE* WITH THE INFINITIVE AFTER NOUNS AND ADJECTIVES

75. A noun or an adjective is generally followed by **à** + an infinitive when the infinitive may be made passive in English.⁴

Son écriture est difficile à lire.	His handwriting is hard to read (to be read).
Cela est facile à faire.	That is easy to do (to be done).
Voici un livre à vendre.	Here is a book for sale (to be sold).

76. A noun or an adjective is usually followed by **de** + an infinitive when the passive construction is not possible in English.

Il est facile de faire cela.	It is easy to do that.
J'ai pris la liberté de vous écrire.	I have taken the liberty of writing to you.
Il est difficile de chanter bien.	It is difficult to sing well.
Vous avez besoin de vous méfier.	You need to be suspicious.

³ Takes indirect object of the person. **Il demande à Jean de l'aider.**

⁴ A is also used with some intransitive verbs to denote use, fitness, etc.; **une chambre à coucher, une salle à manger.**

77. A few adjectives, such as **dernier, prêt,** and **seul,** are regularly followed by **à** + an infinitive.

Je suis prêt à partir.   I am ready to go.

THE INFINITIVE AFTER OTHER PREPOSITIONS

78. All prepositions except **en** are followed by the infinitive in French. **En** is followed by the present participle.

Il est parti sans nous dire adieu.   He left without saying good-by to us.

En entrant dans la classe.   On entering the classroom.

79. Pour is used with the infinitive:

(1) to translate *in order to;*

Il faut travailler pour réussir.   You must work in order to succeed.

(2) after verbs of motion when purpose is stressed;

Etes-vous venu pour travailler?   Have you come in order to work?
But:
Il est venu me voir hier soir.   He came to see me last night.

(3) after **assez** and **trop.**

Il a assez de temps pour vous voir.   He has time enough to see you.
Je suis trop occupé pour aller au théâtre.   I am too busy to go to the theater.

80. Par after **commencer** and **finir** is equivalent to the English *by* with the present participle.

Il a commencé par étudier le français.   He began by studying French.
But:
Il a commencé à étudier le français.   He began to study French.

81. Après requires the perfect infinitive; **sans,** either the present or the perfect infinitive.

Après avoir dîné, nous sommes allés en ville.   After dining, we went to town.

Il est parti sans $\left\{ \begin{array}{l} \text{dire} \\ \text{avoir dit} \end{array} \right\}$ He left without saying good-by to anyone.

adieu à personne.

Une invitation à prendre le thé

—Vous avez l'air de chercher quelqu'un, Raymond.

—Oui, Jane. Albert a promis de me retrouver devant Pons à cinq heures. Le voilà. Mademoiselle Robert, permettez-moi de vous présenter mon ami, Albert.

—Je suis enchanté de faire votre connaissance, mademoiselle. C'est votre première visite à Paris?

—Oui. Et il y a tant de choses à voir qu'il est très difficile de choisir les plus importantes.

—Il faut commencer par visiter les principales curiosités. Ensuite demandez à Raymond de vous montrer quelques-uns des petits coins pittoresques que les touristes ne découvrent pas toujours. Je m'empresse de me mettre à votre disposition, si Raymond est trop occupé pour vous servir de guide.

—Je vous remercie, monsieur. Justement, Raymond et moi, nous allons ce soir à un de ces coins-là. Voulez-vous nous faire le plaisir de nous accompagner?

—Volontiers. En attendant, rien ne nous oblige à rester devant une bonne pâtisserie. Entrons. Je vous invite à prendre le thé.

—Voilà une bonne idée, Albert. Il n'y a rien de plus rafraîchissant qu'une tasse de thé. N'est-ce pas, Jane?

—Surtout après avoir passé tout l'après-midi à courir les magasins, comme je viens de le faire.

—Laissez-moi vous servir.

—Sans citron, s'il vous plaît. Pas de lait non plus. Du sucre et un petit gâteau. C'est ça.

—Maintenant, Raymond, quelle est cette boîte de nuit où vous comptez mener Mlle Robert ce soir?

—Le Lapin Agile. Ce n'est pas précisément une boîte. C'est une petite salle aménagée dans un sous-sol où on entend des chansons d'autrefois et où des poètes viennent réciter leurs vers. On n'y voit en général que des Français, car les cabarets à la mode semblent attirer la plupart des touristes.

—Ça doit être très intéressant. Je ne manquerai pas de vous y accompagner.

Conversation

1. Qu'est-ce qu'Albert a promis à Raymond? 2. Quelle est la formule en français pour faire une présentation? 3. Pourquoi est-il difficile de choisir ce qu'on devrait voir à Paris? 4. Où peut-on aller à Paris sans trouver beaucoup de touristes? 5. Qu'est-ce qu'on vend dans une pâtisserie? 6. Que prend-on ordinairement avec le thé? 7. Comment Jane a-t-elle passé son après-midi? 8. Comment s'appelle la boîte de nuit qu'ils vont visiter? 9. Expliquez la phrase "boîte de nuit." 10. Quelle sorte de divertissement trouve-t-on au Lapin Agile?

Composition

"Is Miss Robert at home?"

"Yes, sir. Please step into the living room, and I'll ask her if she can [5] see you."

"Miss Robert? Permit me to introduce myself. I am Albert Miller. My aunt wrote me that you were to arrive in Paris and asked me to look you up. This is (**voici**) my friend, Raymond Alton."

"It is very nice of you to think of me. You must know Paris very well. Perhaps you will help me to choose the most important things to see. I am sorry that I have only four weeks to spend here."

"We shall be happy to put ourselves at your disposal. Most tourists begin by visiting Notre-Dame, the Louvre, and the Champs-Elysées. They are obliged, of course, to know all the popular night clubs. Many of (**d'entre**) them end by leaving the city without having seen anything (of) [6] truly Parisian."

"You are beginning to worry me. Are you forbidding me to admire the stained-glass windows of the Sainte-Chapelle? Are you advising me not to go to the Bal Tabarin?"

"On the contrary. Don't fail to see all the principal sights. As for cabarets, if you are not too tired to go out this evening, we should like to take you to the Oubliettes."

"Is it a night club?"

---

[5] Future tense. Cf. § 71 (2).
[6] Cf. § 128.

"Not exactly. It is a little hall fitted up in a basement, where, with old furniture, old instruments of torture, and stone walls, they have succeeded in imitating rather well the dungeons of an old castle. In this setting, artists wearing ancient costumes sing eighteenth-century songs and others that the public requests them to sing."

"You need not tell me [any] more.[7] At nine o'clock I shall be ready to accompany you."

Drill Exercise

1. He promised to have a cup of tea with me. 2. It is already beginning to rain; let's go into this pastry shop. 3. After looking at the menu, I have decided to take some tea. 4. I advise you to take some cakes; I am very fond of them. 5. I shall not fail to follow your advice. 6. We should have invited John to come with us. 7. Nothing prevents us from telephoning to him now; that is easy to do. 8. I am sure that he would be very glad to join us here. 9. What do you want to take with your tea: lemon, milk, sugar? 10. Did you know that Henry intends to spend this summer in France? 11. John told me yesterday that at last he has enough money to make the trip. 12. I shall invite him to come to my house, but he will be too busy to spend much time in Paris. 13. He does not want to miss this opportunity to see Southern France, where he has some old friends. 14. However, I shall be glad to act as his guide while he is here. 15. If you succeed in finding him at home, tell him to come and join us at (**chez**) Pons'. 16. I have just telephoned him, and he consented to come here right away. 17. There he is. Hurry and order your tea; Albert has already finished his second cup. 18. Let me light a cigarette first. 19. While shopping this afternoon, I ran across one of your friends.

---

[7] **Davantage.** Cf. page 39, note 2.

Special Uses of
Falloir, Pouvoir, Savoir, *and* Faire

82. Falloir (cf. § 156) has two meanings:

(1) *must, to be necessary, to have to* (**falloir** is the usual translation of the English *must* except where *must* expresses duty or moral obligation, when **devoir** replaces it);

Il faut que je finisse mon travail avant six heures.	I must finish my work before six o'clock.

Falloir is regularly followed by the subjunctive, but an infinitive replaces the subjunctive when the context shows clearly to whom the statement applies.

Il faut que je m'en aille.	I must leave.
Il faut tenir sa parole.	One should keep his word.
Un cadeau pour moi? Il faut me le montrer.	A present for me? You must show it to me.

Used negatively, **falloir** means *must not. It is not necessary* is translated by **il n'est pas nécessaire.**

Il ne faut pas dépenser tant d'argent.	You (one, we) must not spend so much money.
Il n'est pas nécessaire de m'attendre.	It is not necessary to wait for me.

(2) *to need, require, must have, it takes* + an expression of time, measure, price, etc.

Il me faut un nouveau chapeau.	I need (must have) a new hat.
Il lui faut dix minutes pour aller à la gare.	He needs (It takes him) ten minutes to go to the station.

83. Pouvoir (cf. § 156) *to be able, can, may, might, could*. The required tense of **pouvoir** can usually be determined by substituting for *can, may,* etc., the equivalent tense of the verbal phrase *to be able.*

Puis-je partir?	Can (May) I go?
Etant malade, il ne pouvait pas travailler.	As he was sick, he could not (was not able to) work.
J'ai pu (Je pus) le rejoindre.	I was able to (could and did) overtake him.
Pourriez-vous m'accompagner?	Could you (Would you be able to) accompany me?
J'aurais pu vous aider.	I could have (might have) helped you (would have been able to help you).

84. Savoir and Connaître (cf. § 156):

(1) **Savoir** has two meanings: (a) *to know how, can, be able* + infinitive (**savoir** translates *can, to be able* in the sense of *to know how;* **pouvoir** translates *to be able* in all other cases);

Il sait jouer du piano.	He can (knows how) to play the piano.
Il ne peut (pourra) pas jouer ce soir, parce qu'il est malade.	He cannot (won't be able) to play tonight because he is sick.

(b) *to know* (with the mind), *know* (as a fact), *know by heart;* in the past definite and past indefinite tenses, *learned, found out.*

Je sais ce qu'il a fait.	I know what he has done.
Je sais qu'il est ici.	I know that he is here.
Nous savions nos leçons.	We knew our lessons.
J'ai su hier que vous étiez arrivé.	I learned yesterday that you had arrived.

(2) **Connaître** means *to know* in the sense of *to be acquainted with, be familiar with;* in the past definite and past indefinite tenses, *became acquainted with.*

Connaissez-vous M. Hébert?	Do you know Mr. Hébert?
Elle connaît très bien Paris.	She knows Paris very well.

Il l'a connue à Londres.   He became acquainted with her in
London.

85. Faire (cf. § 156) before an infinitive has the meaning *to have,
to make, to cause to be done, to order.*

(1) **Faire** may take a direct object, which is at the same time the
subject of the infinitive.

J'ai fait écrire l'étudiant.   I made the student write.
Je l'ai fait écrire.   I made him write.

(2) The infinitive after **faire** may have a direct object, in which
case the infinitive is best rendered in English by a passive form.

Elle a fait servir le café.   She had (someone) serve the coffee;
she had the coffee served.
Elle l'a fait servir.   She had (someone) serve it; she had
it served.

(3) If **faire** and the infinitive each have an object, the object of
faire is indirect in form.

Il a fait étudier la leçon à [1] l'élève.   He had the pupil study the lesson.
Il lui a fait étudier la leçon.   He had him study the lesson.
Il la lui a fait étudier.   He had him study it.
Faites-la-lui étudier.   Have him study it.

Note that all pronoun objects go with **faire** and that noun objects follow the infinitive, the direct object preceding the indirect.

Cours de vacances

Cher Henri:

Quelle bonne nouvelle vous m'annoncez dans votre dernière lettre.
J'ai su il y a quelque temps par votre sœur que vous vouliez venir en
France mais je ne savais pas que vous deviez partir si tôt. Vous me
demandez si vous pourriez suivre les cours de vacances à la Sorbonne.
Naturellement, mais je ne crois pas que ce soit là ce qu'il vous faut.
Vous ne savez pas assez bien le français pour profiter de ces cours-là.

---

[1] To avoid ambiguity, **par** may replace **à. Elle a fait lire ce livre par les élèves.**
She had the pupils read this book.

Et puis, il ne faut pas passer tout votre temps à Paris. Inscrivez-vous plutôt à l'Institut du Panthéon et allez à son annexe d'été, située à Saint-Quay-Portrieux, une des stations balnéaires les plus pittoresques de la Bretagne. Je connais l'école et je sais qu'elle est bonne. Notre West Point y envoie tous les ans une demi-douzaine d'officiers, qui doivent se perfectionner dans la pratique de la langue française avant de s'inscrire pour le cours de civilisation française à la Sorbonne. Cet arrangement leur fait passer de bonnes vacances, tout en apprenant le français. Les leçons et les cours ont lieu le matin; l'après-midi et la soirée sont consacrées aux sports: promenades, plage, tennis, etc. On travaille et on s'amuse en français, car on fait promettre formellement à chaque étudiant de ne parler que le français durant son séjour à l'école. Il n'est pas nécessaire d'y rester tout l'été. On accepte des inscriptions pour n'importe quelle durée. Si cette idée vous tente, faites-le-moi savoir et je vous ferai retenir une chambre avec eau courante chaude et froide. Vous pourrez vous passer de salle de bain particulière. Cela reviendrait trop cher.

Cordiale poignée de main de votre ami

Raymond

Conversation

1. Quelle bonne nouvelle est-ce qu'Henri annonce à Raymond? 2. Qu'est-ce qu'il lui demande? 3. Pourquoi Raymond lui conseille-t-il de ne pas s'inscrire à la Sorbonne? 4. Où lui conseille-t-il de s'inscrire? 5. Dans quelle partie de la France se trouve la Bretagne? 6. Pourquoi y envoie-t-on des officiers américains? 7. Quand est-ce que les cours à Saint-Quay ont lieu? 8. Que fait-on l'après-midi? 9. Que fait-on promettre à chaque étudiant? 10. Qu'est-ce que Raymond suggère à Henri? 11. Quelle sorte de chambre compte-t-il retenir pour Henri?

Composition

Albert was leaving the Sorbonne, where he had just attended a public lecture, when he met Lieutenant Haynes. He had known him at Madame Bernard's and knew that he had registered for the summer courses at a school in Brittany.

"Hello, (my) Lieutenant. You are looking well. You must have spent a good vacation in Brittany."

"Excellent. I could not have found a more picturesque spot. You know it, don't you? The beach is perfect if you know how to swim, but you must not forget that there are often tides of twenty-five feet that can be dangerous. I must show you some photographs that I took while I was there. I am having them developed now."

"I should like to see them. What do you think of the school itself? Can I recommend it to a friend who might decide to go there next summer?"

"Yes. I found there exactly what I needed. They made us promise to speak only French during our stay at Saint-Quay. Even during our walks and our tennis matches we had to speak French. If your friend wants to perfect himself in the spoken language, he cannot do better than to choose this school. You took the course in (de) French civilization at the Sorbonne this summer, didn't you? Did you find it difficult?"

"Somewhat. I have just taken my examinations, but I shall not know before next week whether I have failed in them or whether I have passed."

"Let's hope that you will pass. I must be off now. I am supposed to be at the Café de la Paix at five o'clock, and it will take me twenty minutes to go there."

Drill Exercise I

1. I learned yesterday that Lieutenant Haynes is to arrive next Monday. Did you know it? 2. Do you know Brittany? 3. You might very well spend a few weeks there. 4. You must not leave France without seeing one or two of the French provinces. 5. Could you recommend to me a good seaside resort? 6. I shall have a room reserved for you at Saint-Quay. 7. How long will it take me to go there? 8. By automobile it will take you twelve hours. 9. It is not necessary to choose an expensive hotel. 10. Must you have a room with [a private] bath? 11. You can have your trunk sent to the hotel. 12. Or shall I have it sent to you? 13. Have it sent to me as soon as it arrives.[2] 14. I could have accompanied you if I had not registered for the summer courses here. 15. You will have to study mornings, but afternoons you can swim or play tennis. 16. You know how to play tennis, don't you?

[2] What tense?

17. Don't forget that you will have to take examinations at the end of the course. 18. You must not fail in them.

Drill Exercise II

1. We must always obey our parents. 2. How long will it take you to go there? 3. We could not go with him last night. 4. If John had the time, he could help you to write the letter. 5. Can you go to the theater with us this evening? 6. They are giving *Cyrano*. Do you know that play? 7. This novel is very interesting; I shall have him read it. 8. In order to make the trip, he needs more money. 9. He will know soon how much money he will need. 10. It was necessary to send the letters to her; he could not have done anything else. 11. They know how to speak French. 12. I shall have him see the doctor immediately. 13. I have to pack my trunk now. 14. We are having them sent to Mary. 15. We could have gone with you if we had not had an appointment with Henry. 16. I did not know that you knew him. 17. It will not be necessary to wait for us. 18. I could have told him what he ought to do. 19. Could you lend me your fountain pen? 20. I must see them before their departure. 21. I am glad that you know it now. 22. They made a trip to Europe last summer. 23. I shall have him read them.

Demonstrative Adjectives and Pronouns — Adverbs

DEMONSTRATIVE ADJECTIVES

86. Table of the demonstrative adjectives:

SINGULAR		PLURAL	
M. **ce, cet**	this, that	**ces**	these, those
F. **cette**	this, that	**ces**	these, those

87. The demonstrative adjectives agree in number and gender with the nouns they modify and are repeated before each noun. The masculine singular form **cet** is used before a vowel or **h** mute.

Cet homme et cette femme.   This man and that woman.

88. To distinguish *this* from *that* and *these* from *those,* **-ci** and **-là** may be added to the noun.

**Ce livre-ci est plus intéressant que   This book is more interesting than
ce livre-là.**   that book.

DEMONSTRATIVE PRONOUNS

89. Forms of the demonstrative pronouns:

(1) Variable forms:

SINGULAR		PLURAL	
M. **celui** ⎱	this one, that one,	**ceux** ⎱	these, those,
F. **celle** ⎰	the one, he, she	**celles** ⎰	the ones, they

Note that these forms are combinations of the demonstrative adjective **ce** and the disjunctive pronouns **lui, eux, elle, elles.**

(2) Invariable forms:

ce this, that, it
ceci this
cela, ça that

90. The variable forms agree in number and gender with a definite antecedent. They are never used alone. They are followed by:

(1) a relative clause;

| Ce livre est celui que vous avez déjà lu. | This book is the one that you have already read. |

(2) a prepositional phrase, generally introduced by **de**;

| Mes amies et celles de ma sœur sont déjà arrivées. | My friends and my sister's (those of my sister) have already arrived. |

(3) **-ci** or **-là**.

| Ceux-ci sont à moi; ceux-là sont à vous. | These are mine; those are yours. |

91. Ceci *this* and cela *that* cannot have a particular word as an
antecedent. They refer to an idea or a thing not specifically mentioned.

| Cela est très important. | That is very important. |
| Je n'aime pas ceci. | I don't like this. |

92. Ce as the subject of être. See § 70.

93. Ce followed by the relative pronoun **qui, que,** or **dont** translates the English *what, that which.*

Dites-moi ce qu'il a fait.	Tell me what he did.
Je sais ce qui est arrivé.	I know what has happened.
C'est ce dont je ne me souviens pas.	That's what I don't remember.

ADVERBS

94. (1) There are in French many simple adverbs such as **ainsi**
thus, **alors** *then,* and **souvent** *often.* In addition, most adjectives
may be converted into adverbs by adding **-ment** to the feminine

singular. Adjectives ending in a vowel in the masculine singular
add **-ment** to the masculine singular.

sûr	sûre	sûrement	surely
facile	facile	facilement	easily
absolu	absolue	absolument	absolutely
doux	douce	doucement	gently

(2) Note the following common exceptions:

constant	constante	constamment	constantly
énorme	énorme	énormément	enormously
nouveau	nouvelle	nouvellement	newly
précis	précise	précisément	precisely
récent	récente	récemment	recently

95. A few common adjectives, such as **bon, cher, ferme,** and
mauvais, are used as adverbs in fixed phrases.

Ces plumes m'ont coûté cher.	Those pens cost me dear.
Cette pipe sent bon (mauvais).	That pipe smells good (bad).
Il travaille ferme.	He is working hard.

COMPARISON OF ADVERBS

96. (1) The comparative of an adverb is formed, like that of an
adjective, by placing **plus, moins, si,** or **aussi** before the adverb.
Than is translated by **que.** The superlative is formed by placing
invariable **le** before the comparative.

Marie parle français plus (moins) correctement que Jean. C'est Pierre qui le parle le plus correctement.	Mary speaks French more (less) correctly than John. Peter speaks it the most correctly.

(2) *More than* and *less than* as adverbs of quantity = **plus de**
and **moins de.**

Il m'a donné plus de dix francs.	He gave me more than ten francs.

97. The following adverbs are compared irregularly:

bien well	**mieux** better	**le mieux** (the) best
mal badly, ill	$\left\{\begin{array}{l}\text{plus mal}\\ \text{pis}\end{array}\right\}$ worse	$\left\{\begin{array}{l}\text{le plus mal}\\ \text{le pis}\end{array}\right\}$ (the) worst

beaucoup much	**plus** more	**le plus** (the) most
peu little	**moins** less	**le moins** the least

Note: **Beaucoup** may never be modified by another adverb except **pas**.

Quel bon vent vous amène?

—Je ne sais pas ce qui m'arrive, dit Albert un jour, mais Paris commence à m'ennuyer.

—Cela se comprend facilement, répondit Raymond. En cette saison Paris est plein de touristes qui parlent français encore plus mal que nous. Nous serions mieux en province.

—Savez-vous ce que nous devrions faire? Louons une auto et faisons une tournée en Touraine. Cela ne coûterait pas bien cher. Nous pourrions visiter le château de Blois et peut-être tous ceux de la région.

Peu de jours après une vieille auto filait par une petite route entre des champs où les vignes poussaient vigoureusement.

—"Chargé. 200 habitants," lisait Raymond dans son guide Taride. Mais ce doit être le village où habite notre ami, le curé.

—En effet. Le voilà, qui se promène devant son église. Bonjour, monsieur le curé, cria-t-il en arrêtant l'auto.

—Tiens! Mes deux Américains! Bonjour, mes amis. Quel bon vent vous amène?

—Mais le vent de votre belle province, monsieur le curé. Il est autrement (*far more*) parfumé que celui de la capitale.

Ils étaient descendus de voiture et se promenaient lentement avec le curé.

—Vous avez raison, dit le vieux curé, mais seulement jusqu'à un certain point. Notre petit vent sent bon les jardins en fleur et les foins coupés mais il flétrit aussi. Tenez! Vous voyez cette paysanne qui s'approche de nous, celle qui porte sur le dos ce gros tas de fagots. Elle paraît avoir plus de soixante-dix ans. Eh bien, non. Elle est moins âgée que vous ne le croyez. Je me rappelle bien le jour de ses fiançailles. Elle était si jolie, si gaie. Et maintenant...

Mais la paysanne entendit ce qu'il disait. Son visage ridé s'illumina d'un doux sourire.

—Ah! monsieur le curé, dit-elle, on ne peut pas être et avoir été.

Conversation

1. Pourquoi est-ce que Paris commence à ennuyer Albert? 2. Que propose-t-il à Raymond? 3. Y a-t-il beaucoup de choses intéressantes à voir en Touraine? 4. Où arrivent-ils enfin? 5. Quel ami retrouvent-ils à Chargé? 6. Comment les reçoit-il? 7. Quelle est l'observation du curé au sujet du vent de son pays? 8. Pourquoi est-ce que la paysanne a l'air si âgée? 9. Qu'est-ce que la vieille dit au curé?

Composition

"This automobile is much better than the one you had last summer."

"Of course. It cost me rather dear, but it is exactly what we need for our little trip in Touraine."

"You were lucky to find what you wanted. How beautiful this country is! Have you ever seen vineyards as green as these? How good the new-mown hay smells!"

"Here's a crossroad. We must not take the wrong road. You have the Taride guidebook, haven't you?"

"Continue straight ahead. Chargé is (at) less than two kilometers from here. That might well be the church that we see over there near that little wood."

"We shall soon see. Yes. There it is. And there's the old curé. Good afternoon, monsieur le curé. We arrive earlier than you thought."

"So much the better. We shall have more time to chat. I was just (justement) saying to one of our peasant women that two Americans were to call on me this afternoon, and you see what has happened. She has sat down on that milestone in order to observe you. You must not be put out with her. Life is rather monotonous here."

"Why! she is old and wrinkled. She does not look strong enough to carry that enormous pile of fagots beside her."

"Oh, she is still hale and hearty in spite of her age and her wrinkles. And once she was the prettiest woman in the village."

The curé had spoken in a low voice, but the peasant woman had heard, nevertheless, what he was saying.

"What is past is past, monsieur le curé," she said, rising and picking up her fagots. "You can't eat your cake and have it."[1]

Drill Exercise

1. I like this novel better than those. 2. What we need is an automobile that does not cost too much. 3. My friends and John's have been studying French for several months. 4. He can easily do that, but this is more difficult. 5. Those tourists over there are the ones we saw at Blois. 6. This château is more beautiful than that of Blois, isn't it? Not much. 7. I don't know what has happened to him. 8. This hat becomes you better than that one. 9. You remember that young Frenchman, don't you? The one to whom I introduced you recently. 10. My room is less expensive than those you saw yesterday. 11. There were more than fifteen persons at dinner. 12. This is (**voici**) the student who speaks French the most correctly. 13. We don't know what we shall say to them. 14. According to my guidebook, this road is the one that leads to Chargé. 15. I will lend you these books, but I can't lend you Mary's. 16. The flowers we bought yesterday still smell good. 17. She does not speak French as fluently as he. 18. He who works will learn more than he who amuses himself. 19. What I remember with the greatest pleasure is our trip to Touraine. 20. Mary's friends and John's will be here early. 21. Less than twenty persons were visiting the château. 22. He gets up at seven o'clock and works hard all day.

Verb Review

tenir to hold; cf. § 156	**venir** to come; cf. § 156
appartenir to belong	**devenir** to become
maintenir to maintain	**revenir** to come back, return
obtenir to obtain, get	**se souvenir de** to remember; cf. p. 45, note 5

1. To whom do these gloves belong? 2. He never remembered names. 3. I am afraid that he may never come back. 4. When will he return? 5. They often came to see us. 6. He would obtain what he wants if he talked to Mr. Martin about it. 7. Do you know what has become

[1] Use the expression given in the French text or the proverb: **On ne peut pas avoir le drap et l'argent.**

of her? 8. That house used to belong to my family. 9. Always remember your parents' advice. 10. He maintains that you are wrong. 11. I am sure that he will remember you. 12. They had just arrived. 13. He got (*p. def.*) what he needed and came back (*p. def.*) immediately.

Possessive Adjectives and Pronouns
Expressions of Time

POSSESSIVE ADJECTIVES

98. Table of the possessive adjectives:

	SINGULAR	PLURAL	
MASC.	FEM.	MASC. AND FEM.	
mon	ma	mes	my
ton	ta	tes	your, thy
son	sa	ses	his, her
notre	notre	nos	our
votre	votre	vos	your
leur	leur	leurs	their

99. (1) Possessive adjectives, contrary to English usage, agree in gender and number with the thing possessed, not with the possessor. They are repeated before each noun modified.

Son livre et son stylo.   His (her) book and his (her) fountain pen.

(2) To avoid ambiguity, the possessive adjective may be supplemented by **à** + a disjunctive pronoun.

Son livre à lui (à elle).   His (her) book.

(3) Emphatic *own* is translated by **propre** or by **à** + a disjunctive pronoun.

Mon propre livre. }
Mon livre à moi. }   My own book.

100. Mon, ton, and **son** are used instead of **ma, ta,** and **sa** before a vowel or **h** mute.

    Mon amie.   My friend.

101. The definite article generally replaces the possessive adjective in referring to parts of the body when there is no ambiguity as to the possessor.

Je me suis coupé le doigt.	I cut my finger.
Ils ont levé la [1] main droite.	They raised their right hands.
Elle a les yeux bleus.	She has blue eyes.

POSSESSIVE PRONOUNS

102. Table of the possessive pronouns:

SINGULAR	PLURAL	
{ le mien, *m.*	les miens	} mine
{ la mienne, *f.*	les miennes	
{ le tien, *m.*	les tiens	} thine
{ la tienne, *f.*	les tiennes	
{ le sien, *m.*	les siens	} his, hers
{ la sienne, *f.*	les siennes	
le (la) nôtre, *m. and f.*	les nôtres	ours
le (la) vôtre, *m. and f.*	les vôtres	yours
le (la) leur, *m. and f.*	les leurs	theirs

103. Possessive pronouns agree in gender and number, as do the adjectives, with the thing possessed, not with the possessor.

Mon auto et la sienne.	My auto and his (hers).
J'ai répondu à ses lettres et aux vôtres.	I have answered his (her) letters and yours.

104. *Mine,* etc. after the verb **être** is translated by **à** + a disjunctive pronoun, except when distinction of ownership is stressed. In this case, a possessive pronoun is generally used.

---

[1] The singular is generally used when each individual possesses but one of the objects named.

Ce livre est à moi.	This book is mine.
Ce livre-ci est le mien; celui-là est le vôtre.	This book is mine; that one is yours.

105. *A friend of mine* (*his,* etc.) is paraphrased by *one of my* (*his,* etc.) *friends.*

Un de mes amis.	A friend of mine.
Un professeur de ses amis.	A professor who is a friend of his.

EXPRESSIONS OF TIME

106. Expressions of time:

Quelle heure est-il?	What time is it?
Il est cinq heures et demie.[2]	It is half past five.
Il est dix heures et (*or* un) quart.	It is a quarter past ten.
Il est midi vingt (minutes).[3]	It is twenty minutes past twelve (noon).
Il est neuf heures moins cinq (minutes).	It is five minutes to nine.
Il est minuit moins le (*or* un) quart.	It is a quarter to twelve (midnight).
A onze heures précises.	At eleven o'clock sharp.
A huit heures du matin (du soir).	At eight A. M. (P. M.).
Quelle heure avez-vous à votre montre?	What time is it by your watch?
Ma montre avance (retarde) de deux minutes.	My watch is two minutes fast (slow).
Il est tard.	It is late.
Je suis en retard.	I am late (behind time).
Je suis en avance.	I am early (ahead of time).
Le train est arrivé à l'heure.	The train arrived on time.
Nous sommes arrivés à temps pour prendre le train.	We arrived in time to catch the train.
Mon train avait (est arrivé avec) une heure de retard.	My train was (arrived) an hour late.

[2] **Demi** standing before a noun is invariable and is joined to the noun by a hyphen. **Une demi-heure,** a half hour.

[3] In timetables and other schedules, 1 P. M. becomes **13 heures,** 2 P. M. **14 heures,** etc. **Rideau à 20 heures 45.** Curtain at 8:45.

J'ai peur

Cela a commencé l'an dernier d'une singulière façon. C'était en automne par un soir humide. Il faisait triste partout. Dans les cafés des gens tristes, assis devant des tables, semblaient n'avoir pas même la force de finir leurs consommations. Sans toucher à la mienne, je me levai et sortis sur le boulevard. J'errai longtemps et vers minuit je rentrai chez moi. Ma concierge, qui se couche avant onze heures, m'ouvrit tout de suite, contrairement à son habitude. Quand je sors de chez moi, je ferme toujours ma porte à clef. Je la trouvai simplement tirée et cela me frappa. Je supposai qu'on avait monté des lettres dans la soirée.

J'entrai. Mon feu brûlait et éclairait un peu l'appartement. J'allais allumer une bougie, quand j'aperçus quelqu'un assis dans mon fauteuil et qui se chauffait les pieds en me tournant le dos.

Je n'eus pas peur. Une supposition très vraisemblable me traversa l'esprit, celle qu'un de mes amis était venu pour me voir, qu'il avait demandé ma clef à la concierge et qu'elle lui avait donné la sienne.

Mon ami, dont je ne voyais que les cheveux, s'était endormi devant mon feu en m'attendant et je m'avançai pour le réveiller. Ses pieds étaient croisés l'un sur l'autre; sa tête penchée sur le côté gauche du fauteuil indiquait bien le sommeil. J'avançai la main pour lui toucher l'épaule.

Je rencontrai le bois du siège! Il n'y avait plus personne! Le fauteuil était vide!

Trois fois depuis j'ai cru revoir l'homme assis dans mon fauteuil. Quand reviendra-t-il? D'aujourd'hui en huit? D'ici un an? Jamais, sans doute. Mais je le sens là derrière moi et j'ai peur. Je ne peux plus rester seul chez moi.

D'après Maupassant

Conversation

1. Quand est-ce que cet incident a eu lieu pour la première fois? 2. Quel temps faisait-il? 3. Comment Maupassant avait-il passé la soirée? 4. A quelle heure est-il rentré chez lui? 5. En trouvant sa porte simplement tirée, qu'a-t-il pensé? 6. Qu'est-ce qu'il a vu en rentrant dans son appartement? 7. Quelle idée lui est venue tout de suite à l'esprit? 8. Comment l'étranger s'était-il installé? 9. Qu'est-ce que Maupassant a

fait ensuite? 10. Qui a-t-il trouvé dans son fauteuil? 11. Est-ce que le souvenir de cet incident a persisté longtemps dans l'esprit de Maupassant? 12. Pourquoi ne veut-il plus rester seul chez lui?

Composition

My grandmother told me this story many years ago. If you don't believe it, please remember that it is her story, not mine. Here it is.

"On (**Par**) a gloomy autumn evening, my cousin Martha and I left the house toward eight o'clock in order to go to say good-by to Aunt Jane, who was to take the 8:20 express. I don't know whether my watch was slow or whether the train arrived ahead of time, but we did not reach the station in time to see Aunt Jane. Instead of going back home, we decided that it was not too late to go to see our friends the Martins. On entering their living room, I noticed someone whom I did not know. He was a man of about sixty (years). I remember that he was very tall and that his hair was gray. Mrs. Martin introduced him to us as one of her relatives who was visiting our city for the first time. He listened to our conversation without taking part in it, and the idea that he was displeased by our visit crossed my mind. He was seated near the fireplace, his feet crossed one over the other, his eyes closed, as if he were asleep. I felt like stretching out my hand and touching his shoulder.

"Suddenly he got up, turned toward me, and, pointing with (**de**) his left hand to the first finger of my right hand, said to me: 'Mary, do you remember that finger? Today is the fifteenth of October.'

"I looked at him astounded. I remembered, indeed, the accident that had spoiled my eighth birthday, how I had broken my finger while playing with my small friends. But how had he learned of (**su**) it, this stranger, who before that evening had never seen me, had never heard of me?"

Drill Exercise

1. Today is the twenty-first of August, and a week from today we must leave. 2. Those books are mine; yours are on the table; where are his? 3. My car is not here; let's take yours; it is at the door. 4. It is half past five; our train leaves at a quarter of six. 5. When does hers leave? It leaves in half an hour. 6. Your brother is eighteen years

old; mine is only fifteen. 7. I met a friend of yours yesterday. 8. We visited the Louvre a week ago; it is a very interesting museum. 9. Your train arrived on time; mine was an hour late. 10. He was to be at the station at 8:30 P. M., but he must have forgotten our appointment. 11. He was here two years ago, when I was in America. 12. My letter, yours, and John's are in the living room. 13. It was late, but we arrived in time to see them. 14. What time is it by your watch? Mine is three minutes slow. 15. I shall be on time, but they are nearly always late. 16. On the sixteenth we arrived in Paris, and the following week we left for London. 17. I am to see him on Monday at six o'clock sharp. 18. I like their rooms better than ours, but ours are less expensive. 19. It is getting late. 20. He cut his finger this morning, but it was not serious. 21. These books are theirs; they are not hers; hers are in her room. 22. She is four years younger than I. 23. She will be fifteen years old next Friday.

Verb Review

écrire to write; cf. § 156   **lire** to read; cf. § 156
  décrire to describe

1. He was reading a detective story while I was writing some letters. 2. Describe to me the town where you stopped. 3. I shall read you what I wrote. 4. He would have written to them if he had known their address. 5. What are you writing? I am writing my French exercise. 6. He wrote (*p. def.*) the letter and read (*p. def.*) it to me. 7. What are you reading? I am reading the advertisements in the newspaper. 8. If I had the opportunity, I should describe our trip to you. 9. After going to bed, I always read for an hour. 10. I should read you that passage if you wanted to listen to it. 11. I am afraid that he doesn't read very well. 12. He wants me to describe to him what I saw in Europe. 13. They will write to you soon. 14. I like Hugo's novels very much, but I have read only two of them. 15. Read me what he says in his letter.

The Relative Pronouns

107. The forms of the relative pronoun are:

	ANTECEDENT A PERSON	ANTECEDENT A THING	
Subject	**qui**	**qui**	who, which, that
Direct object	**que**	**que**	whom, which, that
Object of prepositions	**qui**	M. **lequel,**[1] **lesquels**	whom, which
		F. **laquelle, lesquelles**	
		quoi	what
de + a relative pronoun	**dont**	**dont**	of whom, of which, whose

Relative pronouns are required in French, even though omitted in English.

Les élèves qui sont ici.	The pupils who are here.
Les livres qu'il m'a donnés.	The books (that) he gave me.
Le monsieur à qui vous parlez.	The man to whom you are talking.
Le livre auquel je pense.	The book (that) I am thinking of.

108. Lequel may be used in place of any of the other forms of the relative pronoun when required for clearness and must be used of persons after **parmi** and **entre.**

La sœur de Jean, laquelle vient d'arriver.	John's sister, who has just arrived.
Les invités, parmi lesquels se trouvait son cousin.	The guests, among whom was his cousin.

109. Quoi *what* is used only after a preposition and without a definite antecedent.

Je ne sais pas avec quoi je vais écrire.	I don't know with what I am going to write.

[1] Lequel, lesquels, and lesquelles combine with **de** and **à**, giving **duquel, desquels, desquelles** and **auquel, auxquels, auxquelles.**

110. (1) **Dont,** equivalent to **de** + a relative pronoun, is commonly used in place of **de qui** or **duquel** to translate the English *of whom, of which, whose*. **Dont** must be immediately followed by the subject of the verb in the clause introduced by it. A noun after **dont** in the sense of *whose* must be preceded by the definite article.

Voici le roman dont je vous parlais.	Here is the novel of which I was telling you.
C'est un livre dont le prix est très élevé.	It's a book whose price (of which the price) is very high.
Voici mon cousin, dont vous connaissez déjà la sœur.	This is my cousin, whose sister you already know.

(2) When, in English, *whose* is preceded by a preposition, it cannot be rendered in French by **dont**. Instead, **de qui** (of persons) or **de** + a form of **lequel** (of persons or things) must be used.

Le monsieur avec le fils de qui (duquel) je me promenais.	The man with whose son (with the son of whom) I was walking.

111. The relative pronouns, preceded by the indefinite antecedent **ce** (cf. § 93), are used to translate the English *what, that which*, and, preceded by the demonstrative pronouns **celui, celle,** etc. (cf. § 90), to translate *the one that, he who, those who, whoever*, etc.

Je ne sais pas ce qui vous amuse.	I don't know what is amusing you.
Je me demande ce qu'il me donnera.	I wonder what he will give me.
Ce stylo-là est celui dont je me sers.	That fountain pen is the one I use.
Ces cravates-là ne sont pas celles que j'ai commandées.	Those neckties are not the ones I ordered.
Celui qui dit cela se trompe.	Whoever says that is mistaken.

112. The adverb **où** *where* is often used instead of a relative pronoun preceded by a preposition meaning *to, at, in, on,* etc.

La maison où (dans laquelle) je   The house in which I live.
   demeure.

Le jour où nous sommes arrivés.   The day on which we arrived.

Dans un magasin

Albert donna le dernier coup de brosse au veston qu'il venait de mettre en échange de celui, plus usagé, qu'il portait chez lui. Il se regarda dans la glace, rectifia la position de sa cravate, dont il admira les couleurs voyantes, et se retourna pour prendre sur le lit son pardessus et son chapeau. Le pardessus était un beau vêtement neuf mais le feutre—il s'en apercevait avec horreur—était sale et démodé. Jane, avec qui il devait sortir ce soir-là, ne manquerait pas de le remarquer. Décidément il fallait en acheter un autre. Il ouvrit un tiroir, au fond duquel il gardait son argent, en tira quelques billets qu'il mit dans son portefeuille et se rendit chez un chapelier, dont un ami lui avait donné l'adresse. C'était une chapellerie Mossant, à la devanture de laquelle était exposé un grand choix de modèles de tous les prix. Albert examina l'étalage mais, n'y voyant pas ce qu'il désirait, entra dans la boutique.

—Monsieur désire un chapeau melon? lui demanda le vendeur.

—Non, monsieur. Je désire un chapeau mou en feutre gris foncé dans le genre de celui que je porte. Pointure 7⅛.

—Voici un modèle à 200 francs qui vous ira à merveille.

—Vous n'auriez pas quelque chose de meilleur marché? D'ailleurs, le bord de celui-ci est trop étroit.

Albert se fit montrer beaucoup de chapeaux, en essaya plusieurs et finit par trouver ce qu'il cherchait.

—C'est tout ce qu'il vous faut aujourd'hui? C'est 120 francs alors. Veuillez passer à la caisse.

Content de son achat, Albert descendit le boulevard en flânant, en attendant l'heure de rejoindre Raymond, avec qui il devait aller au cinéma.

Conversation

1. Quels préparatifs Albert fait-il avant de sortir? 2. Son pardessus est-il sale et démodé? 3. A-t-il peur que Jane remarque l'état de son chapeau? 4. Que décide-t-il de faire? 5. Où est-ce qu'Albert garde son

argent? 6. Expliquez en français ce que c'est qu'un chapelier. 7. Que voit Albert à la devanture de la chapellerie? 8. Quelle sorte de chapeau demande-t-il? 9. Que dit-il au vendeur après avoir vu un modèle à 200 francs? 10. Combien paie-t-il le chapeau? 11. Que compte-t-il faire en compagnie de Raymond?

Composition

It was cold in the living room in which Albert was waiting for Jane, for in Paris apartments are not heated, generally, after the first of April.

"This room is an icebox," he said to her when she came in. "You ought to come to my boardinghouse. Madame Bernard always has the furnace lighted when the weather is bad."

But Jane wanted to keep her room, which gave on a public garden. Besides, she liked the other boarders, among whom was a Swedish girl with whom she often went out in the evening.

"Do you know this glove shop?" she asked Albert, as they were strolling down the boulevard. She opened her handbag, at the bottom of which she found a piece of paper on which she had written an address.

"Of course. It's a Perrin glove shop. You'll find there what you need. The Perrin glove is a make whose reputation is world-wide."

"I wish to buy a few pairs of gloves for some friends and for myself also, for I have only those that I am wearing."

"The shop is [but] a few steps (à deux pas) from here. Before going in, let's look at the window."

"I don't see there what I want. Let's go into the shop." (To the clerk) "Will you please show me some suède gloves. Size six."

"Here are some at fifty francs, of a color that is very stylish just now."

"Haven't you some of better quality than those that you have shown me?"

"A kid glove? Or something in doeskin? Doeskin is very soft."

After trying on a dozen gloves, Jane found a suède glove that fitted her well. She also bought three pairs of kid gloves.

"That makes three Christmas presents," she said laughing, "that I won't have to (use avoir à) attend to next winter."

Drill Exercise

1. John's sister, who has been very ill, will not be here today. 2. I did not know the girl to whom he was talking. 3. What he asks is impossible. 4. He has never seen the house in which we live. 5. He knows exactly what he wants. 6. Here are the novels of which I was speaking to you. 7. I will lend you now the ones that I have read. 8. I will send you later those that have just appeared. 9. We found a lot of our friends there, among whom were the Martins. 10. The man with whose son I study is a Frenchman. 11. Put on the necktie whose colors are not loud. 12. I can't imagine what he is thinking of. 13. The flowers I have put in that vase are your sister's. 14. They are the ones John sent to her. 15. Mr. Martin, whose son I used to know when I was young, has left the city. 16. Among those that we saw at the concert were your aunt and your uncle. 17. Ask him what we ought to do. 18. These gloves are not the ones that I ordered. 19. He will know what we need. 20. All those to whom I sent invitations have accepted. 21. Mr. Duval, whose daughter I knew in Paris, is in New York now. 22. It is he with whom I am to go out this evening. 23. Is he the gentleman whose acquaintance I made at the Martins'? 24. Who wrote that novel that everyone is talking about? 25. He's an author of whom I have read several books but whose name I can't recall. 26. Those of whom I think often think also of me.

Verb Review

voir to see; cf. § 156   **s'asseoir** [2] to seat oneself, sit down; cf. § 156

[2] Students will avoid mistakes in the use of **s'asseoir, se coucher, se lever, se promener,** etc., if they note that French has no intransitive verbs corresponding to the English verbs *to sit, to rise, to go to bed,* etc. The ideas contained in the English intransitive verbs are rendered in French by the transitive verbs **asseoir** *to seat,* **coucher** *to put to bed,* **lever** *to raise,* **promener** *to take to (for a) walk,* etc., used reflexively. Thus:

Elle était assise dans le salon.	She was sitting (= was seated) in the salon.
Elle s'asseyait quand je suis entré dans le salon.	She was sitting down (= was seating herself) when I entered the salon.
Elle s'est levée à huit heures.	She arose (= raised herself) at eight o'clock.

1. We had been sitting there for an hour when we saw him. 2. I used to see every day the same old man sitting in the park. 3. I shall see them at half past seven. 4. Let's sit down here. 5. I want you to see my new hat. 6. We shall sit down here if you wish. 7. Do you see that man over there? He always sits down on that bench. 8. They don't want us to sit down there. 9. Sit down beside me; don't sit down over there. 10. We shall see what we can do. 11. How long have you been sitting here? 12. In your place, I should see him at once. 13. We should sit down if we were tired. 14. He saw (*p. def.*) me and sat down (*p. def.*) beside me.

LESSON XVII

Interrogative Pronouns and Adjectives

THE INTERROGATIVE PRONOUNS

113. The forms of the interrogative pronoun are:

REFERRING TO PERSONS			REFERRING TO THINGS	
Subject	qui?	who?	qu'est-ce qui?	what?
Direct object	qui?	whom?	que?	what?
Object of prepositions	qui?	whom?	quoi?	what?

REFERRING TO BOTH PERSONS AND THINGS

SINGULAR	PLURAL	
Masc. lequel? [1]	lesquels?	} which? which one?
Fem. laquelle?	lesquelles?	

Qui est arrivé?	Who has arrived?
Qu'est-ce qui vous intéresse?	What interests you?
Qui avez-vous vu?	Whom did you see?
Qu'avez-vous vu?	What did you see?
Lequel est votre ami?	Which (one) is your friend?
Auquel de ces messieurs parlez-vous?	To which (one) of these gentlemen are you speaking?

114. The interrogative locutions **est-ce que** and **est-ce qui** (cf. § 31) may also be used with the interrogative pronouns.

Qui est-ce qui est arrivé?	Who has arrived?
Qu'est-ce que vous désirez?	What do you wish?

115. The interrogatives **qui** and **quoi** may be used in indirect questions, but **qu'est-ce qui** and **que** are replaced by **ce qui** and **ce que**.

---

[1] Lequel combines with à and de, giving **auquel, auxquels, duquel, desquels, auxquelles, desquelles.**

De qui parlez-vous? Vous savez de qui je parle.	Of whom are you speaking? You know of whom I am speaking.
Dites-moi à quoi vous pensez.	Tell me what you are thinking of.
But:	
Il sait ce qui se passe.	He knows what is happening.

116. *What?* (asking for a definition) is rendered in French by **qu'est-ce que c'est que?** (or **qu'est-ce que?**).[2] This locution should be distinguished from the interrogative adjective **quel? quelle?** etc., meaning *which?* or *what?* in the sense of *which one?*

Qu'est-ce que c'est que le Musée de Cluny?	What is the Cluny Museum?
But:	
Quelle est la leçon?	What (which) is the lesson?

117. *Whose?* in interrogations is translated by **à qui?** to denote mere ownership; in other cases by **de qui? Dont** is never used interrogatively.

De qui êtes-vous le fils?	Whose son are you?
A qui est cette maison?	Whose house is this (i. e., who owns it)?

THE INTERROGATIVE ADJECTIVES

118. The forms of the interrogative adjective are:

	SINGULAR	PLURAL	
Masc.	**quel?**	**quels?**	} what? what a! which?
Fem.	**quelle?**	**quelles?**	

119. The interrogative adjective is followed directly by the noun modified or is used as a predicate adjective with the verb **être.**

Quelle vue superbe!	What a superb view!
Quel est votre sport préféré?	What is your favorite sport?
Quels cours suivez-vous?	What courses are you taking?

[2] In indirect questions ce que c'est que. Je ne sais pas ce que c'est que ce musée-là.

Au théâtre

—Eh bien, Albert, qu'est-ce qu'on fait ce soir? Si on allait au théâtre?

—Je veux bien, Raymond. A quel théâtre irons-nous? Qu'est-ce qui vous intéresse?

—Je ne sais pas ce qu'on donne en ce moment. Regardons les affiches à la colonne Morris là-bas. A l'Odéon on reprend un vieux vaudeville de Feydeau.

—Qu'est-ce que c'est qu'un vaudeville?

—Comment! Vous ne savez pas ce que c'est! C'est une sorte de farce qui n'a rien à voir avec le vaudeville américain, qu'on appelle en France un spectacle de music-hall.

—Cela ne me dit rien. Lesquels des théâtres d'avant-garde sont ouverts?

—Voyons. Il y a relâche au Montparnasse. C'est dommage, parce qu'on y monte des pièces d'une remarquable perfection de mise en scène. Au Vieux Colombier on annonce les dernières d'une pièce américaine.

—Laquelle?

—*La Première Légion*. Il paraît que cette pièce n'a eu qu'un succès d'estime à New York mais ici elle a fait courir tout Paris.

—De qui est-ce?

—D'Emmet Lavery. La version française est de Jean Sylvain. L'action se déroule dans un collège de Jésuites aux Etats-Unis. Il s'agit d'un jeune prêtre tourmenté par le doute qui retrouve sa foi grâce à la guérison miraculeuse d'un jeune garçon paralysé.

—Il y a là de quoi faire un beau sermon mais je préfère quelque chose de plus gai.

—Yvonne Printemps et Pierre Fresnay dans *Trois Valses*, peut-être?

—J'ai déjà vu le film. Avec qui donc suis-je allé le voir? Mais avec vous!

—En effet. Je l'avais complètement oublié. Mais il faut que nous prenions un parti. Voulez-vous voir la pièce de Mauriac au Théâtre Français?

—C'est ce que nous avons de mieux à faire. Allons prendre nos places. La location est ouverte jusqu'à six heures.

Conversation

1. Qu'est-ce que Raymond et Albert décident de faire ce soir-là? 2. Qu'est-ce qu'on joue à l'Odéon? 3. Qu'est-ce que c'est qu'un vaude-ville? 4. Quelle différence y a-t-il entre le vaudeville français et le "vaudeville" anglais? 5. Que veut dire la phrase "théâtre d'avant-garde"? 6. Que donne-t-on au Montparnasse? 7. Que veut dire la phrase "succès d'estime"? 8. Quel est le sujet de la pièce américaine qu'on donne au Vieux Colombier? 9. De qui est-elle? 10. Pourquoi Albert ne veut-il pas aller voir *Trois Valses*? 11. A quel théâtre décident-ils d'aller?

Composition

"What are you thinking about, Albert? You look worried."

"I have invited Jane to go to the theater with me tomorrow night, and I don't know what play to get tickets for."

"What have you seen already? What interests you most? Comedy? Drama? Light opera?"

"I don't know. But something (of) typically French."

"Why don't you go to the Montparnasse?"

"What is the Montparnasse? Who is the director of it? What sort of plays do they put on there?"

"I am surprised that you don't know what the Montparnasse is, for the director of that theater, Gaston Baty, enjoys a world-wide reputation. Just now he is presenting a new version of *Manon Lescaut* with a remarkable staging and original settings and costumes."

"What you say is very interesting, but I should prefer something (of) more modern. Which of the new plays do you recommend?"

"It's too bad that there's no performance tomorrow at the Athénée. They say that Giraudoux's play is fine. To which of the other theaters shall I send you? To the Comédie Française, I think. *Asmodée* is somewhat gloomy but very well played."

"By (de) whom is it?"

"By François Mauriac. The action takes place in an old middle-class home. A young Englishman comes to spend a few weeks with the Barthas family and falls in love with young Miss Barthas. What a drama we witness then! What happens? I shall not tell (it to) you. That would spoil your evening."

"But who is Asmodée?"

"Asmodée is a symbol. He is the lame devil in the novel of LeSage, who lifts up the roofs of the houses in order to see what is going on inside."

"What an ingenious title for a play! I shall get seats this afternoon."

Drill Exercise

1. What marvelous roses! Which ones are you going to choose? 2. What prevents you from doing that? Nothing could prevent me from doing it. 3. Whom did you see in town? I saw nobody. 4. To which one of those ladies were you speaking? 5. Of whom are you thinking? What do you think of him? 6. What is the lesson for today? Which one do we have tomorrow? 7. What is the Sainte-Chapelle? I don't know what the Sainte-Chapelle is. 8. What is he going to do? No one knows what he will do. 9. What time is it? What can (**peut bien**) be detaining him? It is very late. 10. Whose cousin is he? 11. What a beautiful automobile you have there! Whose is it? It is mine. What do you think of it? 12. What is he talking about? I cannot hear what he is saying. 13. Which ones (*f.*) do you know? The ones who have just arrived. 14. What's the matter? What's going on here? 15. Which theater do you want to go to this evening? 16. What play are they giving at the Odéon? 17. Whom have you invited to go with us? 18. Who is the girl to whom you were talking? 19. With whom are we going to the theater? 20. What fine weather! What shall we do? Where shall we go? 21. What is the matter with him? 22. Whose books are these? 23. Of which one is Mauriac the author? 24. From whom did you receive a letter?

Verb Review

> **recevoir** to receive; cf. § 156
>> **apercevoir** to perceive (*with the senses*), notice, see, etc.
>> **s'apercevoir de** to perceive (*with the mind*), become aware of
>> **s'apercevoir que** to perceive that, notice that
> **suivre** to follow; cf. § 156

1. I have received nothing from France since the second of March. 2. We shall follow your advice. 3. Always follow your road map. 4. I

am following exactly the itinerary he gave me. 5. We are afraid that he will not receive our letters. 6. What courses shall I take next year? 7. Which ones were you taking last year? 8. I want you to take a course in (de) French literature. 9. I receive books from Europe almost every week. 10. He would receive the prize in (de) mathematics if he worked more. 11. I shall receive them at once. 12. When he left the movie, he noticed that someone was following him. 13. Louis XIV did not always follow (*p. def.*) the advice of his ministers. 14. When he became aware (*p. def.*) of my presence, he left (*p. def.*). 15. Farther on, you will perceive a small house.

Indefinite Adjectives and Pronouns

120. Indefinite adjectives:

certain certain	**quelque** some; *pl.* a few
chaque each, every	**n'importe quel** any (at all), no matter what

121. Indefinite pronouns:

chacun, chacune each, each one
on one, we, they, people
n'importe qui anyone (at all), no matter who
n'importe quoi anything (whatever), no matter what
personne ... ne [1] nobody, no one
quelqu'un, quelques-uns ⎫
quelqu'une, quelques-unes ⎬ somebody, someone, some
quelque chose something
rien ... ne [1] nothing

122. Forms used either as adjectives or as pronouns:

aucun ... ne [1] no, no one	**plusieurs** several
autre other	**tel, telle** such
même same	**tout, tous** ⎫
nul ... ne no, nobody, none	**toute, toutes** ⎬ all, every, the whole
pas un not one	

USES OF THE INDEFINITES

123. Certain, in the sense of *certain, some,* precedes the noun. After a noun, it means *sure, positive.*

Certaines choses.	Certain things.
Une nouvelle certaine.	Trustworthy news.

[1] For the use of **personne, rien,** and **aucun** in negative sentences, see § 67.

124. Quelques—not the partitive construction—translates *some*, in the sense of *a few*. *Few* in the sense of *not many* is translated by **peu de**.

J'ai des amis à Paris.	I have friends (*no indication as to how many*) in Paris.
J'ai quelques amis à Paris.	I have some (a few) friends in Paris.
J'ai peu d'amis à Paris.	I have few (not many) friends in Paris.

125. On (= *one, we, they, you, people,* etc.) requires the verb in the third person singular. Its corresponding possessive adjective is **son** (= *one's, their, people's,* etc.), and its reflexive forms are **se** and **soi**. A construction with **on** frequently translates an English passive.[2]

Dîner à sept heures. On dansera.	Dinner at seven o'clock. There will be dancing.
Au printemps on porte toujours son imperméable.	In the spring we always wear our raincoats.
On ne doit pas toujours penser à soi.	People should not always think of themselves.

126. Même [3] means *same* before a noun and as a pronoun. After a noun or pronoun, it means *self, very*.

Les mêmes enfants.	The same children.
Moi-même.	Myself.
Ce jour même.	That very day.

127. (1) Autre in the singular is used as in English. In the plural, **les autres** translates *the others;* **d'autres** translates *others*.

Quelques-uns danseront; d'autres joueront au bridge; les autres s'ennuieront.	Some will dance; others will play bridge; the others will be bored.

(2) Distinguish between **un autre** *another* (*a different one*) and **encore un** *another* (*an additional one*).

---

[2] Cf. § 51.

[3] Même is also used invariably as an adverb, meaning *even*. **Il a même gagné le prix.** He even won the prize.

Donnez-moi une autre tasse; celle-ci est fêlée.	Give me another (a different) cup; this one is cracked.
Donnez-moi encore une tasse de thé.	Give me another (an additional) cup of tea.

(3) Note the following idiomatic construction:

Nous autres Américains.	We Americans.

128. **Quelque chose** and **rien** require **de** before an adjective. The adjective is always masculine singular. Although **chose** is feminine, **quelque chose** is construed as masculine.

Quelque chose d'intéressant est arrivé.	Something interesting has happened.
Rien de nouveau n'est arrivé.	Nothing new has happened.

129. **Tel** is preceded (and not followed, as in English) by the indefinite article.

Un tel homme.	Such a man.

130. **Tout** is usually followed by the definite article.

Tous les jours.	Every day.
Toute la journée.	All day, the whole day.

131. **L'un...l'autre** etc. are used in various correlative constructions.

Elles se trompent l'une et l'autre.	They are both mistaken.
Ils se souviennent les uns des autres.	They remember one another.
Ils se parlent l'un à l'autre.	They speak to each other.

132. **N'importe** *it does not matter,* + the interrogative **quel, qui,** or **quoi,** has the force of *any, anyone, anything whatever.*

Dites-lui n'importe quoi.	Tell him anything (at all).
N'importe qui peut faire cela.	Anyone can do that.
Donnez-moi n'importe quel livre.	Give me any book whatever.

Scène de la vie politique

En 1909 Aristide Briand devint pour la première fois président du conseil des ministres. Ancien collaborateur du journal socialiste, *l'Hu-*

manité, où il représentait l'élément révolutionnaire, Briand avait souvent pris le parti du prolétariat. Rien ne faisait prévoir qu'un tel chef, dès qu'il serait au pouvoir, allait changer de camp. C'est donc avec toute confiance qu'au mois d'octobre, 1910, les cheminots se mirent en grève, réclamant le relèvement des salaires et le repos hebdomadaire. Ils n'avaient aucune raison de douter de l'appui de leur ancien camarade. Mais ils se trompaient. Briand, premier ministre, n'était pas le même homme qui avait prêché la grève générale dans les bureaux de *l'Humanité.* Il se rendait déjà compte que la sécurité de l'état importait plus que les droits de n'importe quel groupe. La situation devenait à chaque instant plus dangereuse. Peu de trains marchaient, même sur les grandes lignes, et certains bruits inquiétants commençaient à circuler dans la capitale. Pour éviter quelque chose de désastreux, Briand comprit qu'il fallait agir. Vers le soir on sut de source certaine qu'il avait donné l'ordre d'arrêter les chefs des grévistes.

Ceux-ci étaient réunis dans les bureaux de *l'Humanité.* Quelques-uns jouaient aux cartes, d'autres criaient leur haine du traître, les autres discutaient les mesures nécessaires pour assurer le succès de la grève. A dix heures du soir le chef de la Sûreté arriva, accompagné de plusieurs agents.

—Renault! appela un agent.

—Il est assis dans le fauteuil de monsieur Briand, répondit quelqu'un. Vous pouvez même trouver ici sa table. Nous avons conservé aussi ses plumes comme celles d'un grand homme.

Parmi les huées de tout le monde on emmena les prisonniers.

Ainsi un des premiers actes de Briand ministre fut un désavœu de son passé socialiste.

Conversation

1. Qu'est-ce que M. Briand est devenu en 1909? 2. De quel journal avait-il été collaborateur? 3. Quel parti politique est-ce que *l'Humanité* représentait? 4. Qu'est-ce que les cheminots réclamaient? 5. Selon Briand, qu'est-ce qui importait plus que les droits des grévistes? 6. Pour supprimer le désordre qu'a-t-il décidé de faire? 7. Où se trouvaient les chefs des grévistes? 8. Que faisaient-ils? 9. Qui a opéré les arrestations? 10. Quels souvenirs de Briand conservait-on aux bureaux de *l'Humanité?*

Composition

Aristide Briand, like Clemenceau and so many others, began his political career as [a] member of the Socialist Party. Briand was even a collaborator of the newspaper *l'Humanité,* of which his friend Jaurès was the political director. He had written a pamphlet in which he preached the general strike as something quite legitimate to assure the success of the workers' program. Surely one could have confidence in such a comrade. Nothing would make him change sides. Anyone would tell you that. It was therefore without any mistrust that in October, 1910, the railroadmen went on a strike. No one doubted the support of the former comrade [who had] become now prime minister. The leaders of the strikers, some of whom had known Briand for years, waited quietly in the offices of *l'Humanité,* wondering what Briand would do to help them. Some, seated at the very table where they still kept the pens of the great man, were playing cards. Others were discussing rumors that were beginning to circulate in the city. Not a train was running on the state lines; few trains were running on the other lines. Everything indicated that the railroad companies would be forced to grant the raise in wages demanded by the strikers.

Suddenly there was a knock at the door, and the head of the Sûreté, M. Lepine himself, entered, accompanied by several policemen. The strikers looked at one another astonished, not understanding what was happening. Soon they realized that Briand had betrayed them, and each one began to shout his hatred of the policemen who were carrying out his orders. Amid the hoots of the crowd the prisoners were led away.

The strikers regarded Briand as a traitor. He had simply become a statesman.

Drill Exercise

1. No one of her friends came to greet her. 2. There is nothing more beautiful than a sunset. 3. He works hard the whole day and sees no one. 4. Others have told me the same story. 5. Such things do not happen every day. 6. I should like another cup of coffee. 7. What did they say to each other? Nothing important. 8. One always finds something interesting to do in Paris. 9. Give me another spoon; this one is dirty. 10. There are few Frenchmen in America. 11. Almost all Amer-

icans like Paris, but I know some who prefer London. 12. Each one for himself and may the best one (**le plus fort**) win. 13. You Americans do not always understand us. 14. He can say anything whatever. I shall not believe him. 15. You may take any course whatever; you will learn something useful in it. 16. There are certain things that everyone should know. 17. They remembered each other at once when they met each other by chance in my house. 18. Each day at eight A. M. he is at his office. 19. Such a man ought never to have been chosen. 20. Whom shall I invite to go with us? No matter whom. 21. No one has confidence in him. 22. There are certain picturesque provinces in France, such as Brittany and Normandy, that you ought to visit.

Verb Review

mourir to die; cf. § 156   **naître** to be born; cf. § 156

1. She was born on March 15, 1899. 2. Louis XIV was born (*p. def.*) in 1638 and died (*p. def.*) in 1715. 3. I am afraid that he will die. 4. Born in Havre, she died in Paris in 1905. 5. If the doctor had not come, she would have died. 6. Fewer children will be born during the depression. 7. He will die if we do not take him to the hospital. 8. It's a pity that she died so young. 9. When we got there, he was dead. 10. One is born a poet or one is not a poet.

The Subjunctive Mood (I)

THE SIGNIFICANCE OF THE SUBJUNCTIVE MOOD

133. The indicative mood in French expresses facts. It is the mood of assertion, direct or indirect. Hence all true principal clauses and subordinate clauses that simply make an assertion take the indicative mood. The subjunctive mood, on the other hand, expresses some sort of personal reaction to an assertion. It is rarely used in principal clauses. It is used in dependent clauses after expressions of uncertainty, emotion, necessity, importance, will, etc.

THE SUBJUNCTIVE IN NOUN CLAUSES

134. The subjunctive is used in noun clauses (i. e., clauses introduced by the conjunction **que,** which serve as the logical subject or object of the principal verb) after impersonal verbs and other expressions denoting:

(1) necessity or importance **(il faut, il est nécessaire, il importe, il est important)**;

    Il faut qu'il vienne tout de suite.   He must come at once.

(2) uncertainty or doubt **(il est possible, il se peut, douter; croire and penser** [1] **when negative or interrogative)**;

    Il se peut que vous ayez raison.   It may be that you are right.

---

[1] **Croire and penser,** even when negative or interrogative, are frequently followed by the indicative, particularly when the tense is future or conditional. **Je ne croyais pas qu'il viendrait.** I didn't think he would come. **Croyez-vous qu'il va venir?** Do you think he is going to come?

(But expressions denoting certainty, unless negative or inter-rogative—**être sûr, certain, évident, probable,** etc.; **il paraît;** [2] **croire** and **penser** when affirmative—take the indicative.)

Je suis sûr qu'il viendra.   I am sure he will come.
But:
Il n'est pas sûr qu'il soit nommé.   It is not sure that he is nominated.

(3) emotion [3] (**avoir peur; craindre; s'étonner; c'est dommage; être content, heureux, fâché,** etc.; **regretter**);

Je crains qu'il ne [4] pleuve demain.   I fear it may rain tomorrow.

(4) will (**aimer mieux, commander, défendre, demander, désirer, empêcher, permettre, vouloir, valoir mieux**).

Il veut que nous l'accompagnions.   He wants us to accompany him.

135. An infinitive may be used as well as a subjunctive or in preference to it with most of the verbs and verbal expressions listed in § 134. The infinitive is always used with **aimer mieux, désirer,** and **vouloir** when the subject of the verb in the main clause is also the subject of the verb in the dependent clause. The infinitive construction is preferable with **commander, défendre, demander, empêcher,** and **permettre** even though the verbs in the main and the dependent clauses have different subjects.

Elle a peur de tomber.   She is afraid of falling.
Je lui ai défendu de sortir.   I have forbidden him to leave.
Il veut nous accompagner.   He wishes to accompany us.

SEQUENCE OF TENSES

136. There are four tenses in the subjunctive mood, the present, perfect, imperfect, and pluperfect tenses. They are used as follows:

---

[2] **Il me (lui, nous,** etc.) **semble** takes the indicative. **Il semble** is usually followed by the subjunctive.

[3] **Espérer** *to hope* takes the indicative.

[4] **Avoir peur, craindre,** and **empêcher** may take a redundant **ne** in the dependent clause when the verb in the main clause is affirmative. Cf. § 163.

PRINCIPAL CLAUSE   DEPENDENT CLAUSE

Present		For action taking place at the same time as that of the main verb or after it. (English present, future, or conditional tense)
Future	Present subjunctive	
Conditional [5]		For action occurring before the time of the main verb. (English perfect, past, or future perfect tense)
Imperative	Perfect subjunctive	

Je suis content qu'il vienne.   I am glad that he is coming (will come).

Je regrette qu'il ne soit pas venu.   I am sorry that he did (has) not come.

Je voudrais qu'il vienne.   I wish that he would come.

Vous regretterez qu'il soit venu.   You will be sorry that he has come.

Ne demandez pas qu'il vienne.   Don't ask that he come.

137. If the verb in the principal clause is in a past tense, the verb in the dependent clause is imperfect or pluperfect subjunctive. These two tenses of the subjunctive are rarely used in conversation or in informal writing. They are frequently replaced by the present subjunctive, particularly after a perfect tense in the main clause. For other ways of avoiding their use, see §§ 141 and 142.

Je ne voulais pas qu'il vînt.   I did not want him to come.

Je regrettais qu'il fût venu.   I was sorry that he had come.

J'ai demandé qu'il vînt (vienne).   I asked that he should come.

Un tour sur le boulevard

—Voulez-vous que nous fassions un petit tour sur le boulevard? demanda Albert à son ami Raymond. J'ai besoin de me dégourdir les jambes après avoir passé tout l'après-midi à écrire des lettres.

—J'ai peur que nous ne rentrions trempés. Les ondées sont fréquentes en cette saison-ci.

—Je ne crois pas qu'il pleuve aujourd'hui. Il vaudrait mieux cependant que nous prenions nos imperméables.

[5] The conditional may also be followed by an imperfect or pluperfect subjunctive in literary style.

Au bout d'un quart d'heure le temps se couvre et le soleil se cache derrière de gros nuages.

—Je vous ai bien dit que nous allions avoir une averse, dit Raymond. Réfugions-nous chez le bistro. Tiens! Voilà Pierre qui nous y a devancés. Bonjour, Pierre. Il paraît que vous n'aimez pas la pluie non plus.

—Devinez qui je viens de voir. Le gros Marcel!

—Pas possible! Je croyais qu'il avait quitté Paris.

—Pas encore. Mais il lui est arrivé une aventure des plus amusantes. Seulement il ne faut pas qu'il sache que c'est moi qui vous l'ai racontée. Dimanche passé Marcel est allé à Rouen avec sa fiancée et sa mère assister à je ne sais plus quelle fête. Ils comptaient rentrer à Paris par le dernier rapide du soir, parce qu'il faut absolument que Marcel soit à Paris lundi matin. Par suite d'une panne de taxi ils arrivent à la gare deux minutes avant le départ du train. Marcel, craignant de manquer son train, perd la tête, oublie qu'il n'est pas seul, disparaît dans la gare, emportant dans sa poche les billets de Blanchette et de sa mère. Quand celles-ci arrivent à la barrière, le contrôleur les arrête malgré leurs protestations. Il regrette infiniment de ne pas pouvoir les laisser passer mais elles n'ont pas de billets. Vous croyez que Marcel est revenu les chercher? Mais pas du tout. Le malheureux s'en va tout bonnement à Paris, laissant sa fiancée à Rouen, sans billet, sans argent et sans gîte. Vous pensez bien que Marcel n'aime pas qu'on lui rappelle cet incident-là.

Conversation

1. Qu'est-ce qu'Albert suggère à Raymond? 2. Pourquoi veut-il faire un petit tour sur le boulevard? 3. Pourquoi valait-il mieux prendre leurs imperméables? 4. Est-ce qu'ils s'en sont servis? 5. Où se sont-ils réfugiés pendant l'averse? 6. Qui ont-ils trouvé dans le bistro? 7. Que leur raconte-t-il? 8. Où est-ce que le gros Marcel était allé le dimanche précédent? 9. Avec qui? 10. Qu'est-ce qui leur est arrivé, en retournant à la gare? 11. Qu'est-ce que Marcel a fait en y arrivant? 12. Pourquoi Blanchette et sa mère n'ont-elles pas pu prendre le train? 13. Croyez-vous que Marcel soit content de cette aventure?

Composition

"Hello, Marcel. How does it happen that you are still in Paris? I thought that you had returned to Nantes."

"Unfortunately I shall have to remain here the whole summer."

"It is too bad that you cannot spend the vacation with us as [you did] last year. How is Blanchette?"

"I am afraid that she is at outs with me for the moment. At least, she won't see me."

"What's happened?"

"Something stupid. Two weeks ago she telephoned me. 'Mother and I are going to Rouen Sunday for some sort of fête at the Oliviers'. Madeleine wants you to come with us.' — 'Very well, but it is important that I be back Sunday evening.' — 'We must come back Sunday too. There's an express at 10:45.'

"At Rouen the weather is bad. All day the sky is overcast, and when toward 10:30 we call a taxi to go to the station, the rain is falling in torrents. At some distance from the station we have engine trouble. The chauffeur cannot go any farther. We get out, drenched to the skin. Then I lose my head. Afraid of missing my train and forgetting that I have all the tickets in my pocket, I run to the station and get aboard the train at the last minute. I don't know what happened when Blanchette and her mother reached the gate, but I am glad that I did not hear what they said about me."

"It may be that Blanchette is still angry with you, but I hope that the matter is not as serious as you think (it)."

"I don't think that it is very serious, but when I do a silly thing I don't want to be reminded of it all the time. And that is exactly what Blanchette is going to do."

Drill Exercise

1. It is important that Marcel should be in Rouen tomorrow. 2. They have not yet arrived. It may be that they have had engine trouble. 3. The Oliviers have invited us to spend Sunday with them. 4. They asked me to bring you too. 5. It appears that Marcel and his fiancée will be there, and they want you to meet them. 6. It is too bad that you cannot go there. 7. I am glad that they invited me even if I cannot

accept their invitation. 8. I thought that they had forgotten me. 9. It seems to me that you are spending a lot of time in the cafés. 10. You must not miss your train. Are you sure that it leaves at 10:40? 11. I wish you would take a walk with me this afternoon. 12. I can't prevent you from going out, but I am certain that you will return drenched to the skin. 13. I know that the weather is overcast, but I doubt that it will rain. 14. It would be better for you to take your raincoat anyway. 15. If it rains, we shall have to take refuge in a café. 16. We are sorry that Blanchette did not accompany you. 17. I am afraid that he has already left. 18. I hope that she is not sick. 19. It is possible that the ticket-taker will not let us pass without tickets. 20. I did not think that Marcel would do a silly thing like that.

Grammatical Exercise

1. It is very important that you stay. 2. He does not want us to leave. 3. I am sorry that he has gone away. 4. We doubt that she has arrived. 5. Are you afraid that he will not know you? 6. It is possible that it may rain. 7. We shall not allow them to do that. 8. It is necessary that you learn French. 9. She is glad that he will be there. 10. It is a pity that he has not seen them. 11. They do not want her to come with him, and he does not want to come without her. 12. It is not necessary that he wait for us.

Verb Review

> **conduire** to conduct, take, drive (*an auto*), etc.; cf. § 156
>   **introduire** to show in
>   **construire** to construct, build
>   **reconduire** to see home (to the door, out)
> **vivre** to live; cf. § 156

Note: *Live* in the sense of *to dwell* is translated by **demeurer** or by **habiter**. J'habite (demeure à) New York. I live in New York.

1. I shall drive if you want me to do so. 2. He was still living in 1937. 3. As long as I live, I shall remember her. 4. It is not necessary for you to see me to the door. 5. I built that house three years ago. 6. Louis XIV lived (*p. def.*) in (à) the seventeenth century. 7. Long

live the Republic! 8. He used to drive too fast. 9. I always see my guests to the door. 10. If I knew the road, I would drive. 11. Show them in. 12. They introduced (*p. def.*) that fashion on returning from France. 13. I lived ten years in France. 14. He has never driven an automobile. 15. I shall see them home after the theater.

LESSON XX

The Subjunctive (II)

THE SUBJUNCTIVE IN ADJECTIVAL CLAUSES

138. The subjunctive is used in adjectival clauses (i. e., those introduced by a relative pronoun):

(1) when the clause indicates characteristics desired but not yet attained (the antecedent in the main clause is generally indefinite, i. e., it is accompanied by the indefinite article or the partitive form **du, de la, de l', or des**);

Je cherche une maison qui vous convienne.	I am looking for a house which will (may) suit you.
Il veut choisir des cours qui soient faciles.	He wants to choose courses which are (may be) easy.
But:	
Il a choisi tous les cours qui sont faciles.	He has chosen all the easy courses.
J'ai trouvé une maison qui me convient.	I have found a house which suits me.

(2) when the antecedent in the main clause is qualified by an adjective in the superlative degree or by **seul, premier,** or **dernier,** unless the statement is unreservedly a fact;

C'est la meilleure pièce que j'aie vue.	This is the best play that I have seen.
C'est le seul ami qui me soit fidèle.	He is the only friend who is true to me.
But:	
C'est la dernière fois que je l'ai vu.	That is the last time that I saw him.

(3) after a general negation in the main clause;

| Je ne connais personne qui sache cela. | I do not know anyone who knows that. |
| Il n'y a rien que vous puissiez faire. | There is nothing that you can do. |

(4) in compound relative and indefinite clauses introduced by *whoever, whatever,* etc. (the word order in the following examples should be noted [1]).

Qui que ce soit que vous ayez vu.	Whoever it is that you have seen.
Qui que vous soyez.	Whoever you may be.
Quoi que vous fassiez.	Whatever you do.
Quelles que soient ses raisons.	Whatever his reasons may be.
Quelque difficile que soit ce travail.	However difficult this work may be.
Quelque rapidement qu'il écrive.	However rapidly he writes.
Quelques raisons qu'il ait.	Whatever reasons he may have.

THE SUBJUNCTIVE IN ADVERBIAL CLAUSES

139. The subjunctive is used in adverbial clauses after the following conjunctions of:

(1) time before which or up to which: **avant que** *before*, **jusqu'à ce que** *until;*

| J'étudierai jusqu'à ce que vous arriviez. | I shall study until you arrive. |

(2) purpose: **pour que** *in order that*, **afin que** *in order that*, **de sorte (façon) que** *so that;* [2]

| Pour que vous ne manquiez pas le train, j'ai commandé un taxi. | In order that you may not miss the train, I have ordered a taxi. |
| Conduisez votre auto de sorte que vous n'ayez pas d'accidents. | Drive your auto so that you won't have any accidents. |

---

[1] It should be noted that *whatever* as an adjective is translated by **quel, quelle, quels,** or **quelles** when the verb is **être;** otherwise by **quelque(s).**

[2] De sorte (façon) que takes the indicative in result clauses. **Il a parlé de façon que tout le monde l'a compris.** He spoke so that everyone understood him.

(3) emotion: **de crainte que,**[3] **de peur que** [3] *for fear that, lest;*

Je vous enverrai un chèque, de peur que vous n'ayez pas assez d'argent.	I shall send you a check, for fear that you haven't enough money.

(4) condition: **à moins que** [3] *unless,* **pourvu que** *provided (that)*;

Il viendra, à moins qu'il ne soit malade.	He will come unless he is sick.

(5) concession: **quoique, bien que** *although;*

Quoique la réunion soit importante, je ne peux pas y aller.	Although the meeting is important, I cannot go to it.

(6) negation: **sans que** *without.*

Il est parti, sans que je l'aie vu.	He left without my seeing him.

La légende de la Sainte-Chapelle

—Je viens de passer une heure à la Sainte-Chapelle, dit Raymond. Vous l'avez visitée, n'est-ce pas?

—Plusieurs fois, répondit Albert. A mon avis, c'est la plus belle église gothique qu'on puisse admirer à Paris.

—Il faut alors que je vous raconte une légende qui s'y rattache, à moins que vous ne la connaissiez déjà.

—Je sais seulement que Saint Louis a fait construire cette chapelle pour y conserver la couronne d'épines que le roi de Constantinople, Baudouin II, lui avait offerte en 1239.

—Eh bien, pour que la divine relique trouve [4] en France un sanctuaire digne d'elle, Louis avait fait appel à tous les "ouvriers en pierre" de l'Europe. Or, un soir en 1242 deux hommes, étrangers l'un à l'autre, qui se rendaient au concours ouvert par le roi, sont arrivés à une auberge des Alpes et y ont passé la nuit dans la même chambre. Le plus jeune des deux a montré à son compagnon le plan d'un admirable édifice, surmonté par une flèche d'une élégance et d'une hardiesse incomparables. L'autre a pâli et longtemps avant qu'il ne fasse [4] jour, il est sorti seul de la maison, emportant le précieux parchemin et laissant le jeune artiste baignant dans son sang. Celui-ci, bientôt guéri

---

[8] Usually followed by a redundant **ne.** Cf. § 163.

[4] In formal style the imperfect subjunctive would be used. Cf. § 141.

de sa blessure mais privé de sa raison, a disparu à son tour. Cinq ans plus tard, au moment même où le monument achevé apparaissait dans toute sa splendeur, il est entré à Paris. Devant la réalisation matérielle de son rêve, il a recouvré la raison et a raconté son histoire au chapelain de la Chapelle. Celui-ci, prenant les mains du pauvre artiste, lui a dit: "Mon ami, il n'y a plus ni vengeance ni gloire à espérer. Votre assassin m'a tout confessé. Enfermé au fond d'un cloître sous le nom de Frère Jean du Repentir, il pleurera son crime jusqu'à son dernier soupir."

—Quelque touchante que soit votre légende, il n'y a pas un atome de vérité dedans. Tout le monde sait que Pierre de Montereau a été l'architecte de la Sainte-Chapelle.

—Mais il n'y a personne qui sache qui était Pierre de Montereau. Il se peut que l'assassin-voleur ait été lui. Il est également possible que son nom soit celui du jeune artiste à qui on aurait rendu ses parchemins.

—Quoi qu'il en soit, la légende mérite d'être contée.

Conversation

1. Qu'est-ce que c'est que la Sainte-Chapelle? 2. Qui était le roi de France à l'époque où cet incident a eu lieu? 3. Qu'est-ce que le roi de Constantinople a offert à Saint Louis? 4. A quelle fin voulait-on construire la Sainte-Chapelle? 5. Afin de choisir un architecte, qu'est-ce que Saint Louis a fait? 6. Qu'est-ce qui s'est passé dans la chambre des deux artistes? 7. Qu'est-ce qui est arrivé au blessé? 8. Quand est-il arrivé enfin à Paris? 9. A qui a-t-il raconté son histoire? 10. Qu'est-ce que le chapelain lui a appris au sujet de l'assassin? 11. Qui était en réalité l'architecte de la Sainte-Chapelle?

Composition

"I have just visited the Sainte-Chapelle," said Albert. "Although it is quite small, I have never seen a church which pleases me as much. I should like to find someone who can tell me its history."

"It was built by Louis IX to receive the Crown of Thorns, which he had brought back from the Holy Land."

"The one that is now in the collection of relics of Notre-Dame?"

"The same. Some historians say that the Venetians sold it to Saint

Louis; others claim that the king of Jerusalem gave it to him. Be that as it may, Louis had spent several years in Palestine, and he believed that he had found the Crown of Thorns worn by Our Lord."

"Unless I am mistaken, the architect of the Sainte-Chapelle was a certain Pierre de Montereau."

"You do well to (**de**) say 'a certain Pierre de Montereau,' because no one knows who Pierre de Montereau was."

"It seems impossible that he has remained completely unknown."

"There is a legend that I might relate to you, although it is extremely improbable."

"I like legends, however improbable they are."

"Well, in order to have a sanctuary worthy of the divine relic, Louis opened a competition and invited all 'workers in stone' to submit plans for the new edifice. Two of the competitors met by chance in a country inn and the older of the two stabbed his rival and stole his parchments (from him)."

"And the plan of the dead man was chosen for the construction of the edifice?"

"Yes. But the young artist did not die. Five years later, before they had [5] finished the construction of the chapel, he arrived in Paris."

"In order to denounce his rival?"

"Yes, but the latter had already repented of his crime, had confessed everything to a priest, and had been shut up in a cloister."

"But it is not possible that this legend contains an atom of truth, for then Pierre de Montereau would be the criminal!"

"Or the young artist. Who knows?"

Drill Exercise I

1. There is nothing that I can do. 2. We are looking for a maid who knows how to do the cooking. 3. For fear that he may not have received my letter, I shall send him a telegram. 4. He is the only person that I know in Paris. 5. John will come unless he is sick. 6. We are going to wait until [6] he comes. 7. Although it is raining, we shall go to the movies. 8. In order that he may find us easily, we shall wait here. 9. Whatever you may think of it, the idea is interesting.

[5] For tense, see § 141.
[6] After **attendre** *until* is translated by **que** alone.

10. He studies all day so that his friends may see him in the evening. 11. We are looking for courses that are rather easy. 12. Last quarter we chose courses that were much too hard. 13. Before you visit the chapel, I shall tell you the history of it. 14. It is the most curious legend that I have ever read. 15. I know no one who can help us now. 16. Whoever it is who comes, tell him to wait for us. 17. Whatever your reasons may be, John will not accept your decision. 18. Unless you tell me the whole story, I cannot advise you. 19. However easy your courses are, you will have to study a great deal. 20. He had left London before we arrived so that we did not see him.

Drill Exercise II

1. This is the first time that I have seen that play. 2. Is he going away without our saying good-by to him? 3. They will stay with us until their apartment is finished. 4. Although he is very busy, I am sure that he will come. 5. Don't leave before we arrive. 6. He will be here although he has been very sick. 7. I want a car that my mother can drive. 8. There is no church in Paris that is more beautiful than this one. 9. Whoever [7] built it was an artist. 10. Unless you have visited the Alps, you don't know Switzerland.

Verb Review

craindre (de) to fear, be afraid; cf. § 156
  peindre to paint
  plaindre to pity, feel sorry for
  se plaindre de to complain of (about)

plaire to please; cf. § 156
  se taire to be silent, cease speaking

1. We are afraid that he may not come. 2. What is he complaining about? 3. I am glad that France pleased you. 4. Everyone became silent (p. déf.). 5. I did not pity them. 6. Don't complain; be silent. 7. He will please them if he is silent. 8. I would fear nothing if he were with me. 9. They are sorry that the children are afraid of them. 10. Always try to please your parents. 11. They feared (p. déf.) death and became silent (p. déf.). 12. If he fails in his examination, I shall feel sorry for him. 13. He was silent while they were complaining about the government. 14. I was not afraid of him. 15. That artist paints well. 16. He has painted some beautiful pictures.

[7] Celui qui. Cf. § 111.

The Subjunctive (III)
The Present Participle

THE SUBJUNCTIVE IN PRINCIPAL CLAUSES

140. The subjunctive occurs but rarely in principal clauses. When so used, it expresses a wish or an order.[1]

Vive le roi!	Long live the king.
Que Dieu vous bénisse!	God bless you!
Qu'il vienne, s'il le veut.	Let him come if he wishes.

SUBSTITUTES FOR THE SUBJUNCTIVE

141. The imperfect and the pluperfect subjunctive are rarely used in conversation or in informal writing. Where a subjunctive construction cannot be avoided, they are sometimes replaced, in violation of the rules, by a present or perfect subjunctive.

Je voulais qu'il vienne (vînt).	I wanted him to come.
Il avait peur que je ne le fasse (fisse).	He was afraid that I would do it.

142. It is often possible and preferable to cast sentences in such a way as to avoid using the subjunctive, even in a present sequence.

(1) An infinitive construction may be used as pointed out in § 135.

(2) When the subject of the dependent clause is the same as the subject of the principal clause, the following conjunctions gov-

---

[1] Such clauses are really dependent clauses with a main clause containing the verb *I wish* or a similar expression understood.

erning the subjunctive are replaced by prepositions followed by
an infinitive:

que	is replaced by	**de** *to*
afin que	is replaced by	**afin de** *in order to*
pour que	is replaced by	**pour** *in order to*
à moins que	is replaced by	**à moins de** *unless*
avant que	is replaced by	**avant de** *before*
de peur que	is replaced by	**de peur de** *lest, for fear of*
de façon que	is replaced by	**de façon à** *so as to*
sans que	is replaced by	**sans** *without*

Je regrettais de ne pouvoir y aller.	I was sorry I could not go there.
Il est parti de bonne heure pour ne pas manquer le train.	He left early in order not to miss the train.
Ils s'en sont allés sans me dire adieu.	They left without saying good-by to me.
Nous leur avons dit cela avant de partir.	We told them that before we left.

(3) The dependent clause may be replaced by a noun or an adjective construction.

Quoiqu'il fût riche, il n'était pas avare.	**Quoique riche, il n'était pas avare.**
Je les ai vus avant qu'ils soient partis.	**Je les ai vus avant leur départ.**

(4) The sentence may be rephrased (a) by inserting an infinitive
such as **apprendre, trouver,** or **savoir;**

Il était content que vous gagnassiez le prix.	**Il était content d'apprendre que vous aviez gagné le prix.**
Elle voulait que nous allassions à l'église.	**Elle voulait nous faire aller à l'église.**
Je regrettais qu'il ne fût pas venu.	**Je regrettais de savoir qu'il n'était pas venu.**

(b) by replacing the construction which requires the subjunctive
by a construction which does not require the subjunctive.

Il a fallu que nous restassions ici.	Nous avons dû rester ici.
Il viendrait à moins que nous ne fussions absents.	Il viendrait si nous n'étions pas absents.

THE PRESENT PARTICIPLE

143. The present participle is invariable in French. It is used as an English participle, (a) to introduce a phrase modifying a noun or pronoun, or (b) preceded by **en,** *in, upon, while, during,* to modify a verb. When accompanied by **en,** the present participle always refers to the subject of the sentence.

Prenant sa plume, elle s'est mise à écrire.	Taking her pen, she began to write.
(Tout) en parlant, il examinait ses auditeurs.	While speaking, he examined his hearers.
Tout en travaillant bien, il ne réussit pas.	Although he works hard, he does not succeed.
Je l'ai vue sortant de la maison.	I saw her (as she was) going out of the house.
Je l'ai vu, en sortant de la maison.	I saw him as I was going out of the house.
En partant de bonne heure, vous arrivez à quatre heures.	By leaving early, you arrive at four o'clock.

144. The present participle may also be used as an ordinary adjective. In such a case, it agrees like all adjectives.

Des enfants obéissants.	Obedient children.

Une excursion en auto

6 rue de Tournon,
Paris (VIe).[2]
21 juillet, 1939.

Mon cher Fred:

Voici la dernière fois que je vous écris de Paris. Je ne veux pas quitter l'Europe sans avoir vu l'Angleterre, de sorte que je serai à Londres avant que vous receviez cette lettre.

[2] I. e., le sixième arrondissement (ward).

Il y a quinze jours un Français de mes amis, qui a une Peugeot, m'a invité à faire une randonnée de week-end avec lui et nous sommes allés jusqu'à Lyon, passant par une belle contrée que moi, n'ayant pas de voiture, je n'aurais jamais pu voir autrement. Tout en admirant le pays, nous n'avons pas négligé le côté gastronomique de notre excursion. Avant de quitter Paris, nous nous sommes procuré une carte de la région et une liste des meilleures auberges. Je vous garantis que nous n'en avons pas manqué une seule. Je me souviens surtout de celle de Saulieu où on nous a servi un poulet accommodé d'une sauce épatante. J'ai demandé au maître d'hôtel de m'en donner la recette mais il a refusé, tout en se confondant en excuses. J'ai bien regretté que vous ne soyez pas là pour savourer toutes ces bonnes choses. A Lyon, le beau-frère de mon ami nous a menés dîner chez la Mère Brazier, maison renommée dans toute la France pour son excellente cuisine. En revenant, nous avons fait le trajet de Lyon à Paris sans nous arrêter en route. Quoique Marcel conduise très bien, il conduit trop vite. Je ne lui en ai rien dit, de peur de le froisser, mais il y a certains virages que je n'aime pas me rappeler.

Je n'ai pas pu empêcher Jane de partir le 19. Nous avons fêté ensemble le 14 juillet: feu d'artifice au Pont-Neuf; ensuite, bal en plein air place de la Sorbonne. Cela l'a beaucoup amusée de danser dans la rue.

Je suis très content de savoir que vous êtes entré à la banque de votre père. Vous voilà casé et bien casé. Mes compliments.

J'espère que toute votre famille se porte bien. Ne manquez pas de me rappeler au bon souvenir de tous.

Cordiale poignée de main et à bientôt.

Raymond

Conversation

1. Quelle est la date de cette lettre? 2. Où Raymond compte-t-il aller avant de quitter l'Europe? 3. Où est-il allé faire une randonnée et avec qui? 4. Qu'est-ce qu'ils s'étaient procuré avant de quitter Paris? 5. Que leur a-t-on servi à dîner à Saulieu? 6. Qu'ont-ils demandé au maître d'hôtel? 7. Qui les a menés dîner chez la Mère Brazier? 8. Qu'est-ce que Raymond a fait le 14 juillet? 9. Pourquoi fête-t-on le 14 juillet en France? 10. Où Fred a-t-il trouvé une situation? 10. Comment dit-on en français: "My regards to your family"?

Composition

"Then there's nothing I can say, Albert, to prevent you from leaving next Monday?"

"No, Raymond. You wouldn't want me to return to the United States without having seen London, would you? While I am very fond of France, I can't miss this opportunity to visit the land of my ancestors. By the way, I have just received a letter from Fred, saying that he has taken a position in the Central Bank."

"I am glad that they have finally got a position for him. While he is a good fellow, Fred isn't very clever. Let's hope that he will succeed there. Is Jane still in Paris? I haven't seen her for two weeks."

"She left the day after the national holiday. We celebrated the Fourteenth of July together. After watching the fireworks at the Pont-Neuf, we danced in the street for an hour. Unless you attend one of those open-air dances, you don't know what a popular fête in France is. Before we went home, we took a taxi to the Dôme, but all the tables were taken, and we were not permitted to enter."

"I am sorry that I was not able to see Jane again before she left. Marcel took me to Lyons with him last Thursday in his new Peugeot. We went through a beautiful region, avoiding the main highways and the large towns. Marcel knows all the best inns, and he chose those which are renowned for their regional dishes. I shall not tell you all the good things they served us, lest I make you jealous. It's too bad that you missed this excursion, for you like the country, and, unless you have a car, you never see the prettiest spots."

"I wonder why Marcel did not invite me too."

"After inviting me, he asked me for your number. He telephoned to you several times, but you were always out."

Drill Exercise I

Avoid the use of the subjunctive wherever possible.

1. We were afraid that he had gone without you. 2. He did not permit us to go with him. 3. Although he was once very rich, he has lost his money now. 4. They were sorry that he was no longer in Paris. 5. I did not see them until they arrived here. 6. It was necessary for us to wait for them. 7. We forbade him to come with us. 8.

He did not want us to help him. 9. In order that he should not wait, we telephoned him. 10. Unless he saw us at Auteuil, he does not know that we are in Paris. 11. Before he left, he came to see us.

Drill Exercise II

Translate: (1) using the subjunctive when necessary, and (2) avoiding the subjunctive if possible.

1. We shall wait until they leave. 2. He does not want us to forget his address. 3. I doubt that he can go with me. 4. He will not prevent us from going with them. 5. They will leave without our seeing them. 6. We are sorry that we are not going with you. 7. I am glad that you can go with him. 8. He will be glad that you can dine with us. 9. Although he is very busy, he has promised to spend his vacation with us. 10. I shall help him in order that he may finish his work early.

Drill Exercise III

Use the present participle wherever possible.

1. On entering the café, we found all the tables taken. 2. They saw us leaving the house. 3. By taking a taxi, you will reach the station in twenty minutes. 4. When we left the café, we found John, who was waiting for us. 5. While waiting for his friend, he wrote a letter. 6. He is telephoning to Fred. 7. If you hurry, you will find him there. 8. The young man driving the new Peugeot is Marcel. 9. Although he has an automobile, he does not often go to the country. 10. As we were returning from Lyons, we passed through Saulieu. 11. On seeing me, he stopped. 12. He called to me as I was leaving the house.

Verb Review

rire to laugh; cf. § 156   **courir** to run; cf. § 156
   sourire to smile

1. Why are you laughing? I was not laughing. 2. If you ran, you would arrive in time. 3. He did not smile when I told him that. 4. They ran very fast because it was raining. 5. I shall not laugh. 6. I

should not run so fast if I were not late. 7. Don't run; we have lots of time. 8. I am afraid he will not laugh. 9. He ran (*p. def.*) to the door and opened (*p. def.*) it. 10. When I told (*p. def.*) him the story, he laughed (*p. def.*).

Review Exercises

1. The airplane from London has just arrived in Havre. 2. There is my friend getting out of the plane. 3. He is going to spend a few weeks with me in Normandy, and then he is going to Italy. 4. He needs a few weeks of rest, for he has been working all winter in England. 5. How many days will he spend here? 6. What is his name? What is the name of the Spanish girl who is talking to him? 7. Lindbergh is an aviator. 8. He made the first nonstop crossing of the Atlantic by airplane from America to France. 9. They speak French in New Orleans. 10. Spanish is spoken in most of the islands of the West Indies. 11. I pay thirty cents a dozen for these oranges. 12. Do you know Dr. Dupont? He is an excellent physician. 13. I have three classes at the university on Friday mornings. 14. Will you translate for me this letter written in Spanish? I cannot (**savoir**) read Spanish. 15. She buys a new hat each season, and hats are expensive. 16. There are excellent restaurants in this city. I know several of them. 17. We ordered neither dessert nor coffee. 18. Do you like Italian wines? 19. When I am really thirsty, I prefer cold water. 20. Don't drink too much. 21. Don't forget to order some fruit and some white wine. 22. There were few people in the restaurant. 23. Some Belgians were dining at a small table. 24. While eating, they talked with enthusiasm. 25. I listened attentively, but I heard only a few words of their conversation. 26. I am sure that they were Belgians, however, because of their accent. 27. Most small hotels have no elevator. 28. Let's call a taxi. Taxis are cheap here, and there are many of them. 29. You will pay for it, of course. 30. In this quarter there are streets full of cafés. 31. I have never seen as many in a single street. 32. Do you like French automobiles? Or do you prefer American cars? 33. You accept too many invitations. I have accepted only two this week. 34. I should prefer to remain at home tonight. 35. Can you give me some addresses of furnished apartments? 36. I have no change. Have you any? Can you lend me some? Gladly. 37. Here are some interesting novels. I will give you two of them.

Lessons III and IV, §§ 16–32

1. Trouville is one of the most expensive beaches in France. 2. It is not so pretty as the picturesque little beaches in Brittany. 3. The young man with (à) the white sweater is the best dancer in our crowd. 4. Who is that tall slender girl? She seems very nice. 5. She is the daughter of a very rich old businessman. 6. They live in that beautiful house with the little green windows near the public gardens. 7. Let's go to the Casino. That will be more interesting than to stay here. 8. I am willing. I would rather go there than go to a café. 9. Why does Mr. Dupont spend so much money when times are so hard? 10. He does not spend as much as you think, but he spends a lot more than he earns. 11. Will you tell me the names of the principal newspapers in Paris? 12. *Paris-Soir* has more readers than the other evening papers, but it is not so serious as the *Intransigeant*. 13. I haven't the least idea where you will find him. 14. Perhaps John knows where he went. 15. "This is the worst café in the Quarter," Raymond said. "The ice cream is bad, and the cakes are worse." 16. My friends would rather see plays than visit churches. They have already visited too many. 17. We haven't the slightest desire to study. 18. He will be angry with you if you don't wait for him. 19. Did the Spaniards discover South America? 20. Les Deux Magots is an old café, but it is not so old as the Régence. 21. Will John and Albert continue their walk? 22. That news is false. 23. There are fewer tables on the terrace than inside the café. 24. I have sent for my books, but they have not yet arrived. 25. John is not so good in French as his sister.

Lessons V and VI, §§ 33–45

1. How long has Mr. Parker been in France? 2. He has been here for a month. 3. He is going to Tours tomorrow. 4. He has sent for a taxi, and, when it arrives, he will go to the station to get his ticket. 5. He has asked John to go with him, but John won't go. 6. Will you go to the horse races at Auteuil with me? Where shall I meet you? Be on time, for I won't wait. 7. M. Dupont and his daughter have been waiting for the autobus for half an hour. 8. When it arrives, they will take it to go to the city. 9. When we see our friends during ⁺he Christmas vacation, we shall be very happy. 10. If you should visit

Minorca, what city would you want to see? 11. In 1756 Minorca had belonged to the English for fifty years. 12. The island was small and poor and had only a few thousand inhabitants. 13. When the cook came in with the menu, the duke was in a bad humor. 14. As soon as he had read the menu, he told the cook that he did not like his sauces. 15. If you would tell me what you desire for your dinner, I should be glad to serve it. 16. The duke consented to try the sauce. 17. When we were young, we used to spend our vacations in the country. 18. While the duke was dining, no one dared to enter the dining room. 19. What books did she use in her French course? The same [ones] that you used to use. 20. I wrote a letter to my mother every day while I was at the university. 21. Have you written to her recently? 22. Did you sleep well last night? 23. No. I have not been sleeping well for some time. 24. I did not know that you had been sick. 25. The Martins came to see us last summer. 26. We had not seen them for two years, and we hoped that they would spend several weeks with us. 27. However, they left the next day, because Henry was not feeling very well. 28. They were entering the store when I saw them. 29. I had been looking for them for half an hour.

Lesson VII, §§ 46–53

1. Marcel is a true Parisian, having been born in the quarter of the Bastille. 2. He was eighteen years old when his mother died. 3. His father went to live in Lyons, but Marcel stayed in Paris and went to the medical school. 4. He is now a doctor. 5. What has become of him? 6. When I was at the Sorbonne, we used to see each other every day. 7. He left Paris a year ago, and I have not seen him since. 8. Has my trunk arrived? 9. Yes. The janitor has carried it up to your room. 10. We walked fast because we did not wish to arrive there late. 11. When she saw us, she stopped, and we talked with one another for a quarter of an hour. 12. We got home at five P. M., having stopped on the way to visit the gardens of Versailles. 13. These books were written by a former professor of history. 14. You can buy them everywhere where books are sold. 15. I have read them, and I found them very interesting. 16. John and his sister took a walk with us this afternoon. We had a fine time. 17. Here are the books you lent me. 18. She introduced herself to my mother. 19. Annette fell in the street yesterday, but fortunately she did not hurt herself.

20. Jane returned a week ago from a trip to Italy. 21. John does not like to write letters, but he has written several this morning. 22. Has he mailed them? 23. I bought two volumes of Maupassant that I saw in a bookstore window. 24. They contain short stories that I have read and reread.

Lessons VIII and IX, §§ 54–61

1. Why didn't you give them to us? 2. Who sent them to you? 3. When had he introduced us to them? 4. Why didn't they give some to them? 5. He does not want to present me to her. 6. Don't you remember me? 7. Didn't you remember her? 8. We left without them. 9. John will leave a week from Sunday. Yes, I was just thinking about it. 10. Will you lend me your guidebook? 11. I shall send it to you at once. I don't need it. 12. Why did you ask me to lend it to you? 13. I cannot lend it to you. It is not mine. 14. Albert and I are going to Chevreuse. Don't you want to go with us? 15. The abbey of Port-Royal was destroyed by Louis XIV. 16. You remember the old tower that we visited, don't you? 17. Marcel asked for a leave, and they granted it to him. 18. I am glad of it. 19. To whom did you telephone? To her. 20. She and I are going to visit an old quarter of the city. 21. He got ready to spend the night there. 22. Who is the owner of that superb house? 23. I [am]. Do you want me to show it to you? 24. Have you any relatives in Avignon? Yes, I have (some). 25. My cousin Martha lives there. You remember her, of course. 26. She was married last winter. 27. We saw Paul at the theater, and he introduced me to the girl who was with him. 28. Raymond didn't know her either, and I introduced him to her. 29. Don't telephone to him. I shall telephone to him myself. 30. They are angry with me, but *I* am not angry with them. 31. He has a new automobile, and he is always talking about it. 32. Albert is older than Jane, but he is not so old as Raymond. 33. He is a year older than she and two years younger than he.

Lesson X, §§ 62–70

1. Nothing has happened since you left. 2. I have seen no one. 3. No one has telephoned to me. 4. I hardly need tell you that you have not written me a single letter. 5. Neither Mary nor John has returned from the country. 6. I have received from them neither post cards nor

letters. 7. And yet they are my best friends. 8. Lassailly was a young author who had not had any success. 9. He had written only two or three books. 10. No one of his friends was able to help him. 11. Had he ever worked for Balzac? No. Never. 12. He had a mind not to accept Balzac's offer. 13. How did he like the life at Balzac's? 14. It was very hard, for Balzac almost never slept. 15. Have you read *Le Père Goriot?* It is the best novel of Balzac's. 16. It was not I who called you up. It was she. 17. It was not my fault that you were refused a leave. 18. They are no longer here. 19. Don't say anything to him about it. 20. She is a Canadian, it is true, but she speaks French like a Frenchwoman.

Lessons XI and XII, §§ 71–81

1. You must be tired. 2. You ought to have gone to bed earlier. 3. I know it. But if I begin to read a detective story, I can't go to bed without finishing it. 4. You should not begin a story at night if you have work to do the next day. 5. If I had had work to do the next day, I should not have asked you to lend me that novel. 6. Paul was to join me at the café at ten o'clock. 7. After waiting for him an hour, I decided to go home. 8. May I ask you if you will be able to come tonight? 9. If the policeman should see Deloncle, he would not recognize him. 10. He asked the stranger to get into his automobile, but he would not do it. 11. He must have been suspicious of him. 12. However, the policeman ordered him to accompany him, and he had to do it. 13. I have invited Jane to go to a night club. Are you too busy to accompany us? 14. I am ready to leave now. 15. Where do you intend to go? 16. We shall begin by visiting the Lapin Agile, but we shall doubtless end by going to the Bal Tabarin. 17. I tried to prevent him from spending so much money, but it is very easy to spend money here. 18. Hurry and call a taxi. 19. That is easy to say, but it is not easy to find a taxi at this hour of the night. 20. I saw Guitry play the role of Pasteur. 21. Have you come here to have a good time or to work? 22. She will be obliged to work. Otherwise her father will not permit her to remain at the university. 23. We haven't enough time to visit all the sights of the city. 24. While having tea, they discussed what they intended to do the next day. 25. It is better not to try to see everything. 26. I advise you to see only the most important things. 27. I wondered whether you would send me

an invitation. 28. I remember sending you one. 29. If you did not receive it, it is not my fault. 30. You must have forgotten to mail it.

Lessons XIII and XIV, §§ 82–96

1. Did you know that Henry is to arrive tomorrow? 2. I found it out yesterday through his sister, the one that goes to the Sorbonne. 3. I could have told you that a week ago. 4. He can spend only a few days here. 5. He has had his trunk sent to a beach in Brittany. 6. Do you know Saint-Quay? Couldn't you spend a week or two there with us? 7. I might ask for a week's leave, but they won't give it to me. Of that I am sure. 8. If I had known sooner that you were to go there, I could have arranged to get away from the office for a few days. 9. Who could do all that with so little money? 10. They made him promise to come if he could. 11. It takes a lot of money to buy an American automobile in France, and those that are made in France are not much cheaper. 12. Can you drive an automobile? Fairly well, but my brother drives better than I [do]. 13. You must not remain in Paris all summer. 14. You must see other parts of France. 15. Do you know how to· swim? 16. Do you like to swim? 17. We cannot swim here at high tide. It is too dangerous. 18. She had a room reserved for her in the best hotel. 19. She had John reserve it. 20. This trip has cost her dear. 21. Have you seen him recently? 22. Does he still speak French as badly as he once (**autrefois**) spoke it? 23. It is not necessary to visit all the châteaux of Touraine, but you must visit two or three of them, at least. 24. It takes only a few hours to go by automobile from Paris to Tours. 25. Wait a minute. I'll send for my road map and Raymond's also. 26. You might need them. 27. The Taride map is more useful than the one you have. 28. The map is cheap. It costs less than ten francs. 29. I could have gone. She should have gone. They would go if they could. 30. These are English cigarettes. May I offer you one of them? 31. I had her come in, and then I made her write a letter to her father.

Lessons XV and XVI, §§ 97–112

1. I can't find my fountain pen. Will you lend me yours? 2. I have lost mine also. 3. What time did you get home? 4. It was very late— 1:20 A. M., I think, or perhaps a little later, as my watch is usually

slow. 5. The express is often late, but tonight it arrived on time. 6. Albert spent the evening with a friend of his. 7. He was an artist from the Latin Quarter who wanted to sell Albert some paintings. 8. Some of the paintings were his, and some belonged to an artist friend of his, whose name I don't remember. 9. All the paintings, his [own] and those of his friend, were mediocre. 10. The stranger was warming his feet in front of the fire. 11. He raised his head as I entered, got up from the chair on which he was sitting, and offered me his hand. 12. The janitor, who had not yet gone to bed, had given him my key, with which he had opened my door. 13. That was an experience that I shall long remember. 14. Here is a necktie whose colors you will like. 15. Tell me what you are thinking of. 16. May I introduce to you Mr. Aubin, of whom I have spoken to you so many times? 17. My boardinghouse is better than the one in which you are living. 18. The boarders, among whom are several French girls and a young Swiss student, speak French fluently. 19. There is also an American officer with whom I often go to the theater. 20. He has been here for a year and knows what interests American tourists. 21. The girl with whom you saw me yesterday is a friend of my aunt's who has just arrived in Paris. 22. You will find what you need in that shop. 23. He never received the letter that I sent to him. 24. That gentleman is a famous banker in whose château there is a fine collection of modern paintings.

Lessons XVII and XVIII, §§ 113–132

1. Who was Briand? 2. Of what country was he prime minister? 3. To what political party did he belong? 4. What is la Sûreté? 5. Don't you know what it is? 6. What newspaper do you read? 7. Whose is that newspaper? 8. Which one do you mean? 9. Not a train is running. 10. No one knows why. 11. Something terrible must have happened. 12. With whom are you going to the theater? 13. To which one are you going? 14. Some are closed for the season; others are going to close soon; at the others they are playing classic plays. 15. Which of the new plays do you prefer? 16. I haven't seen any (one) of them. 17. Two have been recommended to me. We shall choose one or the other. 18. Whom did they find in the office, and what were they doing? 19. To whom were you talking and of what? 20. What astonished the strikers? 21. The strikers accused one another.

22. What an amusing scene! 23. Have you ever seen such a film? 24. I have already seen this film. Let's choose another. Any one at all. 25. What evening will you be free? I can arrange to be free any evening. 26. They did not remember each other. 27. I saw the same play in New York with the same actors. 28. He has friends everywhere. He even has a few friends in Russia. 29. Each one must pay for his ticket.

Lessons XIX, XX, and XXI, §§ 133–144

1. I must tell you something that happened to me recently. 2. I hope that you won't make fun of me, although the incident is very amusing. 3. I am even afraid that you will find my story hard to believe. 4. Marcel wants me to go to Rouen with him, but I don't want to go. 5. Do you think that it will rain today? 6. It would be better for you to postpone your trip until tomorrow. 7. I doubt that you will find your friends at home. 8. It may be that you are right. 9. An accident prevented him from arriving at the station on time. 10. I don't believe that he will spend the whole day writing letters. 11. She has forbidden him to come to see her. 12. There is nothing more beautiful than the Sainte-Chapelle. It is essential that you see it. 13. However busy you may be, don't fail to spend a day at Fontainebleau. 14. How does it happen that you know all these things? 15. The stranger asked the young artist to show him his plan. 16. The artist was afraid of losing his plan. 17. He was afraid that the stranger would steal it. 18. Whoever he is, he is a good architect. 19. You cannot leave until you have finished your work. 20. Although the legend is interesting, it cannot be true. 21. That church has the most beautiful spire that I have ever seen. 22. Unless you drive faster, I am certain that we shall be late. 23. I am looking for a book that describes the Sainte-Chapelle. 24. There is no one who knows when Pierre de Montereau died. 25. Whatever the difficulties may be, he will overcome them. 26. Did you see Raymond before he left Paris? 27. No. He left without my seeing him. 28. Although I like Charles very much, I don't like to travel with him. 29. You can't travel with him without spending a lot of money. 30. Before you leave Lyons, dine at Mère Brazier's. 31. I was sorry I could not go there. 32. While returning from Lyons, we had motor trouble. 33. In order really to know France, you must take a trip by automobile, visiting the small towns and the country.

34. I am glad that you stopped at Saulieu. 35. They wanted us to remain longer with them, but we couldn't do it. 36. The weather was fine until we reached Lyons. 37. Write me before you leave. 38. It's too bad that the rain spoiled the holiday. 39. Unless he is sick, he will be here tomorrow. 40. We are looking for the inn that John told us about.

The Verb — Numbers — Redundant Ne

THE REGULAR VERBS

145	**146**	**147**
FIRST	SECOND	THIRD
CONJUGATION	CONJUGATION	CONJUGATION

Infinitive Mood

Present

donn **er** *to give*	fin **ir** *to finish*	vend **re** *to sell*

Participles

Present Participle

donn **ant** *giving*	fin **iss ant** *finishing*	vend **ant** *selling*

Past Participle

donn **é** *given*	fin **i** *finished*	vend **u** *sold*

Indicative Mood

Present

I give	*I finish*	*I sell*
je donn **e**	fin **is**	vend **s**
tu donn **es**	fin **is**	vend **s**
il donn **e**	fin **it**	vend [1]
nous donn **ons**	fin **iss ons**	vend **ons**
vous donn **ez**	fin **iss ez**	vend **ez**
ils donn **ent**	fin **iss ent**	vend **ent**

Imperfect

I was giving	*I was finishing*	*I was selling*
je donn **ais**	fin **iss ais**	vend **ais**
tu donn **ais**	fin **iss ais**	vend **ais**
il donn **ait**	fin **iss ait**	vend **ait**

[1] In **rompre** and its compounds, this form ends in **t: rompt.**

FIRST CONJUGATION	SECOND CONJUGATION	THIRD CONJUGATION
nous donn **ions**	fin iss **ions**	vend **ions**
vous donn **iez**	fin iss **iez**	vend **iez**
ils donn **aient**	fin iss **aient**	vend **aient**

Past Definite

I gave	*I finished*	*I sold*
je donn **ai**	fin **is**	vend **is**
tu donn **as**	fin **is**	vend **is**
il donn **a**	fin **it**	vend **it**
nous donn **âmes**	fin **îmes**	vend **îmes**
vous donn **âtes**	fin **îtes**	vend **îtes**
ils donn **èrent**	fin **irent**	vend **irent**

Future

I shall give	*I shall finish*	*I shall sell*
je donner **ai**	finir **ai**	vendr **ai**
tu donner **as**	finir **as**	vendr **as**
il donner **a**	finir **a**	vendr **a**
nous donner **ons**	finir **ons**	vendr **ons**
vous donner **ez**	finir **ez**	vendr **ez**
ils donner **ont**	finir **ont**	vendr **ont**

Conditional

I should give	*I should finish*	*I should sell*
je donner **ais**	finir **ais**	vendr **ais**
tu donner **ais**	finir **ais**	vendr **ais**
il donner **ait**	finir **ait**	vendr **ait**
nous donner **ions**	finir **ions**	vendr **ions**
vous donner **iez**	finir **iez**	vendr **iez**
ils donner **aient**	finir **aient**	vendr **aient**

Subjunctive Mood

Present

(That) I may give	*I may finish*	*I may sell*
(que) je donn **e**	fin **isse**	vend **e**
tu donn **es**	fin **isses**	vend **es**
il donn **e**	fin **isse**	vend **e**

FIRST	SECOND	THIRD
CONJUGATION	CONJUGATION	CONJUGATION
nous donn **ions**	fin **issions**	vend **ions**
vous donn **iez**	fin **issiez**	vend **iez**
ils donn **ent**	fin **issent**	vend **ent**

Imperfect

(That) *I might give*	*I might finish*	*I might sell*
(que) je donn **asse**	fin **isse**	vend **isse**
tu donn **asses**	fin **isses**	vend **isses**
il donn **ât**	fin **ît**	vend **ît**
nous donn **assions**	fin **issions**	vend **issions**
vous donn **assiez**	fin **issiez**	vend **issiez**
ils donn **assent**	fin **issent**	vend **issent**

Imperative Mood

Give	*Finish*	*Sell*
donn **e** [2]	fin **is**	vend **s**
donn **ons**	fin **iss ons**	vend **ons**
donn **ez**	fin **iss ez**	vend **ez**

The Auxiliary Verbs

Infinitive Mood

148

Pres. avoir *to have*

149

être *to be*

Participles

Pres. ayant *having*

étant *being*

Past eu (aux. avoir) *had*

été (aux. avoir) *been*

Indicative Mood

Present

I have		*I am*	
j' ai	nous avons	je suis	nous sommes
tu as	vous avez	tu es	vous êtes
il a	ils ont	il est	ils sont

[2] This form becomes "donn **es**" when followed by -y or -en.

Imperfect

I was having		*I was being*	
j' avais	nous avions	j' étais	nous étions
tu avais	vous aviez	tu étais	vous étiez
il avait	ils avaient	il était	ils étaient

Past Definite

I had		*I was*	
j' eus	nous eûmes	je fus	nous fûmes
tu eus	vous eûtes	tu fus	vous fûtes
il eut	ils eurent	il fut	ils furent

Future

I shall have		*I shall be*	
j' aurai	nous aurons	je serai	nous serons
tu auras	vous aurez	tu seras	vous serez
il aura	ils auront	il sera	ils seront

Conditional

I should have		*I should be*	
j' aurais	nous aurions	je serais	nous serions
tu aurais	vous auriez	tu serais	vous seriez
il aurait	ils auraient	il serait	ils seraient

Subjunctive Mood

Present

(That) I may have		*I may be*	
(que) j' aie	nous ayons	je sois	nous soyons
tu aies	vous ayez	tu sois	vous soyez
il ait	ils aient	il soit	ils soient

Imperfect

(That) I might have		*I might be*	
(que) j' eusse	nous eussions	je fusse	nous fussions
tu eusses	vous eussiez	tu fusses	vous fussiez
il eût	ils eussent	il fût	ils fussent

Imperative Mood

Have		*Be*	
aie	ayons	sois	soyons
	ayez		soyez

Compound Tenses

150	**151**
Auxiliary **avoir**	Auxiliary **être**

Perfect Infinitive

avoir donné *to have given*   être venu(e) *to have come*

Perfect Participle

ayant donné *having given*   étant venu(e) *having come*

Past Indefinite

j'ai donné *I have given*   je suis venu(e) *I have come*

Pluperfect

j'avais donné *I had given*   j'étais venu(e) *I had come*

Past Anterior

j'eus donné *I had given*   je fus venu(e) *I had come*

Future Perfect

j'aurai donné *I shall have given*   je serai venu(e) *I shall have come*

Conditional Perfect

j'aurais donné *I should have given*   je serais venu(e) *I should have come*

Perfect Subjunctive

j'aie donné (*that*) *I may have given*   je sois venu(e) (*that*) *I may have come*

Pluperfect Subjunctive

j'eusse donné (*that*) *I might have given*   je fusse venu(e) *that I might have come*

Orthographical Changes

152. Verbs in -cer:

placer *to place*

Pres. Part.	Pres. Ind.	Impf. Ind.	Past Def.	Impf. Subj.
plaçant	place	plaçais	plaçai	plaçasse
	places	plaçais	plaças	plaçasses
	place	plaçait	plaça	plaçât
	plaçons	placions	plaçâmes	plaçassions
	placez	placiez	plaçâtes	plaçassiez
	placent	plaçaient	placèrent	plaçassent

153. Verbs in -ger:

manger *to eat*

Pres. Part.	Pres. Ind.	Impf. Ind.	Past Def.	Impf. Subj.
mangeant	mange	mangeais	mangeai	mangeasse
	manges	mangeais	mangeas	mangeasses
	mange	mangeait	mangea	mangeât
	mangeons	mangions	mangeâmes	mangeassions
	mangez	mangiez	mangeâtes	mangeassiez
	mangent	mangeaient	mangèrent	mangeassent

154. Verbs in -yer:

employer *to use,* payer *to pay*

Pres. Ind.	Fut.	Condl.	Pres. Subj.
emploie, etc.	emploierai, etc.	emploierais, etc.	emploie, etc.
paye, } etc. paie, }	payerai, } etc. paierai, }	payerais, } etc. paierais, }	paye, } etc. paie, }

155. Verbs with stem vowel e or é:

mener *to lead*

Pres. Ind.	Fut.	Condl.	Pres. Subj.
mène	mènerai	mènerais	mène
mènes	mèneras	mènerais	mènes
mène	mènera	mènerait	mène

Pres. Ind.	Fut.	Condl.	Pres. Subj.
menons	mènerons	mènerions	menions
menez	mènerez	mèneriez	meniez
mènent	mèneront	mèneraient	mènent

Note: **Appeler** *to call,* instead of changing **e** to **è**, doubles the **l**. Similarly, **jeter** *to throw* doubles the **t**.

appelle	appellerai	appellerais	appelle
jette	jetterai	jetterais	jette

céder *to yield*

Céder retains its stem vowel **é** in the future and conditional.

cède	céderai	céderais	cède

IRREGULAR VERBS

156. All verbs are arranged alphabetically.

(1) Acquérir *to acquire*

1. *Infinitive* **acquérir;** *fut.* acquerrai; *condl.* acquerrais
2. *Pres. Part.* **acquérant;** *impf. indic.* acquérais; *pres. subj.* acquière, acquières, acquière, acquérions, acquériez, acquièrent
3. *Past Part.* **acquis;** *past indef.* j'ai acquis
4. *Pres. Indic.* **acquiers,** acquiers, acquiert, acquérons, acquérez, acquièrent; *impve.* acquiers, acquérons, acquérez
5. *Past Def.* **acquis;** *impf. subj.* acquisse

(2) Aller *to go*

1. *Infinitive* **aller;** *fut.* irai; *condl.* irais
2. *Pres. Part.* **allant;** *impf. indic.* allais; *pres. subj.* aille, ailles, aille, allions, alliez, aillent
3. *Past Part.* **allé;** *past indef.* je suis allé
4. *Pres. Indic.* **vais,** vas, va, allons, allez, vont; *impve.* va, allons, allez
5. *Past Def.* **allai;** *impf. subj.* allasse

(3) Asseoir *to seat*

1. *Infinitive* **asseoir;** *fut.* assiérai; *condl.* assiérais
2. *Pres. Part.* **asseyant;** *impf. indic.* asseyais; *pres. subj.* asseye, asseyes, asseye, asseyions, asseyiez, asseyent

3. *Past Part.* **assis;** *past indef.,* j'ai assis

4. *Pres. Indic.* **assieds,** assieds, assied, asseyons, asseyez, asseyent; *impve.* assieds, asseyons, asseyez

5. *Past Def.* **assis;** *impf. subj.* assisse

(4) Battre *to beat*

Loses one **t** in the present indicative singular: **bats, bats, bat;** otherwise like **vendre.**

(5) Boire *to drink*

1. *Infinitive* **boire;** *fut.* boirai; *condl.* boirais

2. *Pres. Part.* **buvant;** *impf. indic.* buvais; *pres subj.* boive, boives, boive, buvions, buviez, boivent

3. *Past Part.* **bu;** *past indef.* j'ai bu

4. *Pres. Indic.* **bois,** bois, boit, buvons, buvez, boivent; *impve.* bois, buvons, buvez

5. *Past Def.* **bus;** *impf. subj.* busse

(6) Conclure *to conclude*

1. *Infinitive* **conclure;** *fut.* conclurai; *condl.* conclurais

2. *Pres. Part.* **concluant;** *impf. indic.* concluais; *pres. subj.* conclue

3. *Past Part.* **conclu;** *past indef.* j'ai conclu

4. *Pres. Indic.* **conclus,** conclus, conclut, concluons, concluez, concluent; *impve.* conclus, concluons, concluez

5. *Past Def.* **conclus;** *impf. subj.* conclusse

(7) Conduire *to conduct*

1. *Infinitive* **conduire;** *fut.* conduirai; *condl.* conduirais

2. *Pres. Part.* **conduisant;** *impf. indic.* conduisais; *pres. subj.* conduise

3. *Past Part.* **conduit;** *past indef.* j'ai conduit

4. *Pres. Indic.* **conduis,** conduis, conduit, conduisons, conduisez, conduisent; *impve.* conduis, conduisons, conduisez

5. *Past Def.* **conduisis;** *impf. subj.* conduisisse

(8) Connaître *to know*

1. *Infinitive* **connaître;** *fut.* connaîtrai; *condl.* connaîtrais

2. *Pres. Part.* **connaissant;** *impf. indic.* connaissais; *pres. subj.* connaisse

3. *Past Part.* **connu;** *past indef.* j'ai connu

4. *Pres. Indic.* **connais**, connais, connaît, connaissons, connaissez, connaissent; *impve.* connais, connaissons, connaissez

5. *Past Def.* **connus**; *impf. subj.* connusse

(9) **Courir** *to run*

1. *Infinitive* **courir**; *fut.* courrai; *condl.* courrais

2. *Pres. Part.* **courant**; *impf. indic.* courais; *pres. subj.* coure

3. *Past Part.* **couru**; *past indef.* j'ai couru

4. *Pres. Indic.* **cours**, cours, court, courons, courez, courent; *impve.* cours, courons, courez.

5. *Past Def.* **courus**; *impf. subj.* courusse

(10) **Craindre** *to fear*

1. *Infinitive* **craindre**; *fut.* craindrai; *condl.* craindrais

2. *Pres. Part.* **craignant**; *impf. indic.* craignais; *pres. subj.* craigne, craignes, craigne, craignions, craigniez, craignent

3. *Past Part.* **craint**; *past indef.* j'ai craint

4. *Pres. Indic.* **crains**, crains, craint, craignons, craignez, craignent; *impve.* crains, craignons, craignez

5. *Past Def.* **craignis**; *impf. subj.* craignisse

(11) **Croire** *to believe*

1. *Infinitive* **croire**; *fut.* croirai; *condl.* croirais

2. *Pres. Part.* **croyant**; *impf. indic.* croyais; *pres. subj.* croie, croies, croie, croyions, croyiez, croient

3. *Past Part.* **cru**; *past indef.* j'ai cru

4. *Pres. Indic.* **crois**, crois, croit, croyons, croyez, croient; *impve.* crois, croyons, croyez

5. *Past Def.* **crus**; *impf. subj.* crusse

(12) **Cueillir** *to gather, pick*

1. *Infinitive* **cueillir**; *fut.* cueillerai; *condl.* cueillerais

2. *Pres. Part.* **cueillant**; *impf. indic.* cueillais; *pres. subj.* cueille, cueilles, cueille, cueillions, cueilliez, cueillent

3. *Past Part.* **cueilli**, *past indef.* j'ai cueilli

4. *Pres. Indic.* **cueille**, cueilles, cueille, cueillons, cueillez, cueillent; *impve.* cueille, cueillons, cueillez

5. *Past Def.* **cueillis**; *impf. subj.* cueillisse

(13) Devoir *to owe, must*

   1. *Infinitive* **devoir**; *fut.* devrai; *condl.* devrais

   2. *Pres. Part.* **devant**; *impf. indic.* devais; *pres. subj.* doive, doives, doive, devions, deviez, doivent

      3. *Past Part.* **dû** (*f.* due, *pl.* du(e)s); *past indef.* j'ai dû

      4. *Pres. Indic.* **dois,** dois, doit, devons, devez, doivent; *impve.* ——

      5. *Past Def.* **dus;** *impf. subj.* dusse

(14) Dire *to say, tell*

   1. *Infinitive* **dire**; *fut.* dirai; *condl.* dirais

   2. *Pres. Part.* **disant**; *impf. indic.* disais; *pres. subj.* dise

   3. *Past Part.* **dit**; *past indef.* j'ai dit

   4. *Pres. Indic.* **dis,** dis, dit, disons, dites, disent; *impve.* dis, disons, dites

   5. *Past Def.* **dis;** *impf. subj.* disse

(15) Dormir *to sleep*

   1. *Infinitive* **dormir**; *fut.* dormirai; *condl.* dormirais

   2. *Pres. Part.* **dormant**; *impf. indic.* dormais; *pres. subj.* dorme

   3. *Past Part.* **dormi**; *past indef.* j'ai dormi

   4. *Pres. Indic.* **dors,** dors, dort, dormons, dormez, dorment; *impve.* dors, dormons, dormez

   5. *Past Def.* **dormis;** *impf. subj.* dormisse

(16) Ecrire *to write*

   1. *Infinitive* **écrire**; *fut.* écrirai; *condl.* écrirais

   2. *Pres. Part.* **écrivant**; *impf. indic.* écrivais; *pres. subj.* écrive

   3. *Past Part.* **écrit**; *past indef.* j'ai écrit

   4. *Pres. Indic.* **écris,** écris, écrit, écrivons, écrivez, écrivent; *impve.* écris, écrivons, écrivez

   5. *Past Def.* **écrivis;** *impf. subj.* écrivisse

(17) Envoyer *to send*

   1. *Infinitive* **envoyer**; *fut.* enverrai; *condl.* enverrais

   2. *Pres. Part.* **envoyant**; *impf. indic.* envoyais; *pres. subj.* envoie, envoies, envoie, envoyions, envoyiez, envoient

   3. *Past Part.* **envoyé**; *past indef.* j'ai envoyé

   4. *Pres. Indic.* **envoie,** envoies, envoie, envoyons, envoyez, envoient; *impve.* envoie, envoyons, envoyez

   5. *Past Def.* **envoyai;** *impf. subj.* envoyasse

(18) Faire *to do, make*

1. *Infinitive* faire; *fut.* ferai; *condl.* ferais
2. *Pres. Part.* faisant; *impf. indic.* faisais; *pres. subj.* fasse, fasses, fasse, fassions, fassiez, fassent
3. *Past Part.* fait; *past indef.* j'ai fait
4. *Pres. Indic.* fais, fais, fait, faisons, faites, font; *impve.* fais, faisons, faites
5. *Past Def.* fis; *impf. subj.* fisse

(19) Falloir *must* (impers.)

1. *Infinitive* falloir; *fut.* il faudra; *condl.* il faudrait
2. *Pres. Part.* ——; *impf. indic.* il fallait; *pres. subj.* il faille
3. *Past Part.* fallu; *past indef.* il a fallu.
4. *Pres. Indic.* il faut; *impve.* ——.
5. *Past Def.* il fallut; *impf. subj.* il fallût

(20) Fuir *to flee*

1. *Infinitive* fuir; *fut.* fuirai; *condl.* fuirais
2. *Pres. Part.* fuyant; *impf. indic.* fuyais; *pres. subj.* fuie, fuies, fuie, fuyions, fuyiez, fuient
3. *Past Part.* fui; *past indef.* j'ai fui
4. *Pres. Indic.* fuis, fuis, fuit, fuyons, fuyez, fuient; *impve.* fuis, fuyons, fuyez
5. *Past Def.* fuis; *impf. subj.* fuisse

(21) Lire *to read*

1. *Infinitive* lire; *fut.* lirai; *condl.* lirais
2. *Pres. Part.* lisant; *impf. indic.* lisais; *pres. subj.* lise
3. *Past Part.* lu; *past indef.* j'ai lu
4. *Pres. Indic.* lis, lis, lit, lisons, lisez, lisent; *impve.* lis, lisons, lisez
5. *Past Def.* lus; *impf. subj.* lusse

(22) Mettre *to place, put*

1. *Infinitive* mettre; *fut.* mettrai; *condl.* mettrais
2. *Pres. Part.* mettant; *impf. indic.* mettais; *pres. subj.* mette
3. *Past Part.* mis; *past indef.* j'ai mis
4. *Pres. Indic.* mets, mets, met, mettons, mettez, mettent; *impve.* mets, mettons, mettez.
5. *Past Def.* mis; *impf. subj.* misse

(23) Mourir *to die*

1. *Infinitive* **mourir**; *fut.* mourrai; *condl.* mourrais
2. *Pres. Part.* **mourant**; *impf. indic.* mourais; *pres. subj.* meure, meures, meure, mourions, mouriez, meurent
3. *Past Part.* **mort**; *past indef.* je suis mort
4. *Pres. Indic.* **meurs**, meurs, meurt, mourons, mourez, meurent; *impve.* meurs, mourons, mourez
5. *Past Def.* **mourus**; *impf. subj.* mourusse

(24) Naître *to be born*

1. *Infinitive* **naître**; *fut.* naîtrai; *condl.* naîtrais
2. *Pres. Part.* **naissant**; *impf. indic.* naissais; *pres. subj.* naisse
3. *Past Part.* **né**; *past indef.* je suis né
4. *Pres. Indic.* **nais**, nais, naît, naissons, naissez, naissent; *impve.* nais, naissons, naissez
5. *Past Def.* **naquis**; *impf. subj.* naquisse

(25) Ouvrir *to open*

1. *Infinitive* **ouvrir**; *fut.* ouvrirai; *condl.* ouvrirais
2. *Pres. Part.* **ouvrant**; *impf. indic.* ouvrais; *pres. subj.* ouvre
3. *Past Part.* **ouvert**; *past indef.* j'ai ouvert
4. *Pres. Indic.* **ouvre**, ouvres, ouvre, ouvrons, ouvrez, ouvrent; *impve.* ouvre, ouvrons, ouvrez.
5. *Past Def.* **ouvris**; *impf. subj.* ouvrisse

(26) Plaire *to please*

1. *Infinitive* **plaire**; *fut.* plairai; *condl.* plairais
2. *Pres. Part.* **plaisant**; *impf. indic.* plaisais; *pres. subj.* plaise
3. *Past Part.* **plu**; *past indef.* j'ai plu
4. *Pres. Indic.* **plais**, plais, plaît, plaisons, plaisez, plaisent; *impve.* plais, plaisons, plaisez
5. *Past Def.* **plus**; *impf. subj.* plusse
   Like **plaire**: **taire** (but **il tait** has no circumflex accent)

(27) Pleuvoir *to rain*

1. *Infinitive* **pleuvoir**; *fut.* il pleuvra; *condl.* il pleuvrait
2. *Pres. Part.* **pleuvant**; *impf. indic.* il pleuvait; *pres. subj.* il pleuve
3. *Past Part.* **plu**; *past indef.* il a plu
4. *Pres. Indic.* il **pleut**; *impve.* ——
5. *Past Def.* il **plut**; *impf. subj.* il plût

(28) **Pouvoir** *to be able*

1. *Infinitive* **pouvoir**; *fut.* pourrai; *condl.* pourrais
2. *Pres. Part.* **pouvant**; *impf. indic.* pouvais; *pres. subj.* puisse, puisses, puisse, puissions, puissiez, puissent
3. *Past Part.* **pu**; *past indef.* j'ai pu
4. *Pres. Indic.* **puis** or **peux**, peux, peut, pouvons, pouvez, peuvent; *impve.* ——
5. *Past Def.* **pus**; *impf. subj.* pusse

(29) **Prendre** *to take*

1. *Infinitive* **prendre**; *fut.* prendrai; *condl.* prendrais
2. *Pres. Part.* **prenant**; *impf. indic.* prenais; *pres. subj.* prenne, prennes, prenne, prenions, preniez, prennent
3. *Past Part.* **pris**; *past indef.* j'ai pris
4. *Pres. Indic.* **prends**, prends, prend, prenons, prenez, prennent; *impve.* prends, prenons, prenez
5. *Past Def.* **pris**; *impf. subj.* prisse

(30) **Recevoir** *to receive*

1. *Infinitive* **recevoir**; *fut.* recevrai; *condl.* recevrais
2. *Pres. Part.* **recevant**; *impf. indic.* recevais; *pres. subj.* reçoive, reçoives, reçoive, recevions, receviez, reçoivent
3. *Past Part.* **reçu**; *past indef.* j'ai reçu
4. *Pres. Indic.* **reçois**, reçois, reçoit, recevons, recevez, reçoivent; *impve.* reçois, recevons, recevez
5. *Past Def.* **reçus**; *impf. subj.* reçusse

(31) **Résoudre** *to resolve*

1. *Infinitive* **résoudre**; *fut.* résoudrai; *condl.* résoudrais
2. *Pres. Part.* **résolvant**; *impf. indic.* résolvais; *pres. subj.* résolve
3. *Past Part.* **résolu**; *past indef.* j'ai résolu
4. *Pres. Indic.* **résous**, résous, résout, résolvons, résolvez, résolvent; *impve.* résous, résolvons, résolvez
5. *Past Def.* **résolus**; *impf. sub.* résolusse

(32) **Rire** *to laugh*

1. *Infinitive* **rire**; *fut.* rirai; *condl.* rirais
2. *Pres. Part.* **riant**; *impf. indic.* riais; *pres. subj.* rie, ries, rie, riions, riiez, rient

3. *Past Part.* **ri;** *past indef.* j'ai ri
4. *Pres. Indic.* **ris,** ris, rit, rions, riez, rient; *impve.* ris, rions, riez
5. *Past Def.* **ris;** *impf. subj.* risse

(33) Savoir *to know*

1. *Infinitive* **savoir;** *fut.* saurai; *condl.* saurais
2. *Pres. Part.* **sachant;** *impf. indic.* savais; *pres. subj.* sache, saches, sache, sachions, sachiez, sachent
3. *Past Part.* **su;** *past indef.* j'ai su
4. *Pres. Indic.* **sais,** sais, sait, savons, savez, savent; *impve.* sache, sachons, sachez
5. *Past Def.* **sus;** *impf. subj.* susse

(34) Suffire *to suffice*

1. *Infinitive* **suffire;** *fut.* suffirai; *condl.* suffirais
2. *Pres. Part.* **suffisant;** *impf. indic.* suffisais; *pres. subj.* suffise
3. *Past Part.* **suffi;** *past indef.* j'ai suffi
4. *Pres. Indic.* **suffis,** suffis, suffit, suffisons, suffisez, suffisent; *impv.* suffis, suffisons, suffisez
5. *Past Def.* **suffis;** *impf. subj.* suffisse

(35) Suivre *to follow*

1. *Infinitive* **suivre;** *fut.* suivrai; *condl.* suivrais
2. *Pres. Part.* **suivant;** *impf. indic.* suivais; *pres. subj.* suive
3. *Past Part.* **suivi;** *past indef.* j'ai suivi
4. *Pres. Indic.* **suis,** suis, suit, suivons, suivez, suivent; *impve.* suis, suivons, suivez
5. *Past Def.* **suivis;** *impf. subj.* suivisse

(36) Tenir *to hold*

1. *Infinitive* **tenir;** *fut.* tiendrai; *condl.* tiendrais
2. *Pres. Part.* **tenant;** *impf. indic.* tenais; *pres. subj.* tienne, tiennes, tienne, tenions, teniez, tiennent
3. *Past Part.* **tenu;** *past indef.* j'ai tenu
4. *Pres. Indic.* **tiens,** tiens, tient, tenons, tenez, tiennent; *impve.* tiens, tenons, tenez
5. *Past Def.* **tins,** tins, tint, tînmes, tîntes, tinrent; *impf. subj.* tinsse, tinsses, tînt, tinssions, tinssiez, tinssent

(37) **Vaincre** *to conquer*

1. *Infinitive* **vaincre;** *fut.* vaincrai; *condl.* vaincrais
2. *Pres. Part.* **vainquant;** *impf. indic.* vainquais; *pres. subj.* vainque, vainques, vainque, vainquions, vainquiez, vainquent
3. *Past Part.* **vaincu;** *past indef.* j'ai vaincu
4. *Pres. Indic.* **vaincs,** vaincs, vainc, vainquons, vainquez, vainquent; *impve.* vaincs, vainquons, vainquez
5. *Past Def.* **vainquis;** *impf. subj.* vainquisse

(38) **Valoir** *to be worth*

1. *Infinitive* **valoir;** *fut.* vaudrai; *condl.* vaudrais
2. *Pres. Part.* **valant;** *impf. indic.* valais; *pres. subj.* vaille, vailles, vaille, valions, valiez, vaillent.
3. *Past. Part.* **valu;** *past indef.* j'ai valu
4. *Pres. Indic.* **vaux,** vaux, vaut, valons, valez, valent; *impve.* vaux, valons, valez
5. *Past. Def.* **valus;** *impf. subj.* valusse

(39) **Venir** *to come*

1. *Infinitive* **venir;** *fut.* viendrai; *condl.* viendrais
2. *Pres. Part.* **venant;** *impf. indic.* venais; *pres. subj.* vienne, viennes, vienne, venions, veniez, viennent
3. *Past Part.* **venu;** *past indef.* je suis venu
4. *Pres. Indic.* **viens,** viens, vient, venons, venez, viennent; *impve.* viens, venons, venez
5. *Past Def.* **vins,** vins, vint, vînmes, vîntes, vinrent; *impf. subj.* vinsse, vinsses, vînt, vinssions, vinssiez, vinssent

(40) **Vivre** *to live*

1. *Infinitive* **vivre;** *fut.* vivrai; *condl.* vivrais
2. *Pres. Part.* **vivant;** *impf. indic.* vivais; *pres. subj.* vive
3. *Past Part.* **vécu;** *past indef.* j'ai vécu
4. *Pres. Indic.* **vis,** vis, vit, vivons, vivez, vivent; *impve.,* vis, vivons, vivez
5. *Past Def.* **vécus;** *impf. subj.* vécusse

(41) **Voir** *to see*

1. *Infinitive* **voir;** *fut.* verrai; *condl.* verrais
2. *Pres. Part.* **voyant;** *impf. indic.* voyais; *pres. subj.* voie, voies, voie, voyions, voyiez, voient

3. *Past Part.* **vu;** *past indef.* j'ai vu

4. *Pres. Indic.* **vois,** vois, voit, voyons, voyez, voient; *impve.* vois, voyons, voyez

5. *Past Def.* **vis;** *impf. subj.* visse

(42) **Vouloir** *to wish*

1. *Infinitive* **vouloir;** *fut.* voudrai; *condl.* voudrais

2. *Pres. Part.* **voulant;** *impf. indic.* voulais; *pres. subj.* veuille, veuilles, veuille, voulions, vouliez, veuillent

3. *Past Part.* **voulu;** *past indef.* j'ai voulu

4. *Pres. Indic.* **veux,** veux, veut, voulons, voulez, veulent; *impve.* veuillez

5. *Past Def.* **voulus;** *impf. subj.* voulusse

157. Reference list of irregular verbs. The numbers refer to the model verbs of § 156. For the orthographical changes in verbs of the first conjugation, see §§ 152–155.

accourir	9	craindre	10	inscrire	16
accueillir	12	croire	11	introduire	7
acquérir	1	cueillir	12		
aller	2			joindre	10
apercevoir	30	découvrir	25		
appartenir	36	décrire	16	lire	21
apprendre	29	déplaire	26		
asseoir	3	détruire	7	maintenir	36
		devenir	39	mentir	15
battre	4	devoir	13	mettre	22
boire	5	dire	14	mourir	23
		disparaître	8		
combattre	4	dormir	15	naître	24
comprendre	29				
conclure	6	écrire	16	obtenir	36
conduire	7	endormir	15	offrir	25
connaître	8	envoyer	17	ouvrir	25
consentir	15	éprendre	29		
construire	7			paraître	8
contenir	36	faire	18	parcourir	9
courir	9	falloir	19	partir	15
couvrir	25	fuir	20	parvenir	39

peindre 10	remettre 22	suivre 35
permettre 22	repentir 15	surprendre 29
plaindre 10	résoudre 31	
plaire 26	retenir 36	taire 26
pleuvoir 27	revenir 39	tenir 36
poursuivre 35	rire 32	traduire 7
pouvoir 28		
prendre 29	savoir 33	vaincre 37
prévenir 39	sentir 15	valoir 38
promettre 22	servir 15	venir 39
	sortir 15	vivre 40
recevoir 30	souffrir 25	voir 41
reconduire 7	sourire 32	vouloir 42
reconnaître 8	souvenir 39	
relire 21	suffire 34	

NUMBERS

Cardinal Numbers

158. Table of the cardinals:

1. un, une	14. quatorze	70. soixante-dix
2. deux	15. quinze	71. soixante et onze
3. trois	16. seize	80. quatre-vingts
4. quatre	17. dix-sept	81. quatre-vingt-un
5. cinq	18. dix-huit	90. quatre-vingt-dix
6. six	19. dix-neuf	91. quatre-vingt-onze
7. sept	20. vingt	100. cent
8. huit	21. vingt et un	101. cent un
9. neuf	22. vingt-deux	200. deux cents
10. dix	30. trente	201. deux cent un
11. onze	40. quarante	1000. mille
12. douze	50. cinquante	1001. mille un
13. treize	60. soixante	2000. deux mille

(1) Final consonants of 5, 6, 7, 8, 9, 10, 17, 18, and 19 are pronounced except before a word multiplied by them beginning with a consonant or **h** aspirate.

(2) No elision or linking occurs before **huit** or **onze.** Cf. **le onze juin, les huit livres.**

(3) The **t** of **vingt** is pronounced only in the numbers from 21 to 29; **t** is silent in the numbers from 81 to 99 and in 101, 102, etc.

(4) **Et** is regularly used in 21, 31, 41, 51, 61, and 71.

(5) The hyphen is used in all compound numbers under 100, except where **et** is used.

(6) **Quatre-vingt** and multiples of **cent** take **s** when not followed by another number.

(7) **Mille** is invariable. **Mil** replaces **mille** in dates, but the form in hundreds is more frequently used, as in English.

(8) *A* or *one* are not translated before **cent** or **mille.**

Ordinal Numbers

159. The ordinals, with the exception of **premier** *first* and **second** *second,* are formed in French by adding **-ième** to the last consonant of the cardinals. Final **q** in **cinq** becomes **qu,** and final **f** of **neuf** becomes **v.** The form **deuxième** usually replaces **second** in a series of more than two.

cinquième, neuvième, vingt et unième, trente-deuxième

160. The ordinals are used in general as in English, except that in dates and titles they are replaced by the cardinals for all numbers but **premier** *first.*

Louis XIV; le vingt avril.	Louis Fourteenth; the twentieth of April.
Le premier février; Charles Ier.	The first of February; Charles First.

Collective Numbers

161. The following collectives take **s** in the plural and are construed as ordinary nouns. They require **de** before the word they measure.

une dizaine about ten	**une cinquantaine** about fifty
une douzaine a dozen	**une soixantaine** about sixty
une quinzaine about fifteen	**une centaine** about a hundred
une vingtaine about twenty	**un millier** about a thousand
une trentaine about thirty	**un million** a million
une quarantaine about forty	**un milliard** a billion

Une douzaine de roses.	A dozen roses.
Un million de dollars.	A million dollars.

Fractions

162. Fractions are expressed by cardinals in the numerator and ordinals in the denominator, as in English. But the following forms are irregular: **un demi** *a half,* **un tiers** *a third,* **un quart** *a quarter.*

Les cinq huitièmes de la terre.	Five eighths of the earth.
Les trois quarts des habitants.	Three fourths of the inhabitants.

REDUNDANT *NE*

163. A redundant **ne** without negative force is generally used:

(1) after **avoir peur, craindre, empêcher,** or **redouter,** when both clauses are affirmative in English;

J'ai peur qu'il ne vienne.	I am afraid that he will come.
But:	
Je n'ai pas peur qu'il vienne.	I am not afraid that he will come.
J'ai peur qu'il ne vienne pas.	I am afraid that he will not come.

(2) after **de peur que, de crainte que, à moins que,** or **avant que;**

A moins qu'il ne vienne.	Unless he comes.

(3) with the verb in the second member of a comparison of in-equality;

Il est plus fort que je ne le croyais. He is stronger than I thought.

(4) with compound tenses after **il y a ... que, voilà ... que,** or **depuis que.**

Il y a huit jours que je ne l'ai vu. I have not seen him for a week.

French-English Vocabulary

A

à at, in, to, with
abbaye *f.* abbey
abonné *m.* subscriber
abord *see* d'abord
aborder to accost; — **le théâtre** to try one's hand at the theater
absent absent
absolument absolutely
accepter to accept
acclamer to acclaim
accomoder to fix up, prepare (*cooking*)
accompagner to accompany
accorder to grant, give
achat *m.* purchase
acheter to buy
achever to finish
acte *m.* act
actif, active active
addition *f.* bill
admirable admirable
admirer to admire
adresse *f.* address
adresser to address; **s'— à** to address oneself to, apply to
aérodrome *m.* airport
affaire *f.* affair, matter
affamé famished
affiche *f.* placard, poster
affreux frightful
afin de *prep.* in order to
afin que *conj.* in order that

âgé aged, old
agent *m.* agent; policeman
agir to act; **il s'agit de** it is a question of
agréable agreeable, pleasant
aider to help, aid
aigu sharp, acute
ailleurs elsewhere; **d'—** moreover, besides
aimable amiable, kind; **vous serez bien — de** you will be kind enough to
aimer to love, like
ainsi thus
air *m.* air, appearance; **avoir l'—** to seem, look; **en plein —** in the open air
ajouter to add
alerte *f.* alarm
Alexandrie *f. a city and port of Egypt on the Mediterranean, pop. 400,000*
aller to go, be going; to suit; **s'en — to** go away; **— prendre** to go and get, call for; **billet d'— et retour** round-trip ticket
allo hello (*of telephone*)
allumer to light
alors then
aménager to fit up, arrange
amener to bring, take
américain American
Américain *m.* American
Amérique *f.* America; **l'— du Sud** South America

ami *m.*, **amie** *f.* friend

amitié *f.* friendship; **mes —s à** my regards to

amusant amusing, funny

amuser to amuse; **s'—** to amuse oneself, enjoy oneself, have a good time

an *m.* year

ancien old, ancient; former, ex-

anecdote *f.* anecdote

anglais English

Angleterre *f.* England

année *f.* year (*cf. note 2, p. 4*)

annexe *f.* annex

annoncer to announce

apercevoir to perceive; **s'— de** to perceive, become aware of, notice

apéritif *m.* aperitive

apparaître to appear

appareil *m.* apparatus, telephone

appartement *m.* apartment

appartenir to belong

appel *m.* call; **faire l'—** to call on, call the roll

appeler to call; **s'—** to be named

apporter to bring

apprendre to learn

après *adv.* afterward; *prep.* after; **d'—** according to, after

après-midi *m. or f.* afternoon

apprêter to prepare; **s'—** to get ready

approcher to bring near; **s'— de** to come near, approach

appui *m.* support

Arabie *f.* Arabia

arbre *m.* tree

architecte *m.* architect

argent *m.* money

arrangement *m.* arrangement

arranger to arrange

arrestation *f.* arrest

arrêter to stop, arrest; **s'—** to stop

arrivée *f.* arrival

arriver to arrive

artichaut *m.* artichoke

article *m.* article

artifice: feu *m.* **d'—** fireworks

artiste *m. or f.* artist

aspect *m.* appearance

assassin *m.* assassin, ruffian

asseoir to seat; **s'—** to sit down, be seated

assez enough; quite, rather, fairly

assis seated

assister à to attend, be present at

assurer to assure

atome *m.* atom

attendant: en — meanwhile

attendre to await, wait, wait for; **se faire —** to keep someone waiting, be late

atterrir to land (*of airplanes*)

atterrissage: terrain *m.* **d'—** landing field

attirer to draw, attract

attraper to catch

auberge *f.* inn

aucun *with* **ne** not any, no, none, any

aujourd'hui today; **d'— en huit** a week from today

auparavant before, previously

auprès de near to, with

au revoir good-by

aussi also; as; so; such; too; **— bien que** as well as; **—...que** as ...as

aussitôt immediately; **— que** as soon as

autant as much, as many

Auteuil *a suburb west of Paris famous for its race course*

auteur *m.* author

autobus *m.* autobus

automne *m. or f.* autumn

automobile, auto *f.* automobile

autre other, another; **d'—s** others

autrefois formerly, once; **d'—** of former times, of other times

autrement otherwise, differently

avance *f.* advance; **d'—** in advance; **en —** ahead of time

avancer to advance; (*of a watch*) to be fast

avant *adv.,* **— de** *prep.,* **— que** *conj.* before

avant-garde *f.* van, advance guard; **théâtre d'—** *see* **théâtre**

avec with

aventure *f.* adventure

averse *f.* downpour, shower

aviatrice *f.* aviatrix

avion *m.* airplane

avis *m.* advice, opinion; **à mon —** in my opinion

avoir to have; to get; **— à** to have to; **vous avez beau dire cela** it is useless (in vain) for you to say that; **— besoin** to have need; **— chaud** to be hot; **— envie** to desire; **— faim** to be hungry; **— froid** to be cold; **— honte** to be ashamed; **— lieu** to take place; **— peur** to be afraid; **— raison** to be right; **— soif** to be thirsty; **— sommeil** to be sleepy; **— tort** to be wrong; **il doit y avoir** there must be; **il y a** there is, there are; ago

avouer to admit, confess

B

baigner to bathe

bain *m.* bath; **salle** *f.* **de bain(s)** bathroom

bal *m.* ball

balnéaire bathing

banal banal, commonplace

bande *f.* crowd, set, band

banque *f.* bank

banquier *m.* banker

barrière *f.* gate (*of railroad station*)

bas *m.* bottom; stocking

bâtir to build

battre to beat; **se —** to fight

Baudoin II, *King of Constantinople* (*1217–73*), *the last Latin Emperor of Constantinople*

beau, bel, belle beautiful, fine, handsome; **avoir —** + *infin. see* **avoir**

beaucoup many, much

beau-frère *m.* brother-in-law

Belge *m.* Belgian

berger *m.* shepherd

besogne *f.* task, work, job

besoin *m.* need; **avoir — de** to need, have need of

beurre *m.* butter

bien *adv.* well, indeed, very good, to be sure; very; comfortable; much, many; **— que,** although; **aussi — que** as well as

bientôt soon; **à —** see you soon

bière *f.* beer

bifteck *m.* beefsteak

billet *m.* ticket; bill (*of money*); **prendre un —** to buy or get a ticket; **— d'aller et retour** round-trip ticket

Birmanie *f.* Burma, *a province of British India, capital Rangoon*

bistro *m.* small restaurant, café; owner of same

blanc, blanche white

blessure *f.* wound

boire to drink

bois *m.* wood; **Bois** *m.* Bois de Boulogne, *large park on outskirts of Paris*

boisson *f.* drink, beverage

boîte *f.* box; — **de nuit** night club

bon, bonne good, kind; (*exclamation*) all right!

bond *m.* bound, jump

bonjour *m.* good morning

bonnement innocently, simply

bord *m.* shore; board; brim (*of a hat*); edge

bougie *f.* candle

boulevard *m.* boulevard

bourgeois bourgeois

Bourget, le (*Seine*), *Paris airport, northeast of Paris*

bout *m.* end; bit; **au — de** at the end of, after

bouteille *f.* bottle

boutique *f.* shop

boutonnière *f.* buttonhole

brave good, worthy, brave

Brésil *m.* Brazil

Bretagne *f. one of the old provinces of France, capital Rennes*

brise *f.* breeze

brosse *f.* brush

bruit *m.* noise; rumor

brûler to burn

bureau *m.* desk; office; ticket office

C

ça that; *see* **cela**

cabaret *m.* cabaret

cabinet *m.* study, office

cacher to hide

café *m.* coffee; café; **prendre le —** to have coffee

camarade *m.* comrade

camp *m.* camp

campagne *f.* country; **à la —** in (to) the country

Canada *m.* Canada

capitale *f.* capital

car for

caractéristique characteristic

caravane *f.* caravan

cardinal *m.* cardinal

carré square

carte *f.* card; bill of fare; map

cas *m.* case; **en tout —** in any case

caser to find a place for, fix

casino *m.* casino, club

cathédrale *f.* cathedral

cause *f.* cause; **à — de** because of

causer to cause; to chat

ce, cet, cette this, that; **ces** these, those

ce *pron.* it, that; **— qui, — que** that which, what

céder to yield, give up

cela (*contracted to* **ça** *in familiar speech*) that

célèbre famous

celui, celle the one, he, that, this; **ceux, celles** those; **celui-ci** this one, the latter; **celui-là** that one, the former

cent hundred

cependant however

certain certain, sure

certainement certainly

ces these, those

cesser to cease, stop

ceux *see* **celui**

chacun each, each one, everyone

chambre *f.* room, bedroom

chameau *m.* camel

champ *m.* field

chance *f.* chance, luck; **bonne —** good luck

chandail *m.* sweater

changer to change

chanson *f.* song

chanter to sing

chapeau *m.* hat; — melon derby

chapelain *m.* chaplain

chapelier *m.* hatter

chapelle *f.* chapel; **Sainte-Chapelle** *see* **Sainte**

chapellerie *f.* hat store

chaque each, every

Chargé (*Indre-et-Loire*) *small village north of Tours*

Chartres (*Eure-et-Loire*) *famous for its cathedral, about 60 miles southwest of Paris*

château *m.* château, castle

chaud warm

chaud *m.* warmth, heat; **avoir —** to be warm (*of persons*); **faire —** to be warm (*of weather*)

chauffer to heat, warm

chef *m.* chef, chief

cheminot *m.* railroad workman

cher, chère dear, expensive

chercher to look for, seek, search, get; **envoyer —** to send for

cheval *m.* horse

cheveux *m. pl.* hair

Chevreuse (*Seine-et-Oise*) *town about 22 miles from Paris. Former seat of Port-Royal des Champs, headquarters of the Jansenists ("les Solitaires"), destroyed by Louis XIV in 1710*

chez to, at, with, in, at the house of

Chine *f.* China

chinois Chinese

choisir to choose, select

choix *f.* choice, selection

chose *f.* thing

ciel *m.* (*pl.* cieux) sky, heavens

cinéma *m.* "movies," motion-picture theater

cinq five

cinquante fifty

circuler to circulate, pass

citron *m.* lemon

civilisation *f.* civilization

clair *adj.* clear; *noun m.* **— de lune** moonlight

clef *f.* key; **fermer à —** to lock

cliché *m.* picture

client *m.* patient; customer

cloître *m.* cloister, monastery

club *m.* club

Cochinchine *f.* Cochin-China, *one of the provinces of French Indo-China, capital Saïgon*

coin *m.* corner

collaborateur *m.* collaborator

collège *m.* college

Colomb *m.* Columbus

colonie *f.* colony

colonne *f.* column, pillar

combien how many, how much

comédie *f.* comedy

comique comic

commander to order, command

comme how! as, like, as if

commencer to begin, start

comment how, in what manner

commerçant *m.* merchant

commissaire *m.* **de police** superintendent (inspector) of police

commodément comfortably

compagnon *m.* comrade, companion

complet full (*of autobus or streetcar*); complete

complet *m.* suit of clothes

complètement completely

compliment *m.* compliment

complot *m.* plot
comprendre to understand
concierge *m. and f.* janitor
concours *m.* competition, contest
conduire to lead, drive, conduct, accompany
confesser to confess
confiance *f.* confidence
confondre to confuse; **se — en excuses** to make profuse apologies
congé *m.* leave, absence, day off
connaissance *f.* acquaintance, acquaintanceship; **faire la — de** to make the acquaintance of, meet
connaître to know, be acquainted with
consacrer to devote
conseil *m.* piece of advice, counsel
conseiller to counsel, advise
consentir to consent, agree
conséquent: par — consequently
conserver to preserve, keep
consommation *f.* drink
conspirateur *m.* conspirator
construire to construct, build
content glad, content, satisfied
contenter to content, satisfy
conter to tell, relate
continuer to continue
contrairement contrary
contre against
contrée *f.* country, region
contrôleur *m.* controller, inspector, check- or ticket-taker
convenir to agree, admit
convenu agreed
conversation *f.* conversation
coque *f.* shell; **des œufs à la —** boiled eggs
cordial cordial
correct correct
corse Corsican

côté *m.* side; **à —** beside it, next door; **à — de** beside
coucher to put to bed; **se —** to go to bed; **envoyer —** to send to bed
couleur *f.* color
coup *m.* blow; **— d'œil** glance; **— de téléphone** ring, call; **tout à —** suddenly
couper to cut; (*of telephone*) to cut off
couramment fluently
courant *m.* current; **mettre au —** to inform
courir to run; **— les magasins** to shop
couronne *f.* crown
cours *m.* course; **— de vacances** summer courses; **faire un —** to give a course; **suivre un —** to take (attend) a course; **au — de** during the course of
course *f.* race; errand
cousin *m.*, **cousine** *f.* cousin
couteau *m.* knife
coûter to cost
couvrir to cover; **se —** (*of weather*) to cloud over
craindre to fear, be afraid of
cravate *f.* necktie, tie
cri *m.* cry
crier to cry, shout
crime *m.* crime
crinière *f.* mane
critique critical
croire to believe, think
croisé crossed; **veston** *m.* **—** double-breasted coat
cuisine *f.* kitchen; cooking; **faire la —** to cook
cuisinier *m.* cook, chef
curé *m.* curé, priest, curate

curieux curious
curiosité *f.* curiosity; sight

D

d'abord first, at first
dangereux dangerous
dans in, into, within
danser to dance
date *f.* date
Dauphiné *m. one of the old French provinces, capital Grenoble*
davantage more (*cf. p. 39, note 2*)
de of, from, by, with, than
débiter to recite
debout *adv.* standing, erect
décidément decidedly, certainly
décider de to decide; se — à to make up one's mind, decide
décision *f.* decision
découverte *f.* discovery
découvrir to discover
décrire to describe
décrocher (*of telephones*) to unhook, take off (*receiver*)
dedans in it, inside
défiler to parade
définitif definitive
dégourdir to stretch (*one's legs*)
déjà already
déjeuner *m.* breakfast; lunch; petit — breakfast
déjeuner to breakfast; to lunch
délicatement delicately
demain tomorrow; de — en huit a week from tomorrow; à — goodby until tomorrow
demande *f.* request
demander to ask, ask for
demeurer to live, dwell, remain (*cf. Verb Review, p. 117*)

demi half; —-douzaine *f.* half-dozen; —-heure *f.* half-hour
démodé out of fashion, antiquated
demoiselle *f.* miss, young lady
dénouement *m.* solution, conclusion
départ *m.* departure
dépêcher: se — to hurry
dépenser to spend
depuis since, for, from; — quand since when, how long
dernier last, latter
dernières *f. pl.* last performances
dérouler to unfold
derrière behind
désastreux disastrous
désaveu *m.* disavowal
descendre to descend, go *or* come down, get out; to stop (*at a hotel*); *trans.* to bring down
description *f.* description
désert deserted; *m.* desert
désolé very sorry, grieved
désordre *m.* disorder
dès que as soon as
détruire to destroy
deux two
deuxième second
Deux Magots, les *famous café on the Left Bank of the Seine, in Paris* (magot: *a grotesque porcelain figure*)
devancer to precede, anticipate
devant before, in front of
devanture *f.* show window
devenir to become
deviner to guess
devoir to owe; must, ought, is to
diable *m.* devil; —! *exclamation indicating surprise or impatience*
Dieu *m.* God
différence *f.* difference
difficile difficult, hard, hard to please

difficulté *f.* difficulty
digestif digestive
digne worthy
dimanche *m.* Sunday
dîner *m.* dinner
dîner to dine; **— en ville** to dine out
dire to say; **c'est à —** that is to say; **vouloir —** to mean
diriger to direct, guide
discuter to discuss
disparaître to disappear
disperser to disperse, scatter
disposé disposed
disposition *f.* disposition
distance *f.* distance
distraction *f.* distraction, diversion
divin divine
dix ten
dix-huit eighteen
dix-neuf nineteen
dix-sept seventeen
docteur *m.* doctor
doigt *m.* finger
domestique *m.* servant
dommage *m.* damage, loss; **c'est —** it's a pity, it's too bad
donc therefore, then; *used after an imperative to emphasize a command or request*
donner to give; **— sur** to open on, give on
dont whose, of which, of whom
dormir to sleep
dos *m.* back; **à — de** on the back of
dot *f.* dowry
doucement softly
doute *m.* doubt
douter to doubt
doux, douce sweet, soft, gentle, pleasant, mild
douze twelve

droit *m.* right; *adj.* straight
duc *m.* duke
durant during
durée *f.* duration
durer to last

E

eau *f.* water; **— courante** running water
échange *m.* exchange
éclairer to light
école *f.* school; **— de médecine** medical school
écouter to listen
écrier: s'— to exclaim
écrire to write
écrivain *m.* writer, author
écu *m.* écu (*old French coin*), shield
Ecu de France *m. a famous restaurant near the Gare de l'Est*
écurie *f.* stable (*for horses*)
édifice *m.* building
effet *m.* effect; **en —** indeed, that is true
effort *m.* effort
effroi *m.* fright
également likewise, equally
église *f.* church
Egypte *f.* Egypt
élégance *f.* elegance
élégant elegant, stylish, well dressed
élément *m.* element
élève *m. and f.* pupil, student
élever to raise; **s'— à** to amount to
elle she, her; **—-même** herself
émissaire *m.* emissary
emmener to take away, take along
emparer: s'— de to seize, get hold of
empêcher to prevent
employée des téléphones *f.* telephone girl

emporter to carry away

empresser: s'— to be eager, hasten

emprunter to borrow

en *pron.* of it, of them, some, any

en *prep.* in, while, upon, as

enchanté delighted

enclos *m.* enclosure

encore still, yet, besides; — un another; — une fois once more

endormir: s'— to go to sleep

endroit *m.* place

enfant *m.* child

enfermer to enclose, confine

enfin at length, at last, finally

enfoncer: s'— to sink

enfuir: s'— to flee

enlever to carry off, remove

ennuyer to bore, tire

énorme enormous

enseigner to teach

ensuite next, then, afterward

entendre, to hear; — parler de to hear of; bien entendu of course

entre between, among, in

entrer to enter, come in

envers toward, to

envie *f.* desire; avoir — de to desire, want, have a mind to

envoyer to send; — chercher to send for; — coucher to send to bed

épatant splendid, marvelous

épaule *f.* shoulder

épinards *m. pl.* spinach

épine *f.* thorn

époque *f.* period, time

épouser to marry

errer to wander

escalader to scale (*a wall*)

escale *f.* landing, stop (*of airplanes*)

escalier *m.* stairway

Espagne *f.* Spain

espérer to hope

esprit *m.* mind, wit

essayer to try

est *m.* east

estime *m.* esteem; succès d'— indifferent or moderate success

et and

étage *m.* story (*of a building*); au deuxième — on the third floor

étalage *m.* display

étape *f.* landing, stop (*of airplane or ship*)

état *m.* state

Etats-Unis *m. pl.* United States

été *m.* summer

étoile *f.* star

étonner to astonish

étranger *m.* foreigner, stranger; *adj.* foreign, strange

être *m.* being

être to be; — à to belong to; — bien to be comfortable; n'est-ce pas? is it not so? soit! agreed! so be it!

étroit narrow

étudiant *m.*, étudiante *f.* student

étudier to study

Europe *f.* Europe

eux them, they

éveiller to wake up; s'— to wake up

évidemment evidently, of course

éviter to avoid

examen *m.* examination; passer un — to take an examination

examiner to examine

excellent excellent

excepté except

excursion *f.* excursion

excuse *f.* excuse

exemple *m.* example

expédier to send

expliquer to explain

exposer to display

extrême extreme; **Extrême Orient** *m*. Far East

F

facile easy

facilement easily

façon *f*. way, manner

fade insipid, tasteless

fagot *m*. fagot

faim *f*. hunger; **avoir —** to be hungry

faire to make; to do; to have, cause; **— attention** to pay attention; **— beau (temps)** to be fine weather; **— la connaissance de** to make the acquaintance of, meet; **— la cuisine** to cook; **— froid** to be cold (*of the weather*); **— jour** to be light; **— venir** to send for; **— voir** to show; **se — à** to get used to; **se — attendre** to keep people waiting; **se — tard** to get late

falloir must, be necessary, need

fameux famous

famille *f*. family; **en —** informally

farce *f*. farce

farci stuffed

fasciste *m*. fascist

fatigant fatiguing, tiring

fatiguer to tire

fauteuil *m*. armchair

faux false

favori favorite

féminin feminine

femme *f*. woman

fendre to split, slice

fenêtre *f*. window

fermer to shut; **— à clef** to lock

fête *f*. festival, fête, entertainment

fêter to celebrate

feu *m*. fire; **— d'artifice** fireworks

feuille *f*. leaf; sheet of paper

feuilleter to turn the pages of, run through (*conjugated like* **jeter**)

feutre *m*. felt, felt hat

fiançailles *f*. *pl*. betrothal

fiancée *f*. fiancée, betrothed

figure *f*. face, figure

filer to run along

filet *m*. dash (*in cooking*)

fille *f*. daughter; **jeune —** girl, young lady

film *m*. film, "movie"

fils *m*. son

fin *f*. end; **à la —** finally, at last

finir to finish, end

flanelle *f*. flannel

flâner to saunter, stroll

flèche *f*. spire

flétrir to wither, cause to fade

fleur *f*. flower; **en —** in bloom

foi *f*. faith

foin *m*. hay

fois *f*. time; **une —** once

foncé dark (*of colors*)

fond *m*. bottom; further end; **à —** thoroughly

force *f*. strength

formellement formally

fort *adj*. strong, clever; *adv*. much, very; **être — en** to be good at, know very well

fortement firmly, fast

fortune *f*. fortune; **faire —** to make one's fortune

fou, fol, folle crazy, mad

fournir to furnish

fourrer to stuff, cram

fours *m*. *pl*.: **petits —** cakes, cookies

franc *m*. franc

français French

Français *m*. Frenchman

France *f.* France; — **Méridionale** southern France

frapper to strike, knock

fréquent frequent, often

fréquenter to frequent

frère *m.* brother

friand: être — de to be fond of

froid *m.* cold; **avoir** — to be cold (*of persons*); **faire** — to be cold (*of weather*)

froisser to offend, hurt (*the feelings*)

fruit *m.* fruit

fumer to smoke

G

gagner to win, earn

gai gay

gaîment gayly

gant *m.* glove

garantir to guarantee

garçon *m.* boy; waiter

garder to keep

gare *f.* railroad station; — de l'Est *station of the Compagnie de l'Est in Paris;* — d'Orléans *station of the Compagnie Paris-Orléans in Paris*

gastronomique gastronomic

gâteau *m.* cake

gauche left; awkward

geler to freeze

général *adj.* general; *m.* general

genre *m.* type, sort

gens *m. pl.* people; **jeunes** — young people, young men

gentil nice

gérant *m.* manager

gilet *m.* vest

gîte *m.* shelter, place to stay

glace *f.* ice; mirror, glass; **une** —, **des** —s ice cream

glacière *f.* icebox, refrigerator

gloire *f.* glory

gourmand *m.* glutton

gourmet *m.* epicure

goût *m.* taste

goûter to taste

gouverneur *m.* governor

grâce *f.* grace, charm; — à thanks to

grammaire *f.* grammar

grand great, big, tall

grand-oncle *m.* great-uncle

grève *f.* strike; **en** — on strike

gréviste *m.* striker

gris gray

gros, grosse big, large, coarse, heavy

grotesque grotesque

groupe *m.* group

guère: ne ... — hardly

guérir to cure

guérison *f.* cure

guide *m.* guide; guidebook

H

(* indicates aspirate h)

habitant *m.* inhabitant

habiter to inhabit, live in, dwell in (*cf. Verb Review, p. 117*)

habitude *f.* habit; **d'**— usual, usually

habitué *m.* habitué

* haine *f.* hatred

* hardiesse *f.* daring, boldness

* hasard *m.* chance; **par** — by chance

* haut high; loud; tall

* Havre, le (*Seine-Inférieure*) *French port on the English Channel*

hebdomadaire weekly

* héros *m.* hero

hésitation *f.* hesitation

hésiter to hesitate

heure *f.* hour, o'clock, time; **de bonne —** early; **tout à l'—** presently

heureusement happily, fortunately

heureux happy, pleased

hier yesterday; **— soir** last night, last evening

histoire *f.* history, story

historique historical

hiver *m.* winter

homme *m.* man

* honte *f.* shame; **avoir —** to be ashamed

horreur *f.* horror

* hors-d'œuvre *m.* hors-d'œuvre

hôtel *m.* hotel; mansion; **Hôtel de Ville** City Hall

hôtelier *m.* innkeeper, hotelkeeper

* huée *f.* hoot, shout

huile *f.* oil

* huit eight

Humanité *f.*: **L'—** *a socialist newspaper in Paris*

humeur *f.* humor, mood

humide damp

I

ici here

idée *f.* idea

identité *f.* identity

ignorer to be ignorant of, not know

il he, it

île *f.* island

illuminer: **s'—** to light up

imaginer to imagine, conceive, devise; **s'—** to imagine to oneself

impatiemment impatiently

impatience *f.* impatience

imperméable *f.* raincoat

important important

importer to matter; **n'importe** no matter

impossible impossible

impression *f.* impression

incident *m.* incident

incommoder to put out, incommode

incomparable incomparable

inconnu *m.* unknown

Inde *f.* India

indifférent indifferent

indiquer to indicate

Indochine *f.* French Indo-China

infiniment infinitely

influence *f.* influence

informer to inform; **s'— de** to inquire about

inquiet uneasy, anxious

inquiétant disquieting

inscription *f.* registration (*for a course*)

inscrire: **s'—** to register (*for a course*)

insister to insist

installer to install, settle, seat

instant *m.* instant; **à l'—** immediately

instruction *f.* instruction

intéressant interesting

intéresser to interest

intérieur *m.* interior

interroger to question

interrompre to interrupt

interview *m.* interview

Intransigeant *m.*: **L'—** *a liberal newspaper in Paris*

inutile useless

inutilisable useless, unusable

inventer to invent

invention *f.* invention

invitation *f.* invitation

inviter to invite

J

jamais never; ever
jambe *f.* leg
janséniste *m.* Jansenist
Jardies, les Villa des Jardies, *between Versailles and Paris near Ville-d'Avray, belonged once to Balzac and later to Gambetta*
jardin *m.* garden
jaune yellow; *m.* yolk (*of an egg*)
jésuite *m.* Jesuit
jeter to throw, cast; to throw away
jeune young; — **fille** *f.* (young) girl
joli pretty
jouer to play; — **à** to play (*a game*); — **de** to play (*a musical instrument*)
jour *m.* day; **huit —s** a week; **pointe** *f.* **du —** dawn; **quinze —s** two weeks, fortnight; **faire —** to be light
journal *m.* newspaper
journalier daily
journaliste *m.* journalist
journée *f.* day (*cf. note 2, p. 4*)
juillet *m.* July
juin *m.* June
jusque even to; — **là** up to that time; **jusqu'à** *prep.* as far as, up to, until, till; **jusqu'à ce que** *conj.* until
justement precisely, exactly

L

l' *see* **le, la**
la the; her, it
là there; —**-bas** down there, over there; —**-dedans** therein, in it

laisser to leave; to allow, let
lait *m.* milk
laitue *f.* lettuce
lampe *f.* lamp
langue *f.* tongue; language
Lapin Agile, le "The Nimble Rabbit," *a night club in Paris*
latin Latin; **le Quartier Latin** the Latin Quarter
le the; him, it
leçon *f.* lesson
légende *f.* legend
léger light
légion *f.* legion
légume *m.* vegetable
lendemain *m.* next day
lentement slowly
lequel, laquelle which, which one
lettre *f.* letter
leur their; to them
lever to lift, raise; **se —** to rise, get up
libraire *m.* bookseller
librairie *f.* bookstore
lieu *m.* place; **avoir —** to take place; **au — de** in place of, instead of
ligne *f.* line; **grandes —s** main lines (*of railroads*)
lire to read
liste *f.* list
lit *m.* bed
livre *m.* book; *f.* pound
location *f.* ticket office (*of theater*); **prendre des places en —** to buy tickets in advance, get reserved seats
logique *f.* logic
Loire *f. the longest river in France, 650 miles*
Londres *m.* London
longtemps long, a long time
lorsque when
louer to rent

Louis XIV *king of France, 1643–1715*

lui to him, to her, him, he; — -même himself

lune *f.* moon

Lyon (*Rhône*) *famous for its silks, southeast of Paris*

M

madame, Mme *f.* madam, Mrs.

mademoiselle, Mlle *f.* Miss

magasin *m.* store

magnifique magnificent

mai *m.* May

main *f.* hand; à la — in his (her *etc.*) hand

maintenant now

mais but

maison *f.* house; à la — at home

maître *m.* master, teacher; — d'hôtel head waiter

mal *m.* evil, ill; — de mer seasickness

mal *adv.* badly, bad, ill; pas — a good many (deal); il n'est pas trop — he doesn't make a bad appearance

malade sick, ill

malgré in spite of

malheur *m.* misfortune

malheureusement unfortunately

malheureux unfortunate

manger to eat

manière *f.* manner, way

manquer to miss; to fail; il me manque I miss him; — de to almost, come near

marché *m.* market; bargain, deal; meilleur — cheaper

marcher to walk; to run (*of trains, machines*)

maréchal *m.* marshal

mariage *m.* marriage

marque *f.* mark

marquer to mark

Marseille (*Bouches-du-Rhône*) *French seaport on the Mediterranean*

massacrant dreadful

matériel *m.* material

Matin, Le *a newspaper in Paris*

matin *m.* morning; le — in the morning

matinée *f.* morning (*cf. note 2, p. 4*)

mauvais bad, poor

mayonnaise *f.* mayonnaise dressing

méfier: se — de to mistrust

meilleur better; le — best

melon *m.* melon; chapeau — derby (hat)

membre *m.* member

même *adj.* same, very; *adv.* even; tout de —, quand — anyhow, just the same

mener to lead, take

mentir to lie

merci *m.* thanks, thank you, (no) thank you

mère *f.* mother

mériter to deserve, merit

merveille *f.* marvel; à — marvelously

message *m.* message

mesure *f.* measure

mettre to put, place; to put on; se — à to begin; — au courant to inform

meurtrier *m.* murderer

midi *m.* noon

mien (le), mienne (la) mine

mieux better; tant — so much the better

mil thousand
milieu *m.* middle
militaire military; *m.* military man
mille thousand
ministre *m.* minister
Minorque, l'île island of Minorca, *east of Spain*
minuit *m.* midnight
minute *f.* minute
miraculeux miraculous
mise *f.* **en scène** setting
mode *f.* mode, style; **à la —** stylish; popular
modèle *m.* model
moi me, to me
moindre *adj.* less, least, slightest
moins *adv.* less, fewer; **au —** at least; **à — que** unless
mois *m.* month
moment *m.* moment; **en (à) ce —** at this moment
mon, ma, mes my
monde *m.* world; people, crowd; **tout le —** everybody
monseigneur *m.* my lord
monsieur, M. Mr., sir, gentleman
montant *m.* amount
monter to go up, come up, climb, get into; *trans.* to carry up; to put on (*of plays*)
Montereau, Pierre de *architect of the Sainte-Chapelle, 1245-1248*
montrer to show
monument *m.* monument
mot *m.* word; **petit —** note
mou, mol, molle soft
mourir to die
moutarde *f.* mustard
moyen *m.* means, way
mur *m.* wall
musée *m.* museum
mystérieux mysterious

N

nager to swim
naïf, naïve simple
naissance *f.* birth; **marque** *f.* **de —** birthmark
naître to be born
natal native
naturellement naturally, of course
ne ... pas not
nécessaire necessary
négliger to neglect
nettoyer to clean
neuf nine
neuf, neuve new
neveu *m.* nephew; **petit-—** grand-nephew
ni ... ni neither ... nor; **ni vous non plus** nor you either
noir black
nom *m.* name
nombre *m.* number
nommé *m.* by the name of, a person named
nommer to name
non no, not; **— plus** *after neg.* either
notre our; **le nôtre** ours
nous we, us, to us
nouveau, nouvel, nouvelle new; **de nouveau** again
nouvelle *f.* piece of news; **—s** *f. pl.* news
novembre *m.* November
nu naked; **mis à —** bared, exposed
nuage *m.* cloud
nuit *f.* night

O

obliger to oblige
observer to observe
occasion *f.* opportunity

occupé occupied, busy

octobre *m.* October

Odéon *m. a theater in the Latin Quarter of Paris*

odeur *f.* odor

œil (*pl.* yeux) *m.* eye; coup *m.* d'— glance

œuf *m.* egg; —s à la coque boiled eggs

œuvre *f.* work

officier *m.* officer

offrir to offer

olive *f.* olive

on one, you, they, people

ondée *f.* shower

onze eleven

or now

orchestre *m.* orchestra

ordinairement ordinarily

ordonner to order

ordre *m.* order

oreille *f.* ear; prêter l'— to listen

Orient *m.* Orient; Extrême — Far East

origine *f.* origin

orner to decorate

oser to dare

ôter to remove, take off

ou or; — bien or else

où where; (*after expressions of time*) when

oublier to forget

ouest *m.* west

oui yes

ouvert open

ouvrier *m.* workman

ouvrir to open

P

page *f.* page (*of a book*)

pain *m.* bread

pâle pale

pâlir to pale, turn pale

panne *f.* breakdown (*of automobiles etc.*), trouble

pantalon *m.* trousers

papier *m.* paper

par by, in, through, per

paraître to appear, seem

paralyser to paralyze

parce que because

parchemin *m.* parchment

pardessus *m.* overcoat

pardon *m.* pardon, excuse

pareil like, similar

parent *m.* parent, relative

parfaitement perfectly

parfumé perfumed, fragrant

parier to bet

Paris *m.* (*Seine*) *capital of France*

parisien Parisian

Parisien *m.* Parisian

parler to speak; entendre — de to hear of

parti *m.* decision, resolution, side; prendre ce — to decide to do this

particulier private

partie *f.* match, game; party

partir to leave, depart, go away

partout everywhere; un peu — almost everywhere

pas not; no; not any; — du tout not at all

Pascal, Blaise (*1623–1662*) *a famous mathematician and Jansenist leader*

passage *m.* passage; de — transient, passing through, making a short stay

passé *m.* past

passeport *m.* passport

passer to pass, go; to spend time; — un examen to take an examination; se — to happen; se — de to do without

patience *f.* patience

pâtisserie *f.* pastry shop; pastry

pauvre poor

payer to pay, pay for

pays *m.* country

paysanne *f.* peasant woman

peinture *f.* painting

pencher to incline, lean

pendant during; — **que** while

pendule *f.* clock

péninsule *f.* peninsula

penser to think; — **à** to think of (*have one's mind on*); — **de** to think of (*have an opinion about*)

pension *f.* boardinghouse, pension

perdre to lose

père *m.* father

perfection *f.* perfection

perfectionner to perfect

permettre to permit, let

personnage *m.* person, personnage

personne *f.* person; **ne ... —** nobody, no one

petit little, small; **—-neveu** grand-nephew

peu little, few; **un —** a little; **— à —** little by little, gradually; **à — près** almost, nearly; reasonably

Peugeot *f. a famous make of French automobile*

peur *f.* fear; **avoir —** to be afraid

peut-être perhaps, maybe

phrase *f.* phrase, sentence

pièce *f.* room; play (*theater*)

pied *m.* foot; **à —** on foot

pierre *f.* stone

pile *f.* pile

pincée *f.* pinch, small amount

pire *adj.* worse; **le —** the worst

pis *adv.* worse; **tant —** so much the worse

pittoresque picturesque

place *f.* place; seat (*in theater*); room (*space*); square (*in a city*)

placer to place, put

plage *f.* beach

plaire to please; **s'il vous plaît** please, if you please

plaisir *m.* pleasure

plan *m.* plan

plat *m.* plate, dish, platter

plateau *m.* tray

plein full; **en — air** in the open air

pleurer to weep, regret

pleuvoir to rain

pluie *f.* rain

plume *f.* pen

plupart *f.* the greater part, most

plus more; **ne ... —** no longer, no more; **non —** (*after neg.*) either

plusieurs several

plutôt rather

poche *f.* pocket

poète *m.* poet

poignée *f.* shake (*of hand*)

point *m.* point; **sur le — de** on the point of, about to

pointe *f.* point; **— du jour** dawn

pointure *f.* size (*hats, gloves, etc.*)

**pois: petits — *m. pl.* peas

poisson *m.* fish

poivre *m.* pepper

police *f.* police

policier police; **roman *m.* —** mystery novel

politique political

Polonais *m.* Pole

pomme *f.* apple; **— de terre** potato

Pons *a famous tearoom opposite the Luxembourg Gardens*

Pont-Neuf, le *the oldest bridge in Paris, built 1578-1603*

porte *f.* door

portée *f.* reach, range

portefeuille *m.* wallet, purse

porter to carry; to wear; to bear; **se — ** to be (*of health*)

porteur *m.* porter

portière *f.* door (*of a car etc.*)

Port-Mahon *a city on the island of Minorca, east of Spain*

Port-Royal *headquarters of the Jansenist order near Chevreuse*

poser to place, put

position *f.* position

posséder to possess, own

possible possible

potage *m.* soup

poulet *m.* chicken

pour for, in order to; **— que** in order that

pourboire *m.* tip

pourquoi why

pousser to grow

pouvoir to be able, can; **il se peut** it may be

pouvoir *m.* power

pratique *f.* practice

précaution *f.* precaution

prêcher to preach

précieux precious, valuable

précis exact, precise; **à six heures —es** at six o'clock sharp

précisément exactly, precisely

préférer to prefer

premier first; **— ministre** *m.* prime minister

prendre to take, get; to call for; **— le café** to have coffee; **— un billet** to buy (get) a ticket; **aller —** to go and get, call for; **venir —** to come and get, call for

préparatifs *m. pl.* preparations

préparation *f.* preparation

préparer to prepare

près near, near by; **— de** near; **à peu —** almost, nearly; reasonably

présenter to present, introduce

président *m.* president

presque almost

prêt ready

prétendant *m.* suitor

prétendre to claim, wish

prétendu so-called

prêter to lend; **— l'oreille** to listen

prétexte *m.* pretext, excuse

prêtre *m.* priest

prévoir to foresee

prier to pray, ask, beg

principal principal

priver to deprive

prix *m.* price, prize

procès *m.* lawsuit

prochain next

procurer: se — to obtain, procure

professeur *m.* professor, teacher

profiter to profit; **— de** to profit by, take advantage of

projet *m.* plan

prolétariat *m.* proletariat, people

promenade *f.* walk, ride; pleasure trip; **faire une —** to take a walk

promener: se — to walk, promenade

promettre to promise

propos *m.* remark; **à —** by the way

proposer to propose

propre clean, neat; own

propriétaire *m.* owner, proprietor

propriété *f.* estate, property

protestation *f.* protestation, protest

protester to protest

Provence *f. one of the old provinces in southern France, capital Aix-en-Provence*

province *f.* province
puis then, besides
puisque since

Q

quand when; — **même** anyhow; **de-puis** — since when, how long
quarante forty
quart *m.* quarter, fourth
quartier *m.* quarter (*of a city*); **Quartier Latin** *the university quar-ter of Paris on the Left Bank*
quatorze fourteen
quatre four
quatre-vingts eighty
quatre-vingt-dix ninety
que whom, that, which
que? what?
que *conj.* that, than, as; **ne ... —** only
quel, quelle what, what a
quelque some; *pl.* a few; **— ... que** however ...
quelquefois sometimes
quelqu'un someone; *pl.* some
qu'est-ce que? qu'est-ce que c'est que? what is?
qu'est-ce qui? what?
question *f.* question
qui who, whom, that, which
quinze fifteen
quitter to leave
quoi what; **de — vivre** wherewith to live; **il n'y a pas de —** don't mention it, not at all; **— que ce soit** anything at all, no matter what; **— qu'il en soit** be that as it may
quoique although

R

raccrocher to hang up
Racine, Jean (*1639–1699*) *a famous writer of French classical tragedy, educated at Port-Royal*
raconter to relate
rafraîchir to refresh
rafraîchissant refreshing
raid (*final* **d** *pronounced*) *m.* (en-durance) flight (*of an airplane*)
raison *f.* reason; **avoir —** to be right
ramasser to pick up, gather
randonnée *f.* circuit, trip
Rangoon *capital of Lower Burma, a province of British India*
rapide rapid, fast; *m.* express train
rapidement rapidly, fast
rappeler to recall; **se —** to remem-ber, recall; **rappelez-moi au bon souvenir de** remember me to; *cf. p. 45, note 5*
rasseoir: se — to sit down again
rattacher: se — à to be connected with
rayé striped
rayonner to beam, be radiant
réalisation *f.* realization
récepteur *m.* receiver (*of a tele-phone*)
recette *f.* recipe
receveur *m.* conductor (*of a train*)
recevoir to receive; **être reçu à un examen** to pass an examination
rechercher to look for, pursue
réciter to recite
réclamer to demand
recommandation *f.* recommendation
recommander to recommend
recommencer to begin again

récompenser to reward, recompense
reconduire to see home, see out
reconnaissant grateful
reconnaître to recognize
record *m.* record
recouvrer to recover
rectifier to rectify, straighten
redemander to ask again
redevenir to become again
réfléchir to reflect
réfugier: se — to take refuge
refuser to refuse
regagner to regain; to return to
regard *m.* look, glance
regarder to look, look at
régime *m.* regime, rule
région *f.* region
regret *m.* regret
regretter to regret, be sorry (for)
rejoindre to meet again, join
relâche *m.* closed, no performance
(*of the theater*)
relèvement *m.* raise
relique *f.* relic
remarquable remarkable
remarquer to notice
remercier to thank
remettre to put again; to postpone;
se — à to begin again
remonter to go up again
rencontre *f.* meeting; aller à la — de
to go to meet
rencontrer to meet
rendez-vous *m.* appointment, en-
gagement
rendre to render; to give back, return; se — à to go to; se — compte
to realize
renommé renowned
renseignment *m.* piece of information; *pl.* information
rentrer to come *or* go home, return

renverser: se — to lie back, curl up
(*in a chair*)
renvoyer to send back
repartir to leave again
repas *m.* meal
repentir: se — de to repent of
répéter to repeat
répondre to answer, reply
repos *m.* rest, repose
reprendre to take back, recover; to
take up again, resume, pick up
représenter to represent
résoudre to resolve, solve
ressembler à to resemble, look like
restaurant *m.* restaurant
reste *m.* rest, remainder; du — moreover
rester to remain
retard *m.* delay; en — late, behind
time
retenir to retain, reserve
retirer to withdraw; se — to retire,
withdraw
retour *m.* return, return trip; billet
m. d'aller et — round-trip ticket
retourner to return, go back; se —
to turn round
retraite *f.* retreat, retirement; en —
retired
retrouver to find again, join, meet
réunir to unite, bring together
réussir (à) to succeed (in)
rêve *m.* dream
réveiller to awaken; se — to wake
up
revenir to come back, return; to
amount to
revoir to see again; au — good-by
révolution *f.* revolution
révolutionnaire *adj.* revolutionary
revue *f.* review, magazine
riche rich

Richelieu, Armand duc de (*1696–1788*) *Marshal of France, grand-nephew of Cardinal de Richelieu*

Richelieu, Armand-Jean du Plessis *Cardinal de Richelieu* (*1585–1642*), *famous minister of Louis XIII*

ridé wrinkled

rien nothing, anything

rire *m.* laughter, laugh

rire to laugh

robe *f.* dress

roi *m.* king

rôle *m.* role

roman *m.* novel

rond round

rôtir to roast

rouge red

route *f.* route, road; en — on the way

rue *f.* street

ruine *f.* ruin

Russie *f.* Russia

S

sa *see* son

sage wise, sensible

Saïgon *m.* *capital of Cochin-China, a province of French Indo-China*

Sainte-Chapelle, la *a famous Gothic church in Paris* (*see* **Montereau**)

saisir to catch, seize

saison *f.* season

salade *f.* salad

salaire *m.* salary

sale dirty

salle *f.* hall, room; — à manger dining room; — de bain bathroom; — de classe classroom

salon *m.* salon, living room

sanctuaire *m.* sanctuary

sang *m.* blood

sans *prep.:* — que *conj.* without

satisfaisant satisfactory

satisfait satisfied

sauce *f.* sauce

Saulieu (*Côte-d'Or*) *a small town southeast of Paris*

Sauternes *a fine French white wine*

sauver to save

savant *m.* savant

savoir to know (*facts*); to know how; to find out; je ne sais quoi + *noun* some + *noun* or other

savourer to relish, enjoy

scène *f.* scene; mise *f.* en — setting

se himself, herself, itself, themselves

séance *f.* session, sitting

sec, sèche dry

second second

sécurité *f.* security

seigneur *m.* lord

seigneurie *f.* lordship

séjour *m.* stay, sojourn

sel *m.* salt

selon according to

semaine *f.* week

sembler to seem, appear

sens *m.* sense; direction

sentir to feel; to smell (of)

sept seven

sergent *m.* de ville policeman

sermon *m.* sermon

servir to serve; se — de to use, make use of; — de to serve, act as

ses *see* son

seul alone, single

seulement only

si if; so

si yes (*contradicting a negative*)

siège *m.* siege

sien (le), sienne (la) his, hers; les siens one's relations and friends siffler to whistle

signe *m.* sign; faire — to motion

simplement simply; tout — simply, merely

singulier singular, strange

site *m.* site, place

situation *f.* situation

situé situated

situer to situate, locate

six six

socialiste socialist

sœur *f.* sister

soif *f.* thirst; avoir — to be thirsty

soigneusement carefully

soir *m.* evening; hier — last night, last evening

soirée *f.* evening, evening party (*cf. note 2, p. 4*)

soixante sixty

soixante-dix seventy

soleil *m.* sun

solennel solemn

solide solid

Solitaires, les *members of the Jansenist order established at Port-Royal*

sombre dark

sommeil *m.* sleep; avoir — to be sleepy

son, sa, ses his, her, its

songer to dream, think

sonner to ring

Sorbonne, la *college of arts and sciences of the University of Paris; so called from its founder, Robert de Sorbon*

sorte *f.* sort, kind; de — que so that

sortir to go out, come out, leave; *trans.* to take out

sot stupid

sou *m.* cent, sou

soucoupe *f.* saucer

souffrir to suffer, permit

soulier *m.* shoe

soupir to sigh

soupir *m.* sigh

source *f.* source; spring

sourire to smile

sous under

sous-sol *m.* cellar, subbasement

souvenir *m.* remembrance, souvenir, memory

souvenir: se — de to remember (*cf. p. 45, note 5*)

souvent often

spécialité *f.* specialty

spectacle *m.* spectacle, performance

spectre *m.* specter, ghost

splendeur *f.* splendor

sport *m.* sport

station *f.* station; — balnéaire seaside resort

stopper to stop (*of an automobile*)

succès *m.* success; — d'estime indifferent or moderate success

sucre *m.* sugar

sud *m.* south

suggérer to suggest

suite *f.* succession, series, continuation; tout de — right away, at once; par — de in consequence of

suivant following

suivre to follow; to attend (*a course*)

superbe superb, splendid

supplier to ask, beg

supposer to suppose

supposition *f.* supposition

sur on, upon

sûr sure, trustworthy

Sûreté, la *Paris police headquarters*

surgir to rise, spring up

surlendemain *m.* day after, second day

surmonter to surmount

surtout especially, above all
svelte slender, slim
sympathique congenial, likeable
synonyme *m.* synonym

T

table *f.* table
tâcher to try
taire: se — to be silent
tandis que while, whereas
tant so much, so many; — mieux so
much the better; — pis so much
the worse
tard late; se faire — to be getting
late
tarder to delay, be long in
tas *m.* pile, heap
tasse *f.* cup
taxi *m.* taxi
tel, telle such, like
téléphone *m.* telephone; donner un
coup de — à to call up
téléphoner to telephone
tellement so, so much
tempête *f.* storm, tempest
temps *m.* time; weather; à — in
time; combien de — how long; de
— en — from time to time
tenez *exclam.* look here!
tenir to hold, keep
tennis *m.* tennis
tenter to attempt, try; to tempt
terminer, se — to end, finish
terrain *m.* (piece of) ground; —
d'atterrissage landing field (*for
airplanes*)
terrasse *f.* terrace; sidewalk (*where
tables are placed in front of a
café*)
terre *f.* earth, ground; par — on the
ground; à — on the ground

terrible terrible
tête *f.* head
thé *m.* tea
théâtre *m.* theater; — d'avant-garde
*theater where ultramodern plays
are performed*
tiens *exclam.* well!
tirer to draw, get, obtain; to pull to
(*a door*)
tiroir *m.* drawer
titre *m.* title
toast *m.* toast
toilette *f.* toilet
tomate *f.* tomato
tomber to fall
ton *m.* tone
tort *m.* wrong; avoir — to be wrong
tôt soon
touchant touching
toucher to touch
toujours always, still
tour *f.* tower
tour *m.* trip, walk, tour; turn
Touraine *f. one of the old French
provinces, capital Tours*
tourangeau, tourangelle of Touraine
touriste *m.* tourist
tourmenter to torment
tournée *f.* circuit, journey
tourner to turn; to stir (*in cooking*);
se — to turn
Tours (*Indre-et-Loire*) *old capital of
Touraine, center of the château
country*
tout, toute, tous, toutes all, whole,
every; tout *m.* everything
tout *adv.* wholly, quite, very; — à
coup suddenly; — à fait quite,
wholly; — à l'heure presently;
— de même just the same, all the
same; — de suite at once; — en
while; pas du — not at all

traduire to translate

train *m.* train

traître *m.* traitor

trajet *m.* trip, passage

tranchant sharp, cutting

tranquillement quietly

travail *m.* work

travailler to work; — **ferme** to work hard

travailleur *m.* worker, industrious person

traverser to cross, traverse

treize thirteen

trembler to tremble

tremper to soak

trente thirty

très very

tressaillement *m.* start

triste sad, dreary

trois three

tromper to deceive; **se** — to be mistaken

trop too, too much, too many

troubler to trouble

trouver to find; to like; to think; **se** — to find oneself, be; **comment le trouvez-vous?** what do you think of it? how do you like it?

tumulte *m.* tumult

U

université *f.* university

usagé worn

utiliser to make use of

V

vacances *f. pl.* vacation; **cours** *m. pl.* **de** — summer courses

valise *f.* valise, suitcase

vallée *f.* valley

valoir to be worth; — **mieux** to be better

vaste vast, large

vaudeville *m.* vaudeville (*a sort of farce, not like the American vaudeville*)

veau *m.* veal, calf

vendeur *m.,* **vendeuse** *f.* clerk, seller, vender

vendre to sell

vengeance *f.* vengeance

venir to come; — **de** to have just; **faire** — to send for; — **prendre** to come and get, call for

vent *m.* wind

verbe *m.* verb

véritable true, veritable

vérité *f.* truth

verrouiller to bolt

vers *m.* verse, line of poetry

vers toward, about

version *f.* version

veston *m.* coat; — **croisé** double-breasted coat

vêtement *m.* clothes, garment

viande *f.* meat

vide empty

vie *f.* life

vieillard *m.* old man

vieux, vieil, vieille old, aged

vif intense, lively

vigne *f.* vine

vigoureusement vigorously

vigoureux vigorous, energetic

village *m.* village

ville *f.* city; **en** — in town; **sergent** *m.* **de** — policeman

vin *m.* wine

vinaigre *m.* vinegar

vingt twenty

virage *m.* turn (*in a road*)

visage *m.* face

visite *f.* visit
visiter to visit, inspect
vite quick, fast
vitrail *m.* stained-glass window
vivre to live (*cf. Verb Review, p. 117*)
voici here is, here are
voilà there is, there are, behold, there!; me — here I am
voir to see, look at; faire — to show; rien à — avec nothing to do with
voisin *m.* neighbor
voiture *f.* carriage; car, automobile
voix *f.* voice
vol *m.* flight
voler to steal; to fly
voleur *m.* thief
volume *m.* volume
vouloir to be willing; to wish, want; — bien to be willing, be kind enough to; en — à to be angry with, have a grudge against; — dire to mean; veuillez (bien) please, be kind enough to
voyage *m.* voyage, trip, journey; faire un — to have *or* take a trip; bon —! have a good trip!
voyageur *m.* traveler, passenger
voyant brilliant, gaudy (*of colors*)
vrai true, real
vraiment truly, really
vraisemblable probable
vue *f.* view

W

week-end *m.* week end

Y

y there; to, at, in, *etc.* it *or* them
yeux *m. pl.* of œil

English-French Vocabulary

A preposition in parentheses is the preposition required before a dependent infinitive.

A

a, an un, une
abbey abbaye *f.*
able: be — pouvoir
aboard: get — monter dans
about (*concerning*) de, sur, à propos de, au sujet de; (*nearly*) à peu près, environ; **what's it all** —? de quoi s'agit-il?
absorbed in absorbé dans
accent accent *m.*
accept accepter
accident accident *m.*
accompany accompagner
accomplish accomplir
according to selon
accuse accuser
acquaintance connaissance *f.;* **make the** — **of** faire la connaissance de
act acte *m.*
act as servir de; — **as his guide** lui servir de guide
action action *f.*
actor acteur *m.*
add ajouter
address adresse *f.*
admire admirer
adventure aventure *f.*
advertisement annonce *f.*
advice conseils *m. pl.;* **a piece of** — un conseil

advise conseiller (de)
affirm affirmer
afraid: be — craindre (de), avoir peur (de)
Africa Afrique *f.*
after *adv.* après; *prep.* après; *conj.* après que
afternoon après-midi *m. or f.;* —**s** l'après-midi; **good** — bonjour
afterward après
against contre
age âge *m.*
ago il y a
ahead: straight — tout droit; — **of time** en avance
air air *m.;* **(in the) open** — en plein air
Air-France *m. name of a French air line*
airplane avion *m.;* **by** — en avion
airport aérodrome *m.*
all tout(e), tous, toutes
allow laisser, permettre (de)
almost presque; — + *verb* manquer de + *infin.*
alone seul
Alps les Alpes *f. pl.*
already déjà
also aussi
although quoique, bien que *with subj.;* tout en *with pres. part.*
always toujours
A.M. du matin

America Amérique *f.*
American américain
amid parmi
among entre, parmi
amuse amuser; — **oneself** s'amuser
amusing amusant
ancestors ancêtres *m. pl.*
ancient ancien, -ne
and et
anecdote anecdote *f.*
angry fâché; **be** — **with** en vouloir à, être fâché contre *or* avec; **get** — se fâcher
animal animal *m.*
another *adj.* (*different*) autre; (*one more*) encore un; *pron.* un autre
answer réponse *f.*
answer répondre à
any *partitive* de, en; *adj.* quelque, (*with neg.*) aucun, pas un, pas de; — **at all,** — **whatever** n'importe quel; —**way** en tout cas
anyone quelqu'un, (*with neg.*) personne; — **at all** n'importe qui
anything quelque chose *m.*, (*with neg.*) rien; — **else** autre chose; — (*whatever*) n'importe quoi
anyway en tout cas
apartment appartement *m.;* **furnished** — appartement meublé
apology excuse *f.;* **make profuse apologies** se confondre en excuses
appear paraître
appointment rendez-vous *m.*
April avril *m.*
architect architecte *m.*
armchair fauteuil *m.*
army armée *f.*
arrange arranger; — **to** s'arranger pour
arrest arrestation *f.*
arrest arrêter

arrival arrivée *f.*
arrive arriver
article article *m.*
artist artiste *m. and f.*
as *adv.* aussi, (*with neg.*) si; que; — **many** —, — **much** — autant que; —...— aussi (si)...que; — **for** quant à
as *conj.* comme; (*because*) puisque; — **soon** — aussitôt que, dès que
ashamed: be — avoir honte
ask demander (de) *with personal indirect object,* prier (de) *with personal direct object;* — **for** demander; — **someone for something** demander quelque chose à quelqu'un
asleep: be — dormir
Asmodée *m. a play by François Mauriac*
assassin assassin *m.*
assure assurer
astonish étonner
astounded stupéfait
at à, dans, chez; — **first** d'abord; — **last** enfin; — **least** au moins; — **once** tout de suite
Athénée *m. a theater in Paris*
Atlantic Atlantique *m.,* Océan *m.* Atlantique
atom atome *m.*
attend assister à; — **to** s'occuper de
attendant (*of museum*) gardien *m.*
attentively avec attention
August août *m.*
aunt tante *f.*
Austria Autriche *f.*
author auteur *m.*
autobus autobus *m.*
automobile, auto automobile *f.,* auto *f.;* **by** — en auto
autumn automne *m. or f.*

aviator aviateur *m.*, aviatrice *f.*

Avignon *a city on the Rhone in southern France*

avoid éviter

aware: become — of s'apercevoir de

away: get — (from) s'absenter (de)

B

bachelor garçon *m.*

back: be — être de retour; come — revenir; go — rentrer, retourner

back dos *m.;* on camel — à dos de chameau

bad mauvais; it's (that's) too — c'est dommage

bad-looking: he's not — il n'est pas mal (de sa personne)

badly mal

Bal Tabarin *m. a night club in Paris*

band bande *f.*

bank banque *f.*

banker banquier *m.*

bare nu

barmaid (*18th cent.*) limonadière *f.*

basement sous-sol *m.*

Bastille Bastille *f.*

bath bain *m.;* —room salle *f.* de bain(s)

bathing establishment établissement *m.* de bains

be être; se trouver; (*of health*) aller; — back être de retour; — off s'en aller; — that as it may quoi qu'il en soit; it may — il se peut; there is il y a; he is to go il doit aller; if I were you à votre place, si j'étais vous

beach plage *f.*

beautiful beau, bel, belle

because parce que; — of à cause de

become devenir, se faire; (*be be-*

coming) aller; what has — of him? qu'est-il devenu?

bed lit *m.;* go to — se coucher

beefsteak bifteck *m.*

before *adv.* (*time*) auparavant; (*place*) devant

before *conj.* avant que

before *prep.* (*time*) avant; (*place*) devant; (*before infin.*) avant de

beggar mendiant *m.*

begin commencer (à); (*set about*) se mettre à; — by commencer par

Belgian belge

believe croire; — in croire à

belong appartenir, être à

bench banc *m.*

bend pencher

beside à côté de

besides d'ailleurs, et puis

besiege assiéger, faire le siège de

best *adj.* le meilleur; *adv.* le mieux; do one's — faire son possible

betray trahir

better *adj.* meilleur; *adv.* mieux; so much the — tant mieux; be — valoir mieux

between entre

big grand

bill addition *f.*

bill of fare carte *f.*

birthday anniversaire *m.* (de naissance)

birthmark marque *f.* de naissance

black noir

blue bleu

boarder pensionnaire *m. and f.*

boardinghouse pension *f.*

boat bateau *m.*

Bohemian (*artist*) bohème *m.*

book livre *m.*

bookseller libraire *m.*

bookstore librairie *f.*

born né; be — naître
borrow (from) emprunter (à)
both (tous) les deux; —...and et
    ...et; à la fois
bottom fond *m.*
boulevard boulevard *m.*
bourgeois bourgeois
Bourget, Le *airport near Paris*
bow saluer
box boîte *f.,* caisse *f.*
boy garçon *m.*
brave brave, courageu-x, -se
Brazil Brésil *m.*
bread pain *m.*
break casser; — out éclater
breakfast petit déjeuner *m.*
breakfast déjeuner
brilliant brillant
bring (*of persons*) amener; (*of
    things*) apporter; — back rap-
    porter
Brittany Bretagne *f.*
brother frère *m.*
build bâtir, construire
businessman commerçant *m.*
busy occupé
but mais
butter beurre *m.*
buy acheter (from = à)
by par, de; (*with pres. part.*) en

C

cabaret cabaret *m.*
café café *m.*
cake gâteau *m.;* little —s petits fours
    m. pl.
call appeler; — for (*a person*) aller
    (*or* venir) chercher (*or* prendre);
    — upon aller (*or* venir) voir;
    faire une visite à; — up (*tele-
    phone*) téléphoner à

camel chameau *m.;* on — back à
    dos de chameau
can pouvoir, savoir (*see* § *84*)
Canada Canada *m.*
Canadian canadien, -ne
candy bonbons *m. pl.*
car voiture *f.*
caravan caravane *f.*
card carte *f.;* play —s jouer aux
    cartes
cardinal cardinal *m.*
career carrière *f.*
carefully avec soin, soigneusement
carry porter; — down descendre;
    — out exécuter; — up(stairs)
    monter
Casablanca *a port in French Morocco*
case cas *m.;* in any — en tout cas
casino casino *m.*
castle château *m.*
cause causer, faire
celebrate célébrer, fêter
celebrated célèbre
cent sou *m.*
center centre *m.*
central central
century siècle *m.*
certain certain
certainly certainement
chair chaise *f.*
chamber chambre *f.*
Champs-Elysées, les *m. pl. an avenue
    in Paris*
chance hasard *m.;* by — par hasard
change monnaie *f.*
change changer; — sides changer de
    camp
chapel chapelle *f.*
character (*in play*) personnage *m.*
Charles Charles
charming charmant
chat causer

château château *m.*
chauffeur chauffeur *m.*
cheap bon marché, pas cher
cheaper meilleur marché, moins cher
chef chef *m.*
chess player joueur *m.* d'échecs
chin menton *m.*
choose choisir
chop côtelette *f.*
Christmas Noël *m.;* — present cadeau *m.* de Noël; — vacation vacances *f. pl.* de Noël
church église *f.*
Cid, Le *a tragedy by Corneille*
cigarette cigarette *f.*
circulate circuler
city ville *f.*
civilization civilisation *f.*
claim prétendre
class classe *f.; (course)* cours *m.;* —room salle *f.* de classe; French — classe de français
classic classique
classmate camarade *m.* de collège
clean nettoyer
Clemenceau, Georges *a French statesman (1841–1929)*
clerk vendeur *m.,* vendeuse *f.*
clever intelligent
cloister cloître *m.*
close *tr.* fermer; *intr.* se fermer
coat veston *m.;* double-breasted — veston croisé; dinner — smoking *m.*
coffee café *m.;* have — prendre le café
coin pièce *f.* de monnaie
cold froid; I am — j'ai froid; it is — il fait froid
collaborator collaborateur *m.*
collection collection *f.;* — of relics trésor *m.*

colony colonie *f.*
color couleur *f.*
Columbus Christophe Colomb
come venir; — back revenir; — down descendre; — in entrer; — out sortir
Comédie Française (*or* Théâtre Français) *French national theater in Paris*
comedy comédie *f.*
comic comique
commend recommander
company compagnie *f.*
competition concours *m.*
competitor concurrent *m.*
complain (of, about) se plaindre (de)
completely complètement, tout à fait
comrade camarade *m.*
concern regarder, intéresser
concert concert *m.*
concoct confectionner
confess confesser
confidence confiance *f.;* have — in avoir confiance en, se fier à
consent consentir (à)
construction construction *f.*
contain contenir, renfermer
continue continuer (à)
contrary: on the — au contraire
conversation conversation *f.*
cook cuisinier *m.,* chef *m.*
cook faire la cuisine
cooking cuisine *f.;* do the — faire la cuisine
correctly correctement
cost coûter; — a lot coûter cher
costume costume *m.*
could pouvoir (*see* § *83*)
count compter; — on compter sur
country (*political division*) pays *m.;*

(*not city*) campagne *f.; (region)* pays *m.*, région *f.;* in the — à la campagne; *adj.* de campagne

courageous courageu-x, -se

course: of — naturellement, bien entendu

course cours *m.;* **summer —s** cours de vacances; **take a —** suivre un cours

court cour *f.*

cousin cousin *m.*, cousine *f.*

cover couvrir

covered couvert

create créer

creditor créancier *m.*

crime crime *m.*

criminal criminel *m.*

cross traverser; (*the legs*) croiser

crossing traversée *f.*

crossroad carrefour *m.*

crowd foule *f.;* (*set*) bande *f.*

crown couronne *f.*

cry cri *m.*

cry crier; (*exclaim*) s'écrier

cup tasse *f.*

curé curé *m.*

curious curieu-x, -se

cursed maudit

curtain rideau *m.*

customer client *m.*

cut couper

Cyrano de Bergerac *a play by Edmond Rostand*

D

Dakar *a city in Senegal*

dance bal *m.*

dance danser

dancer danseur *m.*

dangerous dangereu-x, -se

dare oser

date (*appointment*) rendez-vous *m.*

date from dater de, remonter à

daughter fille *f.*

day jour *m.*, journée *f.* (*see p. 4, note 2*); **all —** toute la journée; **every —** tous les jours; **the — after** le lendemain de; **the next —** le lendemain; **ten francs a —** dix francs par jour

daybreak pointe *f.* du jour

dead mort; **— man** mort *m.*

deal: a great — beaucoup

dear cher, chère; *adv.* cher

debt dette *f.*

decide décider (de)

decision décision *f.*, parti *m.*

defend défendre

defender défenseur *m.*

delicious délicieu-x, -se

demand demander, réclamer

denounce dénoncer

departure départ *m.*

depression crise *f.* économique

derby (*hat*) chapeau *m.* melon

describe décrire

desert désert *m.*

deserted désert

desire désir *m.*, envie *f.;* **have a — to** avoir envie de

desire désirer

desperate désespéré

dessert dessert *m.*

destroy détruire

detain retenir

detective policier *m.;* **— play** pièce *f.* policière; **— story** roman *m.* policier

develop developper

devil diable *m.*

dictaphone dictaphone *m.*

dictate dicter

die mourir
difficult difficile
difficulty difficulté *f.*
dine dîner; — out dîner en ville
dining room salle *f.* à manger
dinner dîner *m.;* at — à dîner
dinner coat smoking *m.*
director directeur *m.*
dirty sale
disappear disparaître
discourage décourager
discover découvrir
discuss discuter
dish plat *m.*
displeased (with) mécontent (de)
disposal disposition *f.*
distance distance *f.*
disturb déranger
divine divin
do faire; — one's best faire son possible
doctor (*physician*) médecin *m.;* (*title*) docteur *m.*
doeskin peau *f.* de daim, daim *m.*
dog chien *m.*
Dôme, le *a café in the Montparnasse quarter of Paris*
done: well — (*of meats*) bien cuit
door porte *f.*
double-breasted croisé
doubt doute *m.*
doubt douter de
doubtless sans doute
dowry dot *f.*
dozen douzaine *f.;* half — demi-douzaine *f.*
drama drame *m.*
draw tirer
drenched (to the skin) trempé (jusqu'aux os)
dress robe *f.*
dress habiller

dressing sauce *f.;* **mayonnaise —** sauce mayonnaise
drink consommation *f.*
drink boire
drive (*an automobile*) conduire
duke duc *m.*
Dumas, Alexandre (Père) *a French novelist and dramatist (1803–1870)*
dungeons oubliettes *f. pl.*
during pendant
duty devoir *m.*
dwelling logis *m.*

E

each *adj.* chaque; *pron.* chacun; — other se, l'un l'autre
earlier de meilleure heure, plus tôt
early de (très) bonne heure
earn gagner
easily facilement
east est *m.*
easy facile
eat manger
écu (*coin*) écu *m.*
Ecu (*shield*) de France *m. a restaurant in Paris*
edge bord *m.*
edifice édifice *m.*
egg œuf *m.;* **boiled —** œuf à la coque
eight huit
eighteen dix-huit
eighth huitième
eighty quatre-vingts
either ou; (*after neg.*) non plus
elegant élégant
elevator ascenseur *m.*
eleven onze
else: anything — autre chose
emperor empereur *m.*

empty vide

end (*time*) fin *f.;* (*space*) bout *m.;*
at the end of au bout de, à la fin
de

end finir; — by finir par

ending (*of play*) dénouement *m.*

endurance flight raid *m., final d*
pronounced

engine trouble: have — avoir une
panne

England Angleterre *f.*

English anglais

Englishman Anglais *m.*

enjoy jouir de

enormous énorme

enough assez; — to + *infin.* de
quoi + *infin.*

enter entrer

enthusiasm enthousiasme *m.*

entire enti-er -ère

essential essentiel, -le

establishment: bathing — établissement *m.* de bains

Eugene Eugène

Europe Europe *f.*

even même

evening soir *m.,* soirée *f.* (*see p. 4,*
note 2)*; adj.* du soir; good — bon-
soir; in the — le soir

ever jamais

every chaque, tout

everybody, everyone tout le monde

everything tout *m.*

everywhere partout

evidently évidemment

exactly exactement, précisément

examination examen *m.;* fail in an
— échouer à un examen; pass an
— être reçu (réussir) à un examen; take an — passer un examen

examine examiner

excellent excellent

except excepté

exclaim s'écrier

excursion excursion *f.,* randonnée *f.*

execrable exécrable

expect (*await*) attendre; (*intend*)
compter, espérer, avoir l'intention
de; be —ed to devoir; what do
you —? que voulez-vous?

expensive cher, chère

experience expérience *f.*

explain expliquer

explanation explication *f.*

express (train) rapide *m.*

extra *adj.* de plus, supplémentaire

extravagant dépensi-er, -ère

extremely extrêmement

eye œil (*pl.* yeux) *m.*

F

fact fait *m.;* in — en effet

fagot fagot *m.*

fail manquer (de); — (in an examination) échouer (à un examen)

fairly assez; — well assez bien

Faisan *m.* d'Or (Golden Pheasant)
name of a hotel

fall tomber; — in love with tomber
amoureux de, s'éprendre de

family famille *f.*

famous fameu-x, -se

far loin; as — as jusqu'à

farther, — on, any — plus loin

fascist fasciste *m.*

fashion mode *f.*

fast vite

father père *m.*

fault faute *f.*

fear crainte *f.;* for — that de peur
que

fear craindre (de), avoir peur (de)

feat fait *m.;* **military —** fait d'armes
feel sentir; (*of health*) se sentir; — **like** (*doing something*) avoir envie de
fellow garçon *m.;* **a good —** un brave garçon
fête fête *f.*
few (*not many*) peu de; **a —** *adj.* quelques, *pron.* quelques-uns; **the — ** les quelques
fewer moins
fiancée fiancée *f.*
fifteen quinze
fifth cinquième
fifty cinquante
film film *m.*
finally enfin, finir par + *infin.*
financier financier *m.*
find trouver; **— out** apprendre, savoir
fine beau, bel, belle; épatant
finger doigt *m.;* **first —** index *m.*
finish finir (de), terminer
fire feu *m.*
fireplace cheminée *f.*
fireworks feu *m.* d'artifice
first premi-er, -ère; *adv.* **—, at —** d'abord
fit (*of clothes*) aller à
fit up aménager
five cinq
flannels: in white — en flanelle blanche
flight vol *m.;* **endurance —** raid *m.,* *final d pronounced;* **nonstop —** vol sans escale
floor (*story*) étage *m.*
flower fleur *f.*
fluently couramment
fly aller en avion, voler
follow suivre
following suivant

fond: be — (*of persons*) aimer beaucoup; (*of food*) être friand de, aimer beaucoup
Fontainebleau *a town famous for its château and its forest*
foot pied *m.;* **on —** à pied
for *prep.* pour; (*during*) pendant; (*since*) depuis
for *conj.* car, parce que
forbid défendre (à quelqu'un de faire quelque chose)
force forcer (à); **be —d to** être forcé de
forget oublier
former ancien, -ne
fort fort *m.*
fortunately heureusement
fortune fortune *f.;* **seek one's —** aller chercher fortune
forty quarante
forward en avant
fountain pen stylo *m.,* stylographe *m.*
four quatre
fourteen quatorze
fourth quatrième
franc franc *m.*
France France *f.*
free libre
freeze geler
French français
Frenchman Français *m.*
Frenchwoman Française *f.*
fresh frais, fraîche
Friday vendredi *m.*
friend ami *m.,* amie *f.;* **a — of his** un de ses amis
frightened effrayé
frivolous frivole
from de
front: in — of devant
fruit fruits *m. pl.;* **a —** un fruit

full plein
fun: make — of se moquer de
furnace chauffage *m.* central
furnish meubler
furniture meubles *m. pl.*

G

garden jardin *m.*
gate (*at station*) barrière *f.*
Gautier, Théophile *a French poet and novelist (1811-1872)*
gay gai
general général; in — en général
general général *m.*
generally généralement
gentleman monsieur *m.*
George Georges
German allemand
get prendre; — aboard monter dans; — angry se fâcher; — away from s'absenter de; — into monter dans; — home rentrer; — late se faire tard; — out (*of a vehicle*) descendre; — ready to s'apprêter à; — tickets prendre des places; — to (*a place*) arriver à; — up se lever; — used to se faire à
Giraudoux, Jean *a contemporary French dramatist and novelist*
girl jeune fille *f.;* little — petite fille, fillette *f.*
give donner; — on donner sur; — up (*a room*) abandonner, quitter
glad content, heureu-x, -se
gladly volontiers, avec plaisir
gloomy triste, sombre
glove gant *m.,* kid — gant de chevreau; suède — gant de suède
glove shop ganterie *f.*
go aller; — away partir, s'en aller;

— back rentrer, retourner; be going on se passer; — to bed se coucher; — for a walk aller faire une promenade, se promener; — home rentrer chez soi; — into entrer dans; — out sortir; — to sleep s'endormir; — up, — upstairs monter; — through traverser, passer (*with* être) par
God Dieu *m.*
good bon, bonne, brave (*before noun*); (*in a study*) fort; — morning bonjour; *adv.* bon
good-by au revoir, adieu
gourmand gourmand
gourmet gourmet
government gouvernement *m.*
grandmother grand'mère *f.*
grant accorder
gray gris
great grand
great-nephew petit-neveu *m.*
green vert
greet saluer
grotesque grotesque
ground terre *f.*
grumble grogner
guest invité *m.,* invitée *f.*
guide guide *m.;* act as a — (to someone) servir de guide (à quelqu'un)
guidebook guide *m.*

H

habitué habitué *m.*
hair cheveux *m. pl.*
hale and hearty solide
half demi (*invariable before noun and joined to it by hyphen; variable in gender after noun*); —

(an) hour demi-heure *f.;* — **a dozen** demi-douzaine *f.;* — **past ten** dix heures et demie

hall salle *f.*

hand main *f.;* **in the** — à la main

handbag sac *m.* à main

handle manier

hang up raccrocher

happen arriver, se passer; — **to arriver à; how does it** — **that . . . ?** comment se fait-il que . . . ? *with subj.*

happy heureu-x, -se, content

hard *adj.* dur, difficile; — **times** les temps difficiles

hard *adv.* dur, ferme

hardly à peine, ne . . . guère

hat chapeau *m.;* **derby** — chapeau melon; **take off one's** — ôter son chapeau, se découvrir

hatred haine *f.*

have avoir; *(cause to)* faire; — **a good time** s'amuser bien; — **just** venir de + *infin.;* — **to** devoir, falloir, avoir à

Havre Le Havre

hay foin *m.;* **new mown** — les foins coupés

he il, lui

head tête *f.;* chef *m.*

hear entendre; — **of** entendre parler de

heat chauffer

heating chauffage *m.;* **central** — chauffage central

hello bonjour *m.;* *(at telephone)* allo

help aider (à)

Henry Henri

her la, lui, elle

her *possess. adj.* son, sa, ses

here ici; — **is** voici

heroic héroïque

hers le sien *etc.*

hesitate hésiter

hide *trans.* cacher (**from** = à); *intrans.* se cacher

high haut

highway, main — grande route *f.*

him le, lui; —**self** lui-même

his son, sa, ses; *pron.* le sien *etc.*

historian historien *m.*

history histoire *f.*

holiday fête *f.*

Holy Land, The la Terre Sainte

home maison *f.;* **at** — chez moi *etc.,* à la maison; **get** —, **go (back)** — rentrer chez soi

hoot huée *f.*

hope espérer

Horla, le *the monster in Maupassant's story of the same name*

hors-d'œuvre hors-d'œuvre *m. invar.*

horse cheval *m.;* — **races** courses *f.* de chevaux

hospital hôpital *m.*

hot chaud; **be** — avoir chaud, *(of weather)* faire chaud

hotel hôtel *m.*

Hôtel de Sens *an ancient residence in Paris, constructed by the bishop of Sens about 1500*

hotelkeeper hôtelier *m.*

hour heure *f.;* **half** — demi-heure *f.*

house maison *f.;* **at (to) her** — chez elle; **boarding**— pension *f.*

how *(in what manner)* comment; *(exclamation)* comme! combien! que! — **much,** — **many** combien; — **long** combien de temps, depuis quand; — **long does it take?** combien de temps faut-il?

however cependant; *(with adj. or adv.)* quelque + *adj. or adv.* que + *subj.*

Hugo, Victor (*1802–1885*) *a French poet, novelist, and dramatist*

human humain

humor humeur *f.;* **in a bad —** de mauvaise humeur

hundred cent

hungry: be — avoir faim

hurry se dépêcher (de)

hurt faire mal à; **— oneself** se faire mal; (*wound*) blesser

I

I je, moi

icebox glacière *f.*

ice cream glaces *f. pl.;* (*one portion*) une glace

idea idée *f.*

if si

ill malade

ill-disposed mal disposé

imagination imagination *f.*

imagine s'imaginer; (*invent*) imaginer

imitate imiter

immediately tout de suite

implore implorer

important important

impossible impossible

impregnable imprenable

improbable invraisemblable

in *of place* (*specific location*) dans; (*less definite and figurative*) en; *of time* (*at the end of*) dans, au bout de; (*during the course of*) en; *with dates* en; *with names of countries, see* § 6

incident incident *m.*

indeed en effet

indicate indiquer

Indo-China Indochine *f.*

influence influence *f.*

inform informer, faire savoir (quelque chose à quelqu'un); **he was —ed that** on lui a fait savoir que

ingenious ingénieu-x, -se

inhabitant habitant *m.*

inn auberge *f.*

inside dedans, à l'intérieur; **— of** à l'intérieur de

inspector: police — commissaire *m.* de police

instead of au lieu de

instruction instruction *f.*

instrument instrument *m.*

intelligent intelligent

intend avoir l'intention de, compter

intention intention *f.*

interest intéresser

interesting intéressant

interview interview *m.*

into dans

introduce présenter; (*a fashion*) introduire; (*show in*) introduire

invent inventer

invitation invitation *f.*

invite inviter (à)

island île *f.*

it il, elle, ce; le, la

Italian italien, -ne

Italy Italie *f.*

itinerary itinéraire *m.*

its son, ses

itself elle-même, lui-même

J

Jane Jane, Jeanne

janitor concierge *m.*

Jardies, les *f. pl. country house of Balzac*

Jaurès, Jean (*1859–1914*) *a French socialist statesman, assassinated in 1914*

jealous jalou-x, -se; **make —** rendre jaloux

Jerusalem Jérusalem *m.*

jewel bijou *m.*

John Jean

join aller trouver, venir trouver; retrouver

Joseph Joseph

July juillet *m.*

June juin *m.*

just justement; **— now** actuellement, en ce moment; **have (had) —** venir de *with infin.* (venir *in present and imperfect only*); **I was — saying** je disais justement

K

keep conserver, garder; **— on** continuer à

key clef *f.*

kid chevreau *m.*

kilometer kilomètre *m.*

kind espèce *f.*, sorte *f.*, variété *f.*

king roi *m.*

knock frapper; **there is a — at the door** on frappe à la porte

know (*a fact*) savoir; (*be acquainted with*) **connaître**; (*recognize*) reconnaître; **— how** savoir (*see § 84*)

L

lack manquer de

lady dame *f.*

lame boiteu-x, -se

land terre *f.*

land débarquer; (*of airplane*) atterrir

landing (*aviation*) atterrissage *m.*

language langue *f.;* **the spoken —** la langue parlée

large grand; (*bulky*) gros, -se

last derni-er, -ère; passé; **at — enfin; — night** hier soir; **— Thursday** jeudi dernier; **— week** la semaine dernière; **— year** l'année dernière, l'année passée

late tard; (*behind time*) en retard; **be an hour —** (*of trains*) avoir une heure de retard; **get —** se faire tard

Latin latin

latter celui-ci, ce dernier

laugh rire

lawyer avocat *m.*

lead conduire, mener; **— away** emmener

leader chef *m.*

leaf feuille *f.;* **turn the leaves of** feuilleter (*conjugated like* jeter)

learn apprendre (à); **— of** savoir

least *adj.* le moindre; *adv.* le moins; **at —** au moins

leave congé *m.*

leave (*go away from*) *trans.* quitter; *intrans.* partir, s'en aller; (*go out of*) sortir; **— (behind)** laisser

lecture conférence *f.*

left gauche

left: I have one franc — il me reste un franc

legend légende *f.*

legitimate légitime

lemon citron *m.*

lend prêter

LeSage, Alain-René *an 18th cent. French novelist, author of* Le Diable boiteux.

less moins

lesson leçon *f.*

lest *conj.* de peur que; *prep.* de peur de

let laisser, permettre (de)

letter lettre *f.;* — **paper** papier *m.* à lettre

lieutenant lieutenant *m.*

life vie *f.*

lift (up) soulever

light allumer

like *adv.* comme

like aimer, désirer; **I should like +** *infin.* j'aimerais (beaucoup), je voudrais (bien); **how do you like?** comment trouvez-vous?

line ligne *f.*

listen (to) écouter

literature littérature *f.*

little petit; *adv.* peu

live vivre; (*dwell in*) demeurer (à *or* dans), habiter; **long —!** vive!

living room salon *m.*

local du lieu

London Londres *m.*

long *adj.* long, -ue

long *adv.* longtemps; **a — time** long-temps; **as — as** tant que; **how —** ... ? depuis quand ... ?, combien de temps ... ?

longer *adv.* plus longtemps; **no —** ne ... plus

look, **— at** regarder; **— for** cher-cher; **— up** (*a person*) aller (ve-nir) voir; **— well** avoir bonne mine; (*seem*) avoir l'air, sembler

lord seigneur *m.;* **Our Lord** Notre-Seigneur

lose perdre; **— one's temper** se fâcher

lot: **a —, —s** beaucoup

loud (*of colors*) voyant

louis (*coin*) louis *m.*

Louvre, le *a museum in Paris*

love aimer

love: **fall in — with** s'éprendre de, tomber amoureux de

low bas, -se

lucky: **be —** avoir de la chance

Lyons Lyon *m.*

M

madam madame *f.*

maid bonne *f.*

mail mettre à la poste

main *see* highway

maintain maintenir

make marque *f.*

make faire; (*earn*) faire, gagner; **— fun of** se moquer de; **— + adj.** rendre

man homme *m.;* **old —** vieillard *m.;* **young —** jeune homme (*pl.* jeunes gens)

manager gérant *m.;* **theater —** di-recteur *m.* de théâtre

Manon Lescaut *a famous novel by Abbé Prévost* (*1731*)

many beaucoup; **as —** autant; **so —** tant; **too —** trop

map carte *f.;* **road —** carte routière

March mars *m.*

Marguerite de Valois *daughter of Henry II and Catherine de Medici. She married Henry IV, who re-pudiated her in 1599.*

marriage mariage *m.*

marry (*take in marriage*) épouser, se marier à *or* avec; (*give in mar-riage*) marier; **be (get) married** se marier

Marseilles Marseille *f.*

Martha Marthe

marvelous merveilleu-x, -se

Mary Marie

master maître *m.*

match partie *f.*, match *m., pl.*
matches; **tennis —** partie de tennis

material étoffe *f.*

mathematics mathématiques *f. pl.*

matter chose *f.;* what's the —? qu'-
est-ce qu'il y a? what's the — **with
him?** qu'est-ce qu'il a?

matter importer; **no — who** n'importe qui

Maupassant, Guy de (*1850–1893*) *a
French short-story writer*

Mauriac, François *a contemporary
French novelist and dramatist*

May mai *m.*

may pouvoir; **it — be** il se peut

mayonnaise dressing sauce *f.* mayonnaise

me me, moi

meal repas *m.*

mean vouloir dire

means moyen *m.*

meantime: **in the —** en attendant

meat viande *f.*

medical school école *f.* de médecine

mediocre médiocre

meet (*by chance*) rencontrer; (*by
appointment*) retrouver, aller trouver, venir trouver; (*make the acquaintance of*) faire la connaissance de

member membre *m.*

memory mémoire *f.*, souvenir *m.;*
in — of en mémoire de

menu menu *m.*

meter mètre *m.*

middle-class bourgeois

midnight minuit *m.*

might pouvoir

milestone borne (kilométrique) *f.*

military militaire; **— feat** fait *m.*
d'armes

milk lait *m.*

mind esprit *m.;* **have a — to** avoir
envie de

mine le mien *etc.*

minister ministre *m.*

Minorca Minorque *f.*

minute minute *f.*

miserable misérable

Miss mademoiselle, Mlle *f.*

miss manquer

mistake: **make a —** se tromper; **be
—n** se tromper

mistrust méfiance f.

modern moderne

moment moment *m.*

Monday lundi *m.*

money argent *m.*

monotonous monotone

monster monstre *m.*

month mois *m.*

Montparnasse *m. a theater in Paris*

more plus; davantage (*see p. 39,
note 2*); **not any —** ne ... plus

morning matin *m.*, matinée *f.* (*see
p. 4, note 2*); **—s** le matin; **good
—** bonjour *m.*

Morocco Maroc *m.*

most le plus; **—, — of, the — of**
la plupart de (*takes plural verb*)

mother mère *f.*

motor trouble: **have —** avoir une
panne

movie(s) cinéma *m. sing.*

Mr. monsieur, M.

Mrs. madame, Mme

much, **very —** beaucoup; **as — autant; how —** combien; **so — tant;
so — the better** tant mieux; **too —**
trop

murderer meurtrier *m.*

museum musée *m.;* **— attendant**
gardien *m.* du musée

must devoir, falloir (*see Lesson XIII*)

my mon, ma, mes; **—self** moi-même

mysterious mystérieu-x, -se

N

name nom *m.;* **his — is** il s'appelle

name: be —d s'appeler

Nantes *a city near the mouth of the Loire*

narrow étroit

Natal Natal *m.*

national national

native natal

near *adv.* près; *prep.* près de

nearly presque

necessarily forcément

necessary nécessaire; **be —** être nécessaire, falloir

necktie cravate *f.*

need besoin *m.*

need, have — of, be in — of avoir besoin de, il me (lui *etc.*) faut + *noun or pronoun*

neither ni *with* ne; **— ... nor** ne ... ni ... ni

never jamais; (*with verb*) ne ... jamais

nevertheless néanmoins, tout de même

new nouveau, nouvel, -le; (**brand**) **—** neuf, neuve

new-mown hay les foins coupés *m. pl.*

New Orleans la Nouvelle-Orléans

news nouvelles *f. pl.;* **piece of —** une nouvelle

newspaper journal *m.*

next prochain; (*following*) suivant; **— day** le lendemain; **— Monday** lundi prochain; **— week** la se-maine prochaine; **— year** l'année prochaine

nice gentil, -le; **it is — of you (to)** c'est gentil de votre part (de), vous êtes bien gentil (de), c'est bien aimable à vous (de)

night nuit *f.;* **at —** le soir; **last —** hier soir; **— club** boîte *f.* de nuit

nine neuf

no *adv.* non; pas; *adj.* aucun, pas de; **— one** personne *m. with* ne

nobody personne *m. with* ne

none (*not any*) pas de; (*not one*) aucun, pas un

nonstop sans escale

noon midi *m.*

nor ni *with* ne

Normandy Normandie *f.*

not ne ... pas

note petit mot *m.*

nothing rien; (*with verb*) ne ... rien

notice remarquer, s'apercevoir (de)

Notre-Dame *f. a church in Paris*

novel roman *m.*

now maintenant; **just —** actuelle-ment

number (*quantity*) nombre *m.;* (*telephone*) numéro *m.*

numerous nombreu-x, -se

O

obey obéir à

oblige obliger (à); **be —ed to** être obligé de

observe observer

obtain obtenir, se procurer

ocean océan *m.;* **Atlantic —** Océan Atlantique

o'clock heure *f.*

October octobre *m.*

Odéon *m. a theater in Paris*

of de

off: be — s'en aller

offer offre *f.*

offer offrir

office bureau *m.*

officer officier *m.*

often souvent

oh! oh!

old vieux, vieil, -le; (*former*) ancien, -ne; (*in expressions of age*) âgé; —er plus âgé; be ten years — avoir dix ans; — man vieillard *m.*

on sur; (*with expressions of weather*) par; (*with pres. part.*) en

once une fois; (*formerly*) autrefois; at — tout de suite

one un, une; *indef. pron.* on; — another se, les uns les autres; no — aucun; not — pas un; the — that celui qui

only *adj.* seul; *adv.* seulement, ne . . . que

open ouvert; in the — air en plein air

open *trans.* ouvrir; *intrans.* s'ouvrir

opera opéra *m.;* light — opérette *f.*

opinion avis *m.*

opportunity occasion *f.*

or ou

orange orange *f.*

orchestra orchestre *m.*

order ordre *m.;* in — that afin que, pour que; in — to afin de, pour

order commander

ordinarily ordinairement

original original

Orleans Orléans *m.*

other autre; —s d'autres; the —s les autres

otherwise autrement, si non

Oubliettes, les *f. pl.* (The Dungeon) *a Parisian cabaret*

ought devoir *in condl. or condl. perf.*

our notre, nos; —s le nôtre

out: be — être sorti; get — descendre

outline dessiner

outs: be at — with être fâché avec

over *prep.* sur

overcast couvert

overcome surmonter

over there là-bas

owe devoir

own propre *before noun*

owner propriétaire *m.*

P

pack a trunk faire une malle

page page *f.*

paint peindre

painting peinture *f.*

pair paire *f.*

Palais-Royal *m. a palace, once the residence of the Orleans family. Its gardens were a favorite promenade in the 18th century.*

Palestine Palestine *f.*

pamphlet brochure *f.*

paper papier *m.;* (*newspaper*) journal *m.;* writing — papier à lettre

parchment parchemin *m.*

parent parent *m.*

Paris Paris *m.*

Parisian parisien, -ne

park parc *m.*

part partie *f.;* take — in prendre part à

party (*political*) parti *m.*

pass passer; — an examination être reçu (réussir) à un examen

passage passage *m.*

pastry pâtisserie *f.*

pastry shop pâtisserie *f.*

patience patience *f.;* **have —** avoir patience

pay, pay for payer

pea pois *m.;* **green —s** petits pois

peasant paysan *m.;* **— woman** paysanne *f.*

pen plume *f.*

penny sou *m.*

people (*individuals*) des gens *m. pl.,* des personnes *f. pl.;* (*a group*) du monde *m.;* (*nation*) peuple *m.;* **young —** jeunes gens *m. pl.*

perceive apercevoir, remarquer; (*mentally*) s'apercevoir de, remarquer

per cent pour-cent *m.*

perfect parfait

perfect perfectionner

performance représentation *f.;* **there's no —** il y a relâche

perhaps peut-être

permit permettre (de) *with personal indirect obj.*

Persia Perse *f.*

person personne *f.*

personage personnage *m.*

Peugeot *f. a make of French automobile*

photograph photographie *f.,* photo *f.;* **take a —** prendre une photo

physician médecin *m.*

pick up prendre; (*something that has fallen*) ramasser

picture tableau *m.;* (*movie*) film *m.*

picturesque pittoresque

piece morceau *m.*

pile (*things one above another*) pile *f.;* (*heap*) tas *m.*

pity plaindre; **it is a —** c'est dommage

place endroit *m.,* lieu *m.;* (*position*) place *f.;* **in your —** à votre place; **take —** avoir lieu

plan plan *m.*

play (*theater*) pièce *f.;* **detective —** pièce policière

play jouer; (*a game*) jouer à; **— cards** jouer aux cartes

player joueur *m.;* **chess —** joueur d'échecs

please plaire à; **—, will you —** veuillez, voulez-vous, ayez la bonté de; **if you —** s'il vous plaît

pleasure plaisir *m.*

P.M. du soir

pocket poche *f.*

poet poète *m.*

point of view point *m.* de vue

point to montrer (du doigt)

police police *f.;* **— inspector** commissaire *m.* de police

policeman agent *m.,* sergent *m.* de ville

polite poli

political politique

Pont-Neuf, le *a bridge in Paris*

poor pauvre

popular (*fashionable*) à la mode; (*of the people*) populaire

Portuguese portugais

position place *f.;* **get a — for** caser; **take a — in** entrer à

possible possible

post card carte *f.* postale

postpone remettre (**until** = à)

pound livre *f.*

preach prêcher

prefer préférer, aimer mieux

prepare préparer

presence présence *f.*

present cadeau *m.*

present présenter
pretty joli
prevent empêcher (de)
priest prêtre *m.*
prime minister premier ministre *m.*
prince prince *m.;* **Prince Charming** le Prince Charmant
principal principal
prisoner prisonnier *m.*
private particuli-er, -ère
prize prix *m.*
profession profession *f.,* métier *m.*
professor professeur *m.*
program programme *m.*
promise promettre (de) *with personal indirect obj.*
proud fi-er, -ère
Provence Provence *f.*
province province *f.*
provisions provisions *f. pl.,* vivres *m. pl.*
public publi-c, -que
public public *m.*
pupil élève *m. and f.*
put mettre; **— back** remettre; **— on** (*clothes*) mettre, (*a play*) monter; **be — out with** en vouloir à, être fâché avec *or* contre

Q

quality qualité *f.*
quarter quart *m.;* (*of school year*) trimestre *m.;* (*section of city*) quartier *m.;* **— of an hour** quart d'heure; **Latin —** Quartier Latin
quickly vite
quietly tranquillement
quite (*entirely*) tout à fait; (*rather*) assez

R

race course *f.;* **horse —s** courses de chevaux
railroad chemin *m.* de fer; **— companies** compagnies *f.* de chemin de fer
railroadman cheminot *m.*
rain pluie *f.*
rain pleuvoir
raincoat imperméable *m.*
raise in wages relèvement *m.* des salaires
raise lever
rarely rarement
rash téméraire
rather (*preferably*) plutôt; (*somewhat*) assez; **I should —** j'aimerais mieux
reach arriver à
read lire
reader lecteur *m.,* lectrice *f.*
reading lecture *f.*
ready prêt; **get —** s'apprêter (à)
real réel, -le
realize comprendre, se rendre compte de
really vraiment, réellement
reason raison *f.*
recall rappeler, se rappeler (*see p. 45, note 5*)
receive recevoir
receiver (*telephone*) récepteur *m.*
recently récemment, l'autre jour
recipe recette *f.*
recognize reconnaître
recommend recommander
recommendation recommandation *f.*
recopy recopier
record enregistrer

refuge: take — se réfugier
refuse refuser
regard regarder
Régence, la *a café on the Avenue de l'Opéra in Paris*
region région *f.*
regional régional
register (*at a university*) s'inscrire
regret regretter
relate conter, raconter
relative parent *m.*
relic relique *f.;* **collection of —s** trésor *m.*
remain rester
remarkable remarquable
remember se souvenir de, se rappeler (*see p. 45, note 5*)
remind (**someone of something**) rappeler (quelque chose à quelqu'un)
remove enlever
render rendre
rendezvous rendez-vous *m.*
renowned renommé
rent louer
repent (**of**) se repentir (de)
reply répondre
report compte *m.* rendu
represent représenter
republic république *f.*
reputation réputation *f.*
request prier (de)
reread relire
resemble ressembler à
reserve (*a room*) retenir
resort: seaside — station *f.* balnéaire
respects hommages *m. pl.*
rest repos *m.*
restaurant restaurant *m.*
retired ancien, -ne, en retraite
return retour *m.;* **on her —** à son retour
return (*come back*) revenir; (*go*

back) retourner; — (*home*) rentrer; (*give back*) rendre
review revue *f.*
rich riche
right *adj.* droit; *adv.* — **away** immédiatement, tout de suite
right raison *f.;* **be —** avoir raison
rise se lever
rival rival *m.*
road chemin *m.;* **take the wrong —** se tromper de chemin
road map carte *f.* routière
roast rôti *m.*
role rôle *m.*
roll petit pain *m.*
roof toit *m.*
room pièce *f.;* **bed—** chambre *f.;* **living —** salon *m.;* **— with private bath** chambre avec bain
rose rose *f.*
Rouen *a city 80 miles north of Paris*
rudely rudement
rumor bruit *m.*
run courir; (*of automobile, train*) marcher; **— across** rencontrer, tomber sur
Russia Russie *f.*

S

Saïgon Saigon *m.*
Sainte-Chapelle, la *a church in Paris*
Saint-Quay *m. a seaside resort in Brittany*
salad salade *f.*
salon salon *m.*
same même
sanctuary sanctuaire *m.*
satisfied satisfait, content
Saturday samedi *m.*
sauce sauce *f.*
saucer soucoupe *f.*

save sauver

say dire

scarcely à peine, ne ... guère

scared: be very — avoir très peur

scene scène *f.*

school école *f.*

science science *f.*

seaside resort station *f.* balnéaire

season saison *f.*

seat place *f.;* get —s prendre des places

seat: — oneself s'asseoir; be —ed être assis

second second, deuxième

see voir; — again revoir; — to the door, — home reconduire

seek chercher; — one's fortune aller chercher fortune

seem sembler, avoir l'air

seize saisir; (*take possession of*) s'emparer de

sell vendre

send envoyer, expédier; — for envoyer chercher, faire venir

Senegal Sénégal *m.*

serious sérieu-x, -se

servant domestique *m. and f.*

serve servir

setting décor *m.*

seven sept

seventeenth dix-septième

several plusieurs

sharp (*of time*) précis; at five o'clock — à cinq heures précises

shave se raser

she elle

shirt chemise *f.*

shop boutique *f.,* magasin *m.;* — window devanture *f.*

shop courir les magasins

short court

should (= ought) devoir

shoulder épaule *f.*

shout crier

show montrer, faire voir; — in introduire

shut fermer; — up enfermer

sick malade

side: change —s changer de camp

sight curiosité *f.*

silence silence *m.*

silent silencieu-x, -se; be —, become — se taire; remain — se taire, rester silencieux

silk soie *f.; adj.* de soie

silly: do a — thing faire une bêtise

simply (tout) simplement

since (*time*) *adv.* depuis; *conj.* depuis que; *prep.* depuis

since (*because*) puisque

sing chanter

single seul

sir monsieur, M.

sister sœur *f.*

sit (down) s'asseoir, be —ting être assis

situation situation *f.*

six six

sixty soixante

size (*of gloves etc.*) pointure *f.*

sky ciel *m.* (*pl.* cieux)

sleep sommeil *m.*

sleep dormir; go to — s'endormir

sleepy: be — avoir sommeil

slender svelte

slightest le moindre

slow: be — (*of a watch*) retarder

small petit

smell sentir; — good sentir bon

smile sourire

snow neige *f.*

so *adv.* (*before adj. or adv.*) si; (= *it*) le; (*therefore*) donc, par conséquent; — many, — much tant; (*loose connective beginning a sentence*) ainsi, alors, de sorte que; — that *conj.* (*purpose*) afin que, pour que, de sorte que *with subj.;* (*result*) de sorte que *with indic.*

socialist socialiste *m.*

soft (*of leather*) souple

soldier soldat *m.*

somber sombre

some *partitive* de, en; *adj.* (*a small amount*) quelque; (*a few*) quelques; *pron.* quelques-uns; **—one** quelqu'un

something quelque chose *m.*

somewhat assez

son fils *m.*

song chanson *f.*

soon bientôt, tôt; **as — as** aussitôt que, dès que; **so —** si tôt

Sorbonne, la *see French-English vocabulary*

sorry: be — regretter (de), être désolé; **feel — for** plaindre

sort sorte *f.;* **some — of** je ne sais quel

soup potage *m.*

south sud *m.;* **—** (**of France**) Midi *m.*

South America Amérique *f.* du Sud

Southern France Midi *m.* (de la France)

souvenir souvenir *m.*

Spain Espagne *f.*

Spaniard Espagnol *m.*

Spanish espagnol

speak parler

specialty spécialité *f.*

spend (*money*) dépenser; (*time*) passer; **— an hour writing** passer une heure à écrire

spire flèche *f.*

spite: in — of malgré

spoil gâter

spoon cuiller *f.*

spot endroit *m.*

square carré

stab donner un coup de couteau à

staging mise *f.* en scène

stained-glass window vitrail *m.* (*pl.* vitraux)

stairs escalier *m. sing.;* **carry up—, go up—** monter

stamp timbre *m.*

star étoile *f.*

start (from) partir (de), quitter

state état *m.*

statesman homme *m.* d'état

station gare *f.*

stay séjour *m.*

stay rester

steak biftek *m.*

steal enlever, voler (**from** = à)

step pas *m.;* **but a few —s from here** à deux pas d'ici

step into (*a room*) passer à

still encore, toujours

stocking bas *m.*

stone pierre *f.*

stop arrêt *m.;* (*of airplane*) escale *f.,* étape *f.;* **non—** sans escale

stop *trans.* arrêter; *intrans.* s'arrêter

story histoire *f.;* (*account*) récit *m.;* **detective —** roman *m.* policier; **short —** conte *m.*

straight ahead tout droit

stranger étranger *m.,* inconnu *m.*

street rue *f.*

stretch out avancer

strike grève *f.;* **go on —** se mettre en grève

strike (*of clock*) sonner

striker gréviste *m.*

striped rayé

stroll flâner; — **down** (*a street*) descendre en flânant

strong fort

student étudiant *m.*, étudiante *f.*

study (*room*) cabinet *m.* de travail

study étudier

stupid stupide

stylish chic, à la mode

subject sujet *m.*

submit présenter, soumettre

subscribe to être abonné à

succeed (**in**) réussir (à)

success succès *m.*

such tel, -le, pareil, -le; — **a** un tel; — **as** tel que

suddenly tout à coup

suède suède *m.;* — **glove** gant *m.* de suède

suffer souffrir

sugar sucre *m.*

suggest suggérer

summer été *m.;* — **courses** cours *m. pl.* de vacances

Sunday dimanche *m.*

sunset coucher *m.* du soleil

superb superbe

superintendent: police — commissaire *m.* de police

support appui *m.*

suppose supposer; **be —d to** devoir

sure sûr

surely sûrement

surprise étonner, surprendre; **be —d** s'étonner

surroundings environs *m. pl.*

suspect se douter de

suspicious: be — of se méfier de

sweater chandail *m.*

Swedish suédois

swim nager

Swiss suisse

Switzerland Suisse *f.*

symbol symbole *m.*

T

table table *f.*

tackle aborder

take prendre; (*accompany*) mener, emmener, conduire; (*carry*) porter, emporter; (*a course*) suivre; (*require*) falloir (*see* § 82); — **an examination** passer un examen; — **back home** ramener chez lui; — **from** prendre dans, sur, *etc.* (*see p. 44, note 2*); — **off** enlever, ôter; — **out of** prendre dans; — **place** avoir lieu; — **a walk** faire une promenade; — **the wrong road** se tromper de chemin

talk parler

talkative causeu-r, -se, bavard

tall grand, haut

taxi taxi *m.;* **take a —** prendre un taxi; **take a — to** aller en taxi à

tea thé *m.;* **have (take) —** prendre le thé (une tasse de thé)

telegram dépêche *f.*

telephone téléphone *m.*

telephone téléphoner, donner un coup de téléphone à

tell dire; (*relate*) raconter; — **about** parler de

temper: lose one's — se fâcher

ten dix

tennis tennis *m.;* — **match** partie *f.* de tennis; **play —** jouer au tennis

terrace terrasse *f.*

terrible terrible

terror terreur *f.*

than que; (*before numerals*) de; (*before infin.*) que de

thanks merci; **many —** merci beaucoup (bien)

thank you merci

that *adj.* ce, cet, cette, ces; *indef. pron.* cela, ce; *rel. pron.* qui, que; *conj.* que

the le, la, les

theater théâtre *m.*

their leur; —s le leur

them les, leur; eux, elles

then alors; (*next*) ensuite, puis

there là; y *before verb;* **— is (are)** il y a, (*pointing out*) voilà; **over —** là-bas

therefore donc, par conséquent

these *adj.* ces; *pron.* ceux-ci, celles-ci

they ils, elles; on; eux, elles

thing chose *f.*

think penser, croire; **— of** (*have one's thoughts on*) penser à, (*have an opinion of*) penser de

third troisième

thirsty: **be —** avoir soif

thirty trente

this *adj.* ce, cet, cette; *pron.* ceci; celui-ci, celle-ci; **— is** c'est, voici

thorn épine *f.*

those *adj.* ces; *pron.* ceux-là, celles-là

thousand mille; —s des milliers *m.*

three trois

through par, à travers

throw (away) jeter

thrust fourrer

Thursday jeudi *m.*

ticket (*railway*) billet *m.;* (*theater*) place *f.;* **get —s** prendre des places

ticket-taker contrôleur *m.*

tide marée *f.;* **at high —** à la marée haute

time temps *m.;* (*hour*) heure *f.;* (*occurrence*) fois *f.;* **ahead of —** en avance; **hard —s** les temps difficiles; **a long —** longtemps; **in — to** à temps pour; **on —** à l'heure; **(at) what —** (à) quelle heure; **have a good —** s'amuser

timidly timidement

tip pourboire *m.*

tire fatiguer; **get —d** se fatiguer

title titre *m.*

to à; (*with cities*) à; (*with fem. sing. names of countries*) en; (*with others*) à; (*in order to*) afin de, pour; (*to the house of*) chez

toast pain grillé *m.,* toast *m.*

today aujourd'hui

together ensemble

tomorrow demain; **— night** demain soir

tonight ce soir

too (*also*) aussi; **—, — many, — much** trop

torment tourmenter

torrent: **in —s** à torrents, à verse

torture torture *f.*

touch toucher

Toulouse *f. a city in southern France*

Touraine Touraine *f.*

tourist touriste *m.*

Tours *m. old capital of Touraine*

toward vers; (*behavior, with regard to*) envers

tower tour *f.*

town ville *f.,* village *m.;* **in (to) —** en ville

train train *m.*

traitor traître *m.*

translate traduire

travel voyager

trip voyage *m.;* tournée *f.;* **have a good —!** bon voyage!

trouble mal *m.;* **have motor (engine) —** avoir une panne

trousers pantalon *m. sing.*
Trouville *a French resort on the English Channel*
true vrai
truly vraiment
trunk malle *f.*
truth vérité *f.*
try essayer (de), tâcher (de); — **on** essayer
Tuesday mardi *m.*
turn *trans.* tourner; *intrans.* se tourner; — **the leaves of** feuilleter
twelve douze
twenty vingt
twice deux fois
two deux
typically vraiment

U

ugly laid
unbearable insupportable
uncle oncle *m.*
under sous
understand comprendre
undress se déshabiller
uneasy mal à l'aise
unfortunately malheureusement
United States Etats-Unis *m. pl.*
university université *f.*
unknown inconnu
unless *conj.* à moins que *with subj.; prep.* à moins de
until *conj.* jusqu'à ce que (*after* attendre: que) *with subj.; prep.* jusqu'à, à
up, upstairs: go —, carry — monter
upon sur
us nous
use se servir de; **get —d to** se faire à, s'accoutumer à

use usage *m.;* **make — of** faire usage de
useful utile
usually d'ordinaire, généralement
utter pousser

V

vacation vacances *f. pl.*
valise valise *f.*
valley vallée *f.*
valuable précieu-x, -se
variety variété *f.*
vase vase *m.*
vegetable légume *m.*
Venetian Vénitien *m.*
Versailles, *a town 12 miles west of Paris, famous for its château built by Louis XIV and its parks*
version version *f.*
very très; *adj.* même (*placed after noun*)
vicinity: in the — aux environs
victim victime *f.*
village village *m.*
vineyards vignes *f. pl.*
visit visite *f.*
visit (*persons*) faire une visite à; (*things*) visiter
voice voix *f.;* **in a low —** à voix basse
volume volume *m.*

W

wage salaire *m.;* **raise in —s** relèvement *m.* des salaires
wait (for) attendre
waiter garçon *m.*
walk promenade *f.;* **go for (take)**

a — faire une promenade, se promener

walk aller à pied, marcher; **— fast** marcher vite; **— home** rentrer à pied

wall mur *m.*

want vouloir, désirer; **you are —ed** (*at the telephone*) on vous demande

war guerre *f.*

warm chaud; **be —** (*of persons*) avoir chaud, (*of weather*) faire chaud

warm chauffer

watch montre *f.;* **by your —** à votre montre

watch regarder

water eau *f.*

way route *f.;* **by the —** à propos; **on the —** en route

wear porter

weather temps *m.;* **be bad —** faire mauvais (temps)

Wednesday mercredi *m.*

week semaine *f.,* huit jours; **a — from today** d'aujourd'hui en huit; **last —** la semaine dernière; **next — la semaine prochaine; two —s** quinze jours

well bien; (*introducing a remark*) eh bien

west ouest *m.*

West Indies les Antilles *f. pl.*

what *interrog. adj.* quel; *interrog. pron.* que, quoi; (*asking for a definition*) qu'est-ce que c'est que; *rel. pron.* ce qui, ce que; *exclam.* quoi! comment! **— a** quel

whatever quoi que + *subj.;* quel que + *subj.* (*see § 138*); **any —** n'importe quel; **anything —** n'importe quoi

when, whenever quand, lorsque; *interrog.* quand

where où

whether si

which *adj.* quel; *pron.* qui, que, lequel; **— one** lequel

while (*time*) pendant que, en *with pres. part.;* (*although*) quoique *with subj.,* tout en *with pres. part.*

white blanc, blanche

who qui

whoever celui qui; qui que + *subj.* (*see § 138*)

whole tout

whom *interrog.* qui; *rel.* que, lequel

whose *interrog.* à qui; *rel.* dont, duquel

why pourquoi; *exclam.* mais; **— not?** pourquoi pas?

wife femme *f.*

willing: be — vouloir (bien)

willingly volontiers

win gagner

window fenêtre *f.;* (*of a shop*) devanture *f.*

wine vin *m.*

winter hiver *m.*

with avec; chez

without *conj.* sans que; *prep.* sans

witness assister à

woman femme *f.*

wonder se demander

wood bois *m.*

word mot *m.;* (*spoken*) parole *f.*

work travail *m.*

work travailler; **— hard** travailler ferme

worker travailleur *m.;* (*manual*) ouvrier *m.*

world monde *m.*

world-wide mondial

worried préoccupé

worry inquiéter
worse pire, plus mauvais
worst le pire, le plus mauvais
worthy digne
would (*be willing*) devoir
wrinkle ride *f.*
wrinkled ridé
write écrire
writer écrivain *m.*
writing paper papier *m.* à lettre
wrong: be — avoir tort; take the —
  road se tromper de chemin

Y

year an *m.*, année *f.* (*see p. 4, note
  2*); last — l'année dernière; next
  — l'année prochaine
yes oui; (*contradicting assertion*) si
yesterday hier
yet encore; cependant
you tu, te, toi, vous; *indef.* on
young jeune; — men, — people
  jeunes gens *m. pl.*
your votre, vos; —s le vôtre

Index

Unless preceded by *p.* (page), all numbers refer to paragraphs.